Be Your Best
with NLP

The Power of Ten¹⁰ steps for
living, learning and earning

Terry Carroll

March 2003

TTL

TTL is an imprint of
Take That Ltd.
P.O.Box 200,
Harrogate
HG1 2YR
ENGLAND

email:sales@takethat.co.uk

www.takethat.co.uk

Also by Terry Carroll and published by TTL:
NLP for Traders and Investors (1-873668-81-3)

TTL books are available at special quantity discounts to use as premiums and sales promotions. For more information, please contact the Director of Special Sales at the above address or contact your local bookshop.

Contents

Part 1 Preparing Your Success

Part 2 Creating your success – The Power of Ten[10] Steps to Your Best

Part 3 Enjoying Your Success

Appendices   The Power of Ten[10] steps to success in a fortnight

NLP is a very specific subject. I write and speak using a number of NLP based styles. One of them is called 'Milton Language'. This is a way of communicating to induce a trance like state. It has been shown that trance is the ideal 'learning state'.

As you read this book, you will come across many, very deliberate variations of the traditional grammatical rules on punctuation and mixing up tenses. *Be Your Best with NLP* has been written to work subliminally, as well as consciously to produce an entirely positive set of beliefs and states in the mind of the reader.

Part 1

Preparing Your Success

In the beginning......

ONCE UPON a time...a long time ago...a seed was planted and nourished in green fertile land, among bigger trees that had been around for some time. Some were old and tired; others were sprightly and flexible. Some had been tainted by disease and pests and most were healthy and thriving.

When the wind blew and the weather was rough, many of them creaked and moaned. Only a few believed that every cloud has a silver lining.

Surrounded by the forest, the seed came into the world knowing nothing. It soon became a sapling, curious to learn and eager to grow. It looked up to those around it and learned from their wisdom without question, until big enough, strong enough and wise enough to challenge the views of others. By that time, it was well set, though never entirely secure when the strongest gales blew. Luckily, lightning always seemed to strike elsewhere.

The forest was full of creatures of many kinds, with their own patterns and habits. Each beat with a warm heart, though some were a nuisance or a pestilence, seeking always to take from others whilst offering little or nothing back. The young tree always felt able to learn, as it grew, welcoming these others to its outstretched arms. Some would attack it, or gnaw away at its fabric, while others nested. Some were vagrants and others simply hung around. Not knowing any other way, the tree welcomed the diversity of life and became a haven for many.

Now that it was strong enough to survive on its own, life became more of a challenge. Though its trunk was firm and its branches strong, it was a bigger target for the elements. Needing much more nourishment, it had to compete for both light and water with all those around. As the seasons came and went and the climate became more variable, it needed to draw even more on its strengths and reserves in the competition for survival.

Doubts began to gnaw away even more than the pests. It somehow seemed that as the daily challenges grew, the negative patterns and beliefs it had learned when younger, came more to the fore, becoming almost self-fulfilling. Deep within its very core, something started to eat away the inner strength that had always been so readily available.

It searched and searched all that it knew to find the solutions or even temporary relief from what weighed so much more heavily on its spreading boughs. Sheltering beneath its foliage and mingling deeper among its fellows, it seemed drawn in on itself. It became more easily bent by the wind, more subject to disease. No matter how much nutrition it drew from the ground and the elements, it seemed to weaken by the day.

Having a strong and bold heart, it refused to quit, as it searched and longed for the way out of a seemingly endless downward spiral. It sought the wisdom and advice of many and reflected much. It fought and struggled on, trying always to retain a friendly outward appearance, while the battle continued within.

One day, disaster struck. A bolt of lightning cracked its trunk and its will. It struggled on gamely, refusing to buckle, but was in desperate need of help. Then Merlin appeared...

Terry Carroll has 'reinvented' himself in the last seven years as a motivational speaker and performance coach for teams and individuals. An NLP Practitioner working at the leading edge of personal growth technologies, he is integrating NLP, Emotional Intelligence, Accelerated Learning and other proven techniques into the 'best of the best' for personal and group change. **Hollins *e*plus** specialises in education and sport, **HTBYB** focuses on the world of work.

Terry can be reached at terrycarroll_hollins@lineone.net, or on 01765 620643 (UK).

Chapter 1

Introduction – What this book is about

THIS BOOK is about NLP, and not just NLP. It's about many things which can come together and be interwoven to make the positive patterns of your life... starting from now... Most of all, it is about you... and for you. Why? Because although I wrote it, you are reading it, right now, and interpreting it, through your own, unique, special conscious and unconscious filters, based on the patterns of your existence up to now.

The meaning it has for you is yours, and yours alone. I'm just the tour guide, on your journey to lasting positive change.

When I was young, there was frequently anger in my space. I grew up with part of me apparently accepting this as part of life and occasionally replicating the patterns I had learned...and a growing part of me that repudiated it, hated myself when I did it and wanted no part of it whatsoever.

For 45 years I used my brain to search, for a way to permanently exorcise these demons that were damaging my relationships. I was desperate to change and explored a number of personal development and personal growth tools and techniques. Many of them left me with a temporary feeling of relief or surge of positivism and while I inched forward, nothing produced significant, lasting change. After two broken marriages I was on the verge of resigning myself to years of therapy when I discovered NLP and much more.

In two sessions with a highly skilled NLP Master Trainer, I lost 45 years of anger and started to march forward into a new life.

Around the same time, I read *The Tao of Jung* by David Rosen. It told of how, at a similar age, Karl Jung had 'fallen out' with his teacher, Sigmund Freud, suffering a life crisis in doing so. This was so profound that it felt for him like a death and rebirth. The book also told of how Jung came to understand so much about the mysticism and beliefs of Eastern cultures. The rest of his life became, as much as anything, an integration of East with West, which to me has seemed equivalent to integrating the right brain with the left.

Since then I have studied NLP to Master Practitioner level and along the way discovered so many other tools and techniques, all of which have been integrated into what I do, all have contributed to the growing, lasting, positive change and many have been woven into the fabric of this book.

So it's about much more than NLP. It's about Emotional Intelligence, Accelerated Learning, kinesiology, and much, much more. It's not a textbook and you can use it as a manual for life change if you choose, or you can read it out of absorbed interest, trusting that your unconscious mind takes everything in and never forgets a thing that is congruent with the change you seek to achieve now.

And what is NLP, some of you may ask? Many or most of you may already know, or have some insights. I do not intend to define it here. For me it is the art of communication and the science of excellence. Above all, it is about everything that is about you and what you do. It is about all languaging (verbal and non-verbal) and behaviour. And you cannot not behave…simply by breathing…and being…you exist.

NLP – a model of Excellence

NLP began with Bandler and Grinder studying what made people excellent. Once upon a time, it was believed that only a handful of people on the planet could ski excellently well. Then, we started to film and video these gods of skiing. By freeze framing and breaking down the constituent parts of the skiing process into their basic elements, schools of skiing evolved. Now, my 70-year-old mother can go on a holiday and learn to ski.

Similarly, Bandler and Grinder studied Bateson, Erickson, Satir, Perls and others to understand what made them excellent in their own fields. Primarily, this was based on listening to language patterns and calibrating the neurophysiology that characterized their behaviour patterns. When they had disaggregated the elements of external and internal language and behaviours upon which the excellence was based, they then set about modeling these to achieve similar results.

Personal development through NLP is based on: understanding our own patterns of language and behaviour; their internal meanings; ways in which they can be made more resourceful and effective; and a set of tools and techniques to implement changes we choose to make for ourselves.

In life, there are many role models of excellence. By observing and understanding their patterns of behaviour; by listening to their language patterns and calibrating their neurophysiology, you could gain an understanding sufficient to use as a basis for installing excellent behaviours in your self.

Normally, in performance coaching or counseling, the full NLP based approach is to work with a compliant subject using a patient and detailed questioning process to elicit, understand and where appropriate enhance the strategies and patterns of behaviour that are the basis of excellence. Then, by consciously learning and repeating these elements until they become unconsciously installed, the excellent behaviour can be modeled.

The range of NLP techniques has grown exponentially in its 27 years of life. One of its presuppositions is that continuing flexibility of language and behaviour will produce better and more lasting positive results than merely replicating the previous unresourceful patterns of behaviour.

While it is possible to install or enhance self-confidence, sometimes, especially in the many potentially or actually stressful situations that people may find themselves in, old negative beliefs and patterns may have got in the way. Self-confidence and self-esteem may not always have been sufficient to override irrational patterns of emotions from the past. There are a number of ways to change these permanently. We shall be exploring these more as the book progresses.

In order to create a lasting change, you may wish to use a variety of approaches that best suit you. Modeling can be highly successful. In addition, using positive anchors to utilize powerful resourceful states of achievement from the past, together with reframing apparent negative situations to see the positive aspects and opportunities for learning can lead to a continuous cycle of success.

Finally, you may perceive the possibilities of integrating NLP into a whole new regime of life in general. The regular use of meditation and exercise, together with a balanced diet, can also help you to be more energetic, calmer, more resilient and better able to manage stress and whatever daily challenges may arise.

The world's leading expert on NLP is Richard Bandler who, with John Grinder, originated NLP. He is now taking this a stage further with DHE™ (Design Human Engineering). If you want to get deeply into this subject, read anything with Richard's name on it. He is a very clever person and highly skilled in these things. If you choose to take this further and embark on Practitioner yourself, you must choose your own route and the people who train you must be right for you.

There have been many other clever and artful people along the way, such as Steve and Connierae Andreas, whose book *NLP: The New Technology of Achievement* is not only one of the best, but also one of the most practical I have read. My own journey is converging me towards Robert Dilts, who is not only one of the best practitioners of NLP in the world (and has established a University of NLP in California), and has also introduced completely original thinking and approaches, especially in the area of kinesthetic aspects of the subject.

So, I prefer to answer the question "What is NLP about?" It is about: everything you do and say and how you do and say them; it is about understanding these patterns, processes and behaviours in both yourself and others; it is about making choices to modify, change and improve your own and to learn or model the best in others; it is about a never ending journey towards your magnificent self and your truly limitless potential...which is only limited by your own imagination....

And it's about magic...

Magic

Did you ever feel...you're in the presence of magic? And you know you're in the presence of magic....and you know you know...you're in the presence of magic....when you can be, do or have anything....anything....for your self....right now....

And was there maybe a time, when you were much younger, when there was a magician....and there was a particular trick....and you couldn't see how it worked....and you wondered to yourself "how did they do that?" and you just couldn't grasp it.

How did they do that? Whatever the trick and no matter how hard you concentrated, you just couldn't work it out. It was an illusion. And where did the illusion happen? It seemed to be before your eyes and yet....the illusion happens inside us. That's how magic works.

When I was young and read so many books, my favourite was King Arthur and the Knights of the Round Table. We saw Merlin as the magician. And yet the writer can be a magician too.

The writer takes the plainness and meaninglessness of words on their own and weaves a magic spell in our minds....painting pictures of the sounds and the goings on, stirring our thoughts and feelings. The book in its paper and print is the same for everyone, but the story is for you alone, as only you can put your own interpretation on the words, the phrases, the ink symbols on every page that can create the magic in our minds right now.

The first NLP book I read was *Frogs into Princes* by the originators, Richard Bandler and John Grinder. All my life it seemed I had searched and striven to find a way, a means, a method, a secret, to resolve all that needed to be resolved. I had studied and researched any number of the world's best and best known personal development tools in vain, seeking the holy grail of lasting change. Now here it was.

My personal journey led me to study NLP at Practitioner and Master Practitioner level and the first book I studied was *Magic of NLP Demystified* by Lewis & Pucelik. Now this wasn't a great book, but it introduced me to the wonders of language patterns and eye patterns and I was lost....in a wonderful journey which will never end.

In developing *How to Be Your Best*, our rapidly growing performance coaching and motivational speaking consultancy, I have rediscovered the magic of the written word that I hungered for as an 11-year-old. I'm still looking and now it is no longer a frustrating, never-ending story. My standard is 'the Best of the Best', as NLP and all these other things grow and become interwoven. My sources are in books of all kinds and by many varied authors and also in the rich endlessness and originality of the Internet.

Along the way, I came across someone who for me was also a magician. His name was Milton....Milton Erickson. His lasting memorial is the phenomenal growth of 'Ericksonian' hypnosis and he was arguably the greatest hypnotherapist of all time. The memory is of a grey-haired, kindly eyed man with an intense interest in people and everything about them. His image can live in me forever. And for the last 30 years of his life, he healed people and created lasting change, just by telling stories....

And we live in an age of magic. What would the founding fathers of America make of television? Would they think the images to be ghosts? Might they want to go round behind the back of the 'magic box' to check the rear of the image?

We take so much for granted, thanks to technology. Maybe we have lived in an age of science for too long now. People are searching for spirit. They are asking "is this all there is to life". The New Age has been upon us for some time. We are cosseted by science and technology so sophisticated that many of us cannot even program the video!

It is time for an age of art....and magic.

Choices

This book is also about Choices. We all have choices about everything in our lives....Everything....

I remember being among an audience of 250 listening to the great Lou Tice (Pacific Institute). He said "we have choices about everything." "No we don't," said one chap. "Yes we do" said Lou. "No we don't". "Why not". "Well I can't murder someone". "Why not". "Because I might go to jail for life, or to the chair". "So you have choices...."

And you have a choice about everything in this book. If you have picked it up to look at it, you have a choice that you can read on now. You can buy it or borrow it. You can read it and recommend it. You could have rejected it and put it down and yet somehow the magic can mean that your hands seem glued to the sides and as your mind begins to wander....with all these thoughts....and all these things....then what could be more appealing than to sit down and relax somewhere....to pass the time of day in dreams...to think about all the possibilities that you had not collected together until now.

Was there ever a time when you were sat in a comfy chair? You may have been listening to the strains of heavenly music, like Mozart's clarinet concerto. Maybe a rock band was weaving beat, tune and rhythm in the middle of your head and all the world outside could seem so distant now.

Or was it a film, or theatre, that had you transfixed by the tapestry of its words, the power of its human expression, the colour, the sounds and the feelings...the emotions drawn from deep inside....the tear that inexplicably appeared and welled over....the lump in the throat. And the power and passion of great and enthralling sport.

All these things and these memories can be so entrancing. And what have you wanted to do with your life until now. And what can you do now you know you can change....when you choose.

And I don't mind whether you read or feel or think these things now. I don't mind if you engage your mind...your conscious mind and your unconscious mind in deep rapport now. I promise you that when you do, before you have even read half this book, your whole life can have changed from this moment....

Only you can decide whether to read on....and on....and you're going to have to read some more to find out, if not already. It's your choice....like all those other things....

Excellence in everything

Everybody truly has limitless potential. I know that now. I guess I always sensed it and was looking for the way. It took me six months of chronic illness to find the way. From the moment I was admitted to hospital I started to get better. Two sessions of NLP based therapy rid me of the powerful negative patterns that had been in me for 45 years. Now I have to apologize to some people that I truly am as totally positive as I seem. As you can be....Everybody truly has limitless potential....Let me show you.

(You might want to ask a friend to read out the next section as you can do it.)

- Just stand up for a moment, in a space, with your feet shoulder width apart, nice and relaxed. Raise your right arm and point straight forward. Now swing round to the right, clockwise as far as you comfortably can, noticing where your finger ends up pointing. Now swing back to the front and lower your arm.

- And now, moving your head and your eyes only, if it's alright with you, turn your head to the right, clockwise as far as you comfortably can and notice the furthest possible point you can see out of the corner of your right eye. And in your own time come back to the front.

(The next two steps are best done with your eyes closed, using your imagination only, without moving a muscle.)

- Inside your mind, imagine raising your right arm and swinging round clockwise as far as you possibly can and notice the furthest point you can see out of the corner of your right eye. Now swing back to the front and lower your arm.

● And now, if it's still alright with you, using your imagination only, swing your head and eyes to the right, clockwise and imagine being able to see all the way round to the front, 360°. And in your own time turn back to the front, open your eyes and come back into the room.

● Now finally, if it's alright with you, physically raise your right arm and swing round to the right, clockwise, as far as you can possibly go….and notice how much further you can go than before….

I run that pattern in every *How to be Your Best* session. It always amazes people. Typically they go 15-30° further the second time.

"So how did you do that?".

"I don't know, I guess maybe it was my mind".

"Which part of your mind?"

"My unconscious mind?"

"Yes, you're unconscious mind."

And it's in the unconscious mind that we find our limitless potential.

Let's for a moment distinguish between the mind and the brain. The brain is that grey matter that sits on top of your brain stem. Incidentally, down there is the amygdala, or primitive brain. Not many people realize that our original brain was an emotional brain. You remember 'fight or flight'? Faced with adversity, or a challenge, primitive people had to choose in a hurry. Adrenaline flooded the body and we stood and fought, or ran like hell!

Now, when Fred or Vera gets into an argument... a blinding rage... they can't see straight... it's the old amygdala that has flooded the 'pre-frontal cortex' and it's not until this starts to clear that the rational 'modern' brain can begin to think straight. "I'm sorry, I don't know what came over me." (By the way, did you know that there was a guy who was happily married with kids, had a measured IQ of 120 and when they autopsied him after he died, he was found to have no brain. How did he do that?)

You see, the thing is, the mind is different and especially your unconscious mind, as you will have realized when you will have finished this book.

Everybody truly has limitless potential, now that you can begin to find the way to unlock the power of the unconscious mind.

"So OK, if I accept that this is true now, how come I'm not being my limitless best?"

Well, for some of us, there have been limiting beliefs and negative patterns that were almost always laid down in childhood. When those will have been released, there is no longer any realistic limit to your potential. Add a shot of Motivation and....WHOOSH.....

Leadership and self-leadership

There is much convergence between NLP and Emotional Intelligence. In an excellent, practical and highly readable book *7 Steps to Emotional Intelligence*, Patrick Merlevede, Denis Bridoux and Rudy Vandamme propose: "So, rather than just offering you some topical tips and tricks, as is done by several other books, we have been presenting the very concepts NLP makes available to adults (as well as children) to develop and increase Emotional Intelligence. Hence, applying what you have been learning from this book, and from NLP training in general, will help you to achieve a high score in EQ-tests…"

So an understanding and application of the best of NLP can improve your emotional intelligence. One of the main reasons is that our strongest emotional patterns (and those that may have got in the way in the past) were almost invariably laid down in childhood and usually in the first seven years of our lives.

Emotional intelligence has become important as much as anything because of the problems business and other organizations had been having with people who, while otherwise of reasonable or above average intelligence, sometimes (or even often) displayed inappropriate behaviours, often unaware of the effect they were having on others around them and the organization in general. It is a fair bet that they were also having similar effects in their lives in general.

This book is also about Emotional Intelligence (EQ). For me, EQ is fundamentally about leadership, including self-leadership. It is about instinctively appropriate behaviours in all circumstances, especially in the company of, or aware of the impact on, others.

There is a never-ending debate about whether leaders are born or made. We don't need to consider that here. What I have found in motivational, coaching and personal development work is the possibility of creating the basis of awareness, implementing choice and creating lasting positive change.

My own thesis therefore is that whether someone is a born leader or not, they can learn: (at first consciously and by practice eventually integrated into unconscious patterns of behaviour) the most appropriate and successful attributes of leadership; how to develop and apply an awareness of the impact of one's own behaviour on others; and what is or is not appropriate behaviour accordingly.

A friend had managed to escape an appalling relationship, characterized by systematic verbal and physical abuse over many years. One day, I met someone who had met and knew the perpetrator of this self-indulgent misogynistic behaviour. "He had a very difficult childhood, you know." My response was that, at the age of 50 and assuming him to be totally sane, the subject could not be unaware, either in the moment or in retrospect, of the effects of his behaviour on others, especially his partner and children. He had choices in everything, especially whether to do something about this appalling antisocial and occasionally criminal behaviour.

The alcoholic may claim they cannot do anything about it. They can. The first thing they can do is to go to AA. The second is to stand up in front of peers and announce, "I am an alcoholic." The third is to become aware of the effects their behaviours have on themselves and others. And finally to implement and perpetuate these new choices.

Above all, EQ is about leadership and an awareness of the effect of our behaviours on others. Self-leadership is about the effect on ourselves.

EQ is also about three other key things:
- Self-determination;
- Self-control;
- Empathy.

Self-determination is about the ability to decide a course of action or actions, a life plan or what have you and to implement it, continuously reviewing the feedback available to us and modifying our course for the better. It is also about soundness and being able to start and finish things.

Self-control is about the ability to be aware of and to understand our behaviour in all circumstances. To enhance the positives. To review, understand, work on, change or modify those that are unresourceful or represent less than our magnificent selves. (Note, we are not seeking perfection here, just a growing objective awareness).

Empathy is about an awareness of others, their wishes, needs and behaviours. (Respect the person and change the behaviour).

In reading Goleman's book *Working with Emotional Intelligence*, I was very struck by the 'marshmallow test' and its potential in assessing young people's potential...and much more. You can make up your own mind.

My understanding is that a child of say four years old, is sat in a room at a table. A psychologist or similarly appropriate person places two marshmallows on the table in front of the child. "In a little while I shall leave the room. When I go, you can either have one marshmallow immediately, or, if both are still there when I return, you can have two marshmallows."

The child does not know that the psychologist is going to be away for 20 minutes or so. In Goleman's recounting, when they return, there will either be one or two marshmallows on the table. (One lad in a group of 17 year olds attending *How to Be Your Best* asked, "what happens if there are none left at all?" My response was that we would have a real challenge in that situation...)

Apparently, by tracking these children into their late teens and early twenties, the researchers found that the marshmallow test appeared to be more reliable in predicting success in both career and life in general than any IQ test that had ever been devised.

Why should this be? It seems it might be about gratification...

So, this book is about leadership and all good leadership is self-leadership. By using this book you may begin or continue your journey towards your own magnificent self and limitless potential knowing that if you were even to get only half way there, you can be sound in emotional intelligence, aware of others, a good leader for yourself and others. Why? Because through NLP and these other things you can only improve your objective, conscious and unconscious understanding of your self, having realized the new positive choices you have available for yourself right now...

Balancing IQ and EQ

The ideal universe is a universe in balance. Indeed the universe must always be in balance, otherwise we would not exist. The universe in which we exist is your universe. You exist in it. Only you can perceive it in the unique way that you do, because only you have your own unique patterns. I know how some of those patterns are likely to work, and that is why choice pervades this book, because it is the choices that can work for you that are the ones that matter.

This leads me back to emotional intelligence. Many companies had wondered how extraordinarily intelligent individuals were sometimes capable of stupid or unresourceful decisions or behaviours. Goleman proposed that the emotional component of one's thinking, processing and behaviour was at least as important. For example, if you knew someone who was in the middle of a violent argument, would they ordinarily have been able to sustain rational thinking and behaviour (unless they were a psychopath, for example)?

In the Master Practitioner track of NLP, we talk about achieving self-mastery. This is to be wholly at cause in all things we do. In emotional intelligence terms, I would talk of being able to choose to adopt the language and behaviour most appropriate to each situation. The equation can become:

$$\text{Intelligence} = \text{IQ} + \text{EQ}$$

(and now some writers are talking of SQ, or spiritual intelligence)

In discussing EQ, we are not dismissing IQ. We all have a measurable level of IQ for what it's worth (and to my mind it mainly measures left brain ability). What matters more is your intelligence potential (we were born with much more than we have used so far), what you do with it and how you integrate it with all your other intelligences, especially emotional and spiritual. How many people have you met who had heaps of intelligence, apparently without sufficient ability to appropriately manage their key relationships?

In 1999, Tony Buzan, the originator of the 'Mind Map' was giving a lecture to the BBC. "If this were the 1970s, we would be using less than 20% of our intelligence. Here, at the end of the 1990s, we are using less than 5%..." How can that be? Well, maybe we let TV do too much of our thinking and technology do too much of our doing. (Oh and by the way...weight is increasing and certain diet-related diseases such as obesity, diabetes and heart disease are moving towards epidemic proportions in the Western world).

So it is important to seek balance in everything. IQ can be balanced with EQ. The brain works best when left and right hemispheres are integrated (hence women's apparent greater ability to multitask).

Tools & techniques – the best of the best

As indicated earlier, this book (and indeed the motivational sessions we run) is not just about NLP. It is about much more than that.

In my journey towards personal growth and fulfillment, two of the most persuasive and soundest 'schools' I came across were the Dale Carnegie Institute and the Pacific Institute (Lou Tice). (The latter was substantially focused on leadership). One thing I appreciated about both, in common, and have sought to model my own approach upon, is the ceaseless research for what is best 'out there'. I spend up to 15% of my time researching 'the best of the best' of the modern tools and techniques. In our organization and with the people we coach and motivate, we can have fun with 'tricks and gimmicks' and we are not interested in those or passing fads in the pursuit of lasting growth and change. We are only interested in what works.

And whenever we come across something new and interesting, our approach is to understand and respect it, where appropriate in our chosen context, to understand how it can influence and/or modify our thinking or approach, how it can spark new ideas and how, if at all, these can be integrated to constantly freshen 'the best of the best.' This does not mean we are in a constant dance, hopping from one technique or approach to another. That was what we found in the past had not created what we sought. Instead we are seeking constant understanding, re-interpretation and improvement of the things we know will work... and last...

Visualization

Robert Dilts has brought us a whole new set of variations and choices in his work centred on kinesthetics (touch and feeling). And one of the most powerful single things you can do in your pursuit of how to be your best, is to discover and grow your powers of visualization.

Now, we have come to understand the visualization possibilities that exist beyond making pictures. Our experiences are usually composed of more than just visual elements. Given that every human value and belief has emotion at its seat and that all the patterns which we can be rid of, i.e. the negative and limiting patterns and beliefs, are based on an originating, emotional based experience, the power of visualization also lies in harnessing kinesthetics.

To put it another way, in *The Holographic Universe*, Michael Talbot suggests the possibility that all of our current, let alone past, experience is based on a limitless, constantly evolving, hologram. Even the things we 'touch' may be the products of our own imagination. Indeed, they are the product of the totality of our experience to date. We only know a colour is yellow, because we were told it, or read it. Every textural experience is interpreted through the accumulated textural filters of our past. If we come across a sight, sound, or feeling we have not experienced before, we can either 'guess' or create a new code for the new experience.

Visualization of anything must, by definition, be based on our accumulated experiences also. We create the imagined experience and our mind does not separate the other representational elements if it does not need to (K = kinesthetic; A = auditory; O = olfactory, or smell; G = gustatory, or taste). We want the totality of the future memory, because for us then it is most real.

When we come to the power of *Anchoring* later, you will understand that it is the totality of sensory experience that anchors the memory. So why not with visualization?

For now let us start with making pictures. The power of the human imagination can be such that an imagined experience can be more real than real...While dreams may be a sifting, filtering and sorting process, to most efficiently interpret and store the day's memories, when we dream, our unconscious mind has available the full set of the 'building blocks' (we shall cover 'submodalities' later) of our experience to fabricate what it wishes – and this can be extremely vivid. Did you never have the experience of wondering whether it was real or you were dreaming?

So, through visualization, we can educate our mind to take any of the limitless, minute elements of our experience and compose them into vivid 'daydreams' of experience.

Why would we want to do that? Well, apart from the joy and pleasure of the vivid imagination, we shall be growing, exercising and developing our powers of visualization, just like a muscle, so that they can work better and better. And most of all, because visualized experience can become real experience. There is so much that is happening to me daily now, which seems to flow directly and congruently from the positive, successful, powerful, resourceful future I have visualized and therefore programmed for myself. Especially as we can be open to the learnings that are available to us along the way and the powerful, positive re-interpretations or releases from the past.

So start any future process with visualization. Train your powers of visualization to become the most powerful tool you possess. And if you don't choose to do that, how soon do you choose to be fulfilled and happy. And if not, why not? And for what conceivable positive purpose for yourself would you want to still see the world as a glass half empty?

Some people seek to persuade me of the value of having negative memories or patterns to drive them to positive outcomes. Of course, as we shall discuss later, I respect each person's model of the world, including the patterns for some people where their primary motivation is away from negativity, such as failure, fear, etc.

And whether for myself or clients I can testify over and over to the transformational experience of discovering that you can move towards...anything.

Fear is a future emotion so, if you would persuade me that fear can be a powerful motivator, then presumably you are wanting to move away from fear. By definition, therefore, you are motivated away from the future....And you can choose and change to move inexorably towards a destiny that you can influence and program.

Recall of a picture is in the past. Visualization tends to be of the future. Sometimes of course it can be in the present and indeed in seeking to understand an experience that someone else has had, you can try to picture it, or visualize what it must have been like.

Whether it is in finding a parking space or programming a powerful, positive future, our experience has been that the power of visualization has potentially limitless possibilities. Start to practice it and build it now. By all means integrating it with your other sensory faculties.

Communication

How to 'Be Your Best' is also fundamentally about communication. Not just with others. Not just with your mouth. And especially with yourself.

Do you have 'self-talk'? The good news is that most people do. Do you have a voice inside you that ever berates you or beats you up if things didn't work out the way you hoped, or you let yourself down in some way? Many people do. We shall come back to that.

Understanding NLP has taught us that the totality of effective communication is about everything we do, as well as say. As you become aware of what Desmond Morris once called 'body language' (and non-verbal communication is much, much more than that...), then you will have a whole new set of choices about communication. You see it is about your model of the world and their model of the world. When you are around people you cannot not communicate. The question is whether they are experiencing what you are doing and projecting and how they are interpreting this, consciously and unconsciously through their set of filters. And of course you too, with them.

Beware of two things: the mind read; and projection. When you think you see, hear or feel what someone else is communicating, remember you are probably interpreting this through your own, programmed model of the world. Unless you know enough about that person to calibrate the totality of their sensory and physical communication, you can only come to your own conclusion. And even when you do have exquisite observation and calibration skills, the only way you can get close to knowing what is really happening for them, or what they are really thinking, is to ask confirmatory questions. And even then, you end up interpreting the answer through your model.

I cannot know that my experience of colour is the exact same as yours. We can converge and we are different.

And as you move through your world, consciously and unconsciously interpreting what is happening around you and the totality of communication you are receiving, from outside and inside, remember also that you are constantly communicating beyond yourself also. To put it another way, wittingly or unwittingly, you are projecting yourself outside yourself all the time.

There is a delightfully witty American saying: "Be kind to yourself, because wherever you go, there you are..." There are at least two interpretations for this: first, whatever you believe you are seeing, especially in other people, is a projection of yourself. "I hate her, because she doesn't consider other people..." and you?

The second is that wherever you go, you are ceaselessly communicating yourself beyond yourself, through your non-verbal, as well as verbal behaviours, especially your values.

John Cleese and Robin Skynner co-wrote a series of books, including Life and How to Survive It. The book is in the form of a series of questions posed by Cleese, for Skynner the psychiatrist to answer.

"So, what about love at first sight?" Skynner explains that when you see someone across a room and later, having met them, find that you have so much in common, it is because we are projecting our values (and probably our beliefs) the whole time.

So this book is about Communication, especially with yourself.

How to create rapport with anyone on the planet

In the work we do with organizations and business in the UK, NLP is rapidly coming into the wider public awareness. Where people have heard about NLP, their most common expectation is that it is about Rapport and Communication. It is, and it is about many things besides. In this book, you can learn not only how to create rapport with anyone on the planet (including negative rapport if you wish, so if you wish to get rid of somebody from your space, you can do this without worrying about appearing rude, offending or annoying them by simply using the obverse of creating positive rapport).

NLP is fundamentally about understanding the languaging and behaviour of ourselves and others. It stands to reason therefore, that the most appropriate use for many may be to understand better and enhance the processes of total communication. Given that most of us want to be happy and for most of us that involves getting on with other people, this leads naturally to rapport.

How to sell yourself, to anyone, at any time

How to Be Your Best is also about selling.

Did you, or did anyone you know ever sell anything which was a discretionary purchase for your customer? If you were to do that and you make a successful sale where the customer has choice, what are you really selling? Some people say 'image', others say 'the product' etc. What you are really selling is yourself. Research has suggested that in 80% of cases where a successful sale was made, either the customer already knew the sales person, or already believed or felt that they liked them.

How can you do that? By understanding yourself and the effect you have on other people. By removing negative or limiting patterns or beliefs and replacing them with positive, motivating patterns. By believing in your limitless potential. By understanding other people's model of the world. By understanding the powerful processes of 'total' communication. And by asking questions and noticing everything that happens then...

Now the interesting thing is that many sales training courses that originate from the US seem to focus on 'closing the sale'. And certainly, when all the input coming to you from the client, *based on what you have carefully elicited before that*, suggests that the client is minded to buy – go for it!

However, many sales people seem determined to try and close the sale before they understand much about the prospect, or even before they've actually engaged with them. "I can see you're really interested in that car, sir." (Mind read. Actually, my neighbour's got one, I'm trying desperately to see what he sees in it and anyhow I'm only killing time while my wife is buying a dress next door...)

The trick is in understanding people and asking the right questions. This book will help you to understand people, to create rapport and manage your communication skills. The right questions are: open questions (i.e. they have more than a one-word answer); questions that tease out the person's values (our values underpin every decision we make); questions that consciously or unconsciously elicit respect, and then make use of the client's model of the world; questions that set up the possibility that the client may choose to buy; and then the 'closing' questions.

So why, you might ask, is selling important, if you are not working in sales? Maybe you can already have realized that, whenever you are in the vicinity of, seeking to engage with, or hoping for a result from another person, you are consciously or unconsciously, wittingly or unwittingly, selling yourself. In a meeting or interview; when you meet a prospective friend or love mate; where you want or need a result; etc. you are selling yourself. So when else would you want to be your best if not then?

Living, loving, learning and earning

As you journey through the remainder of this book and however many times you will have read it, then every time you will have realized more and more how being your best can have so many benefits in every aspect of your life now.

Life is for living and will it be by the end of today or maybe tomorrow before you can live your life in the moment? How can you do that?

First, we shall later come across 'peripheral vision'. So, if you were to sit quietly now, focused on a spot across from you and let your 'peripheral' vision spread out around you, all the while focusing on the spot, then you can notice how you can be right in this moment now and everything else can just...drift away...

How do you know this?

Not living in the moment means living in the past, the present or inside your own internal dialogue and self-talk. Practice being able to move your focus outside yourself, so that you can be totally focused on what you are doing, while your awareness becomes that of the things you can really notice outside yourself, that are waiting for your attention.

Karl Jung talks about synchronicity. In simple terms he proposed that if you notice three or more things that seem to be connected (we might have called them coincidences), follow them because they may have a message or a meaning for you. For example, you see the same stranger in three apparently different circumstances over a short period of time. "Wow, what a coincidence" you might say. The thing is that you might have unconsciously noticed that person many, many times, so for what purpose has your unconscious mind brought this person or thing into your conscious awareness now?

So, when you live your life substantially inside your own conscious mind, with your self-talk and constant internal dialogue, not only might you be missing a multitude of opportunities and learnings outside yourself, but also you are cluttering up that tiny gateway of your conscious mind (7 ± 2) into which your unconscious mind wants to bring the really significant bits of the 2.8 million it is processing now. And what room does that leave you to learn and grow?

This is why meditation works so well. It clears the mind, leaving space for the significant messages and learnings to enter your awareness.

If you're not living in the present moment, you may have been living in the past or the future. Now you cannot change the past, only the way you perceive it. The question is, were you living in regret or fear, or basking in the warmth of reflected memories and the anticipation of excitements to come?

Guilt and inappropriate sadness are past feelings. Anger may be a present emotion and it is always based on patterns performed, experienced or learned in the past. Indulging inappropriate anger involved consciously or unconsciously reliving previous angry patterns. Fear is a future emotion and how much of your precious space for living in the moment was ever stalled or paralyzed by fear, foreboding or the other negative emotions.

So, using all these tools and techniques, understand, learn and practice living in the moment. Being your best is in the moment and learning how to be your best means you will want to, and can be more and more in the present moment, and living your life in the way you want it to be and it can be now.

Loving is good. Loving can be in the past, present and future and the very best lovers will tell you that it is best when it is right now. Learning how to be your best will not only make you better and more resourceful around other people, opening the way for new loving possibilities. And it is most of all about learning to love yourself. As George Benson sang "Learning to love yourself is the greatest love of all."

So, as you think of a time, any time in your life when you know you were loved or highly appreciated if only for a moment (including by yourself), then go to that time now. See what you saw, hear what you heard and feel what you felt as you are in that time right now. And be sure that everything you are seeing, hearing, feeling, smelling or tasting is being done through yourself and that you cannot see yourself in the picture as you experience it right now.

And take the picture, sound and feelings and all those things and make them as big and strong and powerful and overwhelming as you can make them now. And know what it is to be loved right now, because when you know that feeling and only that feeling right now then you can be your best now. And try in vain not to be pleasantly surprised that other people are noticing.

Being your best in loving is about being able to be outside yourself and inside yourself with congruent feelings in the same moment. Now I have a clear view that love and relationships are about what you can put into them. The universe is limitless and in perfect balance so as you give out so you will get back. As the bible says 'what you sow you shall reap'.

So many people in the modern world enter relationships for what they can get out of them. I only know one way. "I offer you my whole self, knowing that you won't take all of me." And as Tad James says "anything less than 100% is not enough."

And in every relationship you have ever or will ever have, there is learning. Because perception is projection, everything that is happening to you and for you is both the result of what you are projecting outside and inside yourself and of course how you perceive what is happening in your space.

"He doesn't love me" means "I perceive what he does and says as meaning not love" or "I do not perceive anything that allows me to believe that I am loved" or even "I don't love myself enough or at all to believe that he loves me or can love me" or...you get the picture.

I knew two people, one of whom I loved very much and would have given my whole life to. The problem was that she did not love or even like herself much. She seemed to live inside her mind all the time, based on what she told me, spending many hours just sitting and running the past over and over. It is possible that she even hated herself. It did not stop me reaching out and loving but it did get in the way of her receiving that love and the possibility of being limitlessly happy. And I couldn't change her, she has choices...

The other I did not know directly. He was very aggressive, verbally and physically. He professed to love his partner totally but it was a very jealous, possessive love. He wanted to own her, control her and almost like a leech, suck the lifeblood out of her. Why? Well I don't know and it is possible that he hated himself so much that the only way he could find love was to steal someone else's. He resented her spontaneity and spirituality, her lightness, charisma and ability to get on with almost anyone. So he shut her down and whether intentionally or not, tried to destroy all their and her friendships. He now lives crippled mentally, spiritually and physically, totally on his own, except for the telephone...

So there is so much to learn when you can be your best, because that means that you were no longer preoccupied with the problems and worries and negative patterns that you might have had in the past and you saw only openness and possibilities and life is a lifelong learning process. The question is 'what did you notice?' and 'how can you learn...and grow?'

Deepak Chopra wrote so many good books, only one of which is *The Seven Spiritual Laws of Success*. And as you go through this book, with more new ways of understanding and learning how to be your best then whether you are influencing other people positively or becoming more and more of your limitless potential, it can only succeed in making you more productive and purposeful in every aspect of your life...and work...and earning.

I'll leave you to choose. Do you want to be wealthy...or very wealthy...and it's not just about money. However, in the same way as the values in the stockmarket are an illusion, and inflation is man made, so there is limitless wealth in the world. And are you setting goals, visualizing powerful positive outcomes and projecting your inevitable success, or what have you been waiting for?

Teaching your kids how to learn and be their best

There is so much stress in the world and some of us have worried how our kids can possibly cope. And yet, we may all too easily forget that in the 20th century there were two world conflagrations that threatened to destroy life as we know it. What stress did our parents or grandparents face? How many lost partners, children, relatives or friends and had to rebuild shattered lives? How was it for parents contemplating bringing children into a world that was facing war, at war or had been at war?

And what about the kids? My own origins were pretty normal for a Baby Boomer, I guess. My Dad, however, was brought up in the North East of England, at the time of the Jarrow marches, the Wall Street Crash and the Great Depression. He was born at the end of the First and fought in the Second, World War. When he was at school, he tells that he was only one of two boys that had shoes. When he won a scholarship to Grammar School, his parents could not afford to send his brother.

Despite all this, he and my Mum had us three, starting just after the Second World War and as I write he looks likely to live well beyond his current 83 years.

To be honest, I'm concerned about the degeneration of moral values, especially in the media, TV etc. and the interminable pressure placed on young people to feel unusual if they haven't started sex early. Maybe I'm old-fashioned and I would like a return to the strong traditional values that I believe are held in the spirit of most of us.

And yet, I have limitless belief in the talent, adaptability and survivability of my own children. There is a growing concern for boys. More and more are becoming 'disaffected'. (As if I was never a rebel!) Seriously though, there are some real and valid concerns about the decline in educational achievement and the increase in delinquency, especially among boys.

There is hope, believe me. And yes, NLP is also at the heart of the new possibilities for young and old alike. Older people try to persuade me that memory and mental agility decline with age. Others seem to regard physical degeneration as inevitable also. I will have none of this.

Only today, I was watching a program called 'Fabulous at Fifty' and my goodness there were some beautiful women there and I don't just mean Goldie Hawn or Tina Turner (now over 60). Some of the women in the audience didn't look a day over 30. And then there is Honor Blackman in her 70s...

We shall later come to the mind/body connection and yes, I do believe that aging is an attitude of mind. I teach a memory trick to kids and it works just as well with pensioners to prove that it is not just about memory, it is about recall. Do you know how little of our brain and mind power we are using?

Which brings me back to kids and the words of Tony Buzan I mentioned earlier. Now I have a neutral position on the influences of TV on education. There is more learning available every day of the week on TV than I ever had at school as a kid. The point is to be selective. On the other hand, vocabulary and developing visualization skills must benefit.

I am concerned, however, about the amount of time we all spend watching TV. Not just because it can be degenerative mentally, but also physically. When I was young, we spent that time kicking a ball in a field, exploring the local terrain and generally being in the fresh air.

So of course there are some implicit messages in here and, above all, about taking balanced responsibility for your kids' development. No, I don't mean living their lives for them and especially not reliving your own lives through them. I mean being there when and how they need you to be. I'm talking about 'tough love' (and touch love); listening and understanding; giving them room to be free, explore and learn from mistakes and also setting and being consistent with clearly defined boundaries. And the most important thing is that a child never doubts that they are loved, by someone who is good and kind to them.

And where does NLP fit into all this? Oh, so many ways. First, you could leave this book lying around. They may not want you to tell them to read it, or do it, because they love to explore new ideas and find out for themselves.

My partner's son came to live with us bringing so many unresolved problems and challenges from his past. First, he became curious about what Heather and I do and then set about finding out for himself. Apart from his Mum paying for him to go on an Anthony Robbins weekend, he has discovered all these things for himself and, I recently discovered, has built some formal personal development sessions into every day of his life – at 18. (He has also become preoccupied with healthy eating and exercise, entirely by his own choice, and even cooks his own vegetarian meals.)

So there is hope and much more than that. Many of the *How to Be Your Best* sessions I do are for young people – so far, from ages 10 to 20. Without exception they have been extraordinarily successful (inspirational is one regular description). In these sessions I use many of the techniques and ideas described in this book, with a heavy element of NLP. The response is instant and powerful. Some talk of having changed their lives. Many want to know much more about these things. All see an immediate benefit and new possibilities for the exams they have to take and even months later they will talk about all the changes they have made and the benefits they are getting.

So there are limitless possibilities for young people. And what of the special educational challenges that seem to be growing in society, such as dyslexia, AD/HD, autism, Aspersers syndrome and disaffected behaviours? And why does it seem to be mainly boys?

As I have worked so much with young people and researched intensively on the Internet, I have come to some interim conclusions. First, we are gradually recognizing and respecting the needs and rights of the individual. When I was at school, my educational performance went drastically downhill as soon as I entered Grammar school. I was just bored, as many boys say they are now. Much later I realized that I had an IQ well above average, so what happened?

Education catered for the mainstream and where there are now initiatives such as Special Educational Needs (SEN), or the 'Gifted and Talented', I was just slung into the melting pot. I also now realize that I was much more right brained than many of my male peers. On reflection, my 'dropout' friends appear to have been similarly disposed.

So we now live in a society where young people can be labeled. It is often said that there isn't enough time and money to deal with those who present the greatest challenges. With NLP based techniques and other modern, sophisticated educational approaches that we are now using daily, there is another very different possibility.

I was working with a group of 15 disaffected 13-15 year olds from the worst school in Bradford. We had a wonderful two days and all of them moved forward, sometimes dramatically (even the helpers moved forward). The highlight was a 14 year old lad who most people would have thought was the 'slowest' of the group and rather backward. (By the way, it has been my experience that every SEN child I have worked with has been brighter than the system had concluded they were. One bright lad I worked with had been told he was dyslexic and that this was a disease he would have for the rest of his life!)

Reckoning that the whole group would have learning difficulties of one type or another (statistics in the US show that an extraordinarily high proportion of teenage delinquents have learning disabilities, often not identified or dealt with), I decided to use some NLP techniques, which I knew, would work well for ADHD and dyslexic students. One was teaching them to spell backwards. The 'backward' lad seized on this and asked one of the helpers to think of the biggest word she knew, which was SURREPTITIOUSLY. He took it home that night, worked on the technique and the following morning spelled it backwards perfectly to an astonished group.

He was transformed. Before this event, he didn't even think he could spell, let alone backwards. The group was transformed. For some it was 'if he can do it, I can do it'. All of them improved their spelling and much, much more. We adults were deeply moved and inspired by the whole experience.

So remember, NLP is about all that you are, all that you can do and the whole of your limitless potential. You already have all the tools that you need. You either have the specific tools, or you have the skills to discover, elicit and model those skills in others. Will it be tomorrow or a week's time before you can begin to have realized your limitless potential right now?

So what are you waiting for and there is enough time and there is enough money, for you, and your kids, starting from now...

Nurturing tomorrow's world class human beings

All of us who have children or otherwise have responsibility for or influence over them now have a limitless opportunity to 'create the environment in which their natural talent can flourish'. And it's not just about the things you can understand, learn and apply from reading this book. It's especially about making sure that you are creating this empowering environment and not getting in the way...

And you could have got in the way not just by trying to do it for them, but also by being yourself. Remember, your patterns, values and beliefs were substantially laid down in the first 18 years and especially the first 5-7 years of your life. The 'significant others' in a young person's life can be unwitting teachers of negative or limiting patterns of behaviour by what they do, just as much as by what they say. Childhood should be a time of fun, curiosity and discovery. It would be good to be always a child in some part of you. It will keep you young and always open to new ideas and possibilities.

The person who thinks or behaves as if they know it all can often be the most dangerous, and behave as if they actually know nothing.

Not just parents, teachers and carers, but all of us have a responsibility to positively and constructively create the nurturing environment for tomorrow's world class human beings....including ourselves. Would we not have wished that for ourselves, when we were at an age when we didn't yet know. And it's never too late to change and grow. Notice also, that as you are becoming a positive, empowering influence in the lives of others, especially by becoming so much more of your magnificent self, how your own attitudes can be changing and your choices expanding...

The Power of Ten[10] Steps to Your Best

The core of this book is about Ten Steps to Be Your Best. These have been researched, developed, applied and grown through the now hundreds of sessions of *How to Be Your Best* that we have done, for young people of all ages, from eight to 80.

I do not expect you to slavishly follow either these ten steps or the techniques included in the appendix. I am happy for you to read, discover, play with, understand and apply as many or any of these things in any way that is right for you, knowing that you are unconsciously taking in, analyzing, filtering, shaping and integrating all these things into the patterns you already understand and do.

And by the way, there is no particular order that you need to do them in. Rather, the order was arranged by my wish to create a mnemonic that would enable you to remember, carry and unpack all these ideas, wherever you are and whatever you are doing.

In the index and throughout the book, the core elements are in capitals. Their initials make up a mnemonic:

I CAN BECOME WHAT I'M BEST ABLE
AND THEN GO BEYOND

Above all – having fun!

Several years ago, when I was MD of a Human Resorces company, we were looking for a new bank to deal with. We went through the usual research and eventually drew up a shortlist of three possibles, where we felt the values fit for the people and the bank would work best with our own. We sent each bank a copy of our strategic business plan, at least a week before the meeting. We wanted them to have as much information as they might need to choose whether they wanted to work with us also.

Came the day and we had three one-hour meetings scheduled. Our likely favourite was in the last meeting. We asked each other plenty of questions and everything seemed to be moving towards us choosing each other. Finally, the banker pushed his chair back and, with a serious look on his face said "there's just one other thing…" Our hearts sank and we looked from one to another wondering what disappointment was coming next.

"I've read hundreds of business plans and I must say I have never come across one like yours" he said. "In fact there's one word you've used in your plan which we've never seen in a plan before, and you've used it five times…..it's the word 'fun'…we want to be your bankers."

And I can't imagine it being any other way. No matter how successful we are, or how much money we earn, no value can be put on the pleasure, enjoyment and fun we have in the work we do. In fact, our clients have so much fun that it doesn't even seem like work. If you're not having fun, what are you having and how long do you want to wait?

Whether working with individuals, groups or teams, there is always a point that is reached, where they start to laugh. For some it may be relief, or even release. For others, it may be positivity or even finding what they always believed was there, or was possible and now it can be.

I was driving my son home on his thirteenth birthday.

"What does it feel like to be a teenager?"

"Well, actually, it doesn't seem much different than yesterday, only I'm worried."

"What are you worried about?" I asked.

"I'm worried about losing being a child, Dad."

"Don't ever lose the child in you, Mark. Far too many people seem to reach an age when something inside them says 'it's time to start being an adult' and overnight they seem to age. Keep the child inside you, love it and nurture it. The child inside you is curious and ever hungry to learn. The child will keep you young and you can live a long and healthy life. Most of all, the child inside you can always have fun."

Now this was rich, because it took me 45 years to rediscover and release the child in me, and as each day passes I am getting to know and love and have more fun with my inner child...

Chapter 2

What is your Mission or Purpose in Life?

Lasting levels of CHANGE

ASK YOURSELF THIS? For what purpose, for myself, do I exist on this earth? Have you ever asked that? What do you believe to be your Mission in life in general? Robert Dilts, one of the great NLP teachers of our time has evolved the concept of logical levels of change. They form a pyramid of contexts for choices and behaviours in our lives:

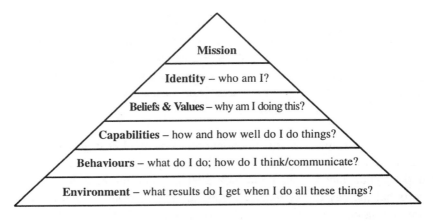

The higher up the pyramid that we make changes in any aspect of our lives, the greater the overall effect. The first four levels influence all of our behaviours. The results we get are experienced in our immediate environment, in which we interact with other people. It is hard to change other people. We all have our own will and model of the world. If you're not getting the results you expect, or want, try different behaviours. The best and most lasting way is to make change at the highest level.

So what is your mission in life? How do all the things you do fit with, facilitate or reinforce it? What is your philosophy in life, or in work? Does anything you are doing go counter to that mission or your stated values? If it does, at the very least, you may be accumulating unconscious stress.

So what's the secret? The secret is in your self. You have all the skills, ability and potential you need. Whether you recognize that you have the specific capabilities or not, the way that you are made means that you have the observation, assimilation, decision and implementation skills to watch and model what works beyond question for others.

After mission comes identity. After you ask yourself the question "for what purpose do I exist" ask yourself "who am I?" Pretty quickly you can define yourself in terms of a set of Values, Beliefs and Attitudes. When we talk about goals for your life later, you will automatically set these in the context of your values, attitudes and beliefs.

What's missing? Is it based on a limiting belief – "oh I couldn't do that because....?" You have independence of thought and action. Life is a voyage of self-discovery. When you will have read this book, what positive thoughts and aspirations do you already sense that you want to have achieved? When you have seen your success, what are you saying to yourself now? That's right....

Ego involvement means emotional attachment. Let it go and learn (later) how to plan and program your success. Put this out into the future and let your unconscious mind look after it, while the conscious mind sorts out the day-to-day details against the predetermined criteria. We are not talking about sloth or procrastination. Professionalism and diligence in the nuts and bolts of all you do in work of any kind is a fundamental prerequisite of success. Meanwhile the unconscious mind creates the 'x-factor' of differentiated success. The conscious mind assembles the data, the unconscious mind notices the patterns, makes the connections and guides your judgment.

We are all one with the universe. Preoccupation with self takes from the rest. "True self-interest teaches selflessness. Heaven and earth endure because they are not simply selfish but exist in behalf of all creation. The wise leader, knowing this, keeps egocentricity in check and by doing so becomes even more effective." (John Heider, *The Tao of Leadership*).

You can be a leader in every aspect of your life. The calm, quiet leader is best, always believing that there is more to learn, more to know. For the now, all that matters is the now. Visualize and program your future and your unconscious mind will sort that out. The past can't be changed and the future is unknowable. You can only do and be the best you can be.

"Prosperity is not defined by money alone; it encompasses time, love, success, joy, comfort, beauty and wisdom... Know what your beliefs are, they can be changed in *this* moment. The power that created you has given you the power to create your own experiences. You can change!" (Louise Hay, *Love Yourself, Heal Your Life*).

Louise Hay also says that the power of the future is in this moment. Féar, of failure, rejection, or whatever, is a future emotion. It may be based on emotional experiences from the past and you may feel the emotion in the present. It is an emotion about something that has not happened yet, and may not. So why worry? Live your life in the present moment and start to visualize your inevitable success and, having done so, enjoy the pleasure of anticipation as you diligently build that success right now.

The Presuppositions of NLP

You can have gained so many insights and meanings in yourself when you will have read this book. Many powerful presuppositions, or fundamental beliefs about ourselves have been identified in NLP. These are summarized in detail in the Appendix. Try them all on to gain an even better understanding of yourself and the possibilities for others.

• Filters – values and beliefs

The filters through which all sensory input are processed include primarily our values and beliefs. These are the basis of our patterns of behaviour, whether resourceful or not.   Having understood these patterns, you can then move towards the goals and achievable outcomes you would like to set yourself.

When we're working with values and beliefs we often uncover limiting decisions and beliefs from childhood. In our experience of life coaching, when we have helped a client make new choices to remove or modify these they can begin to see a way of achieving success. Understanding and applying the tools and techniques of NLP can lead to a state of self-mastery. When this has been achieved, we examine the strategies applied in a particular aspect of the person's life where they would like to achieve change. Unpacking these strategies, reviewing them and modifying them as appropriate can lead to more resourceful behaviour.

Values are your most strongly held beliefs. They will consciously or unconsciously drive many of your behaviours. If you find yourself in conflict with others, or yourself, it may very well be based on a fundamental challenge to your values.

Exercise – Determining your values

What are your values in life? For what purposes for yourself do you work?

Choose one of these, or something else significant in your life such as relationships and ask yourself why is this important for you? Keep asking yourself the question, over and over. Write down whatever comes into mind. You may have five or six values or more, which emerge. Some might include financial gain, others success, yet others fulfillment or respect, etc. What is really, really important for you, and you alone?

Refine your list. Reflect on those values. What do you feel about them? Listen for whether they appear to be driven away from a negative place or towards a positive outcome.

Living your life values

The following day repeat the latter part of the above exercise.

Now you can be confident you have your core values in life or in other things, do the following:

In your own time, place and space, mark out three positions on the floor, perhaps with three blank sheets of paper. Put them no more than a pace apart, wherever seems or feels right for you.

Sitting comfortably in a chair, take the most important value, or the first that comes to mind. Think of a time when you know this value was present in what you were doing, feeling or being. Be in that time now and see, hear and feel what you were experiencing at that time. Use the power of submodalities (see later) to really be in that moment.

Do the same for each of the other two values. Find a way to break the state, by doing or thinking something banal, or imagine a blank screen in your mind.

Now, repeat the process of returning to that time where you were in your first value. Fill yourself up with the experience and, when it is at its height or the strongest, step onto the first sheet of paper.

Keep hold of the feelings and images inside you and think of the time when you experienced your second value. When you are filled up, step onto the second sheet of paper.

Repeat the process for your third value, while keeping hold of the feelings from your second value. Step onto the third sheet of paper.

Break the state and step away from the sheets of paper. When you are ready, repeat the process, stepping through your core values.

Do this as many times as you wish until the experience of associating into your values becomes automatic.

Now, wherever, or whenever you are, you can imagine your three pieces of paper on the floor ahead of you and walk through your core values.

So now, think of a time when you needed to be at your best. As you think of that time now, walk through your core values and notice the changes you may already be experiencing. Maybe you are seeing things in a new light now, feeling more focused, speaking positively to yourself inside.

Finally, plan or review a decision you wish to make. Fill your mind with the factors to consider and then walk through your values, knowing that the answer that pops into your mind is right for you.

Now you can decide with the conviction of your core values, go forward to a real or imagined time in the future, when you are making an important decision. As you see, hear or feel yourself, step into that picture and having walked through your values, did you notice the changes you are experiencing now?

(This exercise is based on and typical of the original work of Robert Dilts).

• *Values, Beliefs and Meta Programs*

As well as our values and beliefs, our filters include what are called in NLP, Meta Programs. These are patterns and programs that were laid down in early life, which have become part of the structure through which we process and unconsciously interpret our whole lives, and everything that happens to us and that we experience.

Some people believe success and failure are a matter of luck. Others believe in the value of a proven methodology, religiously adhered to. Yet others, myself included, believe we are masters of our own destiny while we are in this life.

Success and failure are defined by you and you alone. You set the parameters. If you have been concerned about how others see you, or to be measured by others' measures of performance, how much more can you do when you set the rules of the game. However you see others, or imagine that they see you, you can only process these perceptions through your own model of the world.

If you believe that you can be successful, or, better still, if you believe you are successful, that is all that matters (assuming you are applying rational thought).

Values

Each of us is made up of a set of values and beliefs. What is your values set for life; for relationships; for work? Are your values 'towards' or 'away from' values. When you talk of success, as a value, are you, deep inside, moving towards success, or away from failure? When you have understood your values set; when you have changed or modified these, substantially towards and based on positive language, then you have increased your prospect of success.

We can all choose, whether or not we wish to change. Because you want to succeed, do everything you can to change your internal dialogue and your beliefs to positive... permanently.

We have introduced here the concept of 'logical levels of change'. As we move more towards mission and identity; as we move more towards spirit and abstraction, so we move more towards our higher self. It is in the higher self that we find our essential morality and goodness and the highest motives for achievement, fulfillment and happiness. Are your values aligned with each other?

As you look at your values set, which is the most abstract? Ideally your most important value should be the most abstract. As you look down the list, does each successive value support the fulfillment of the next higher, or highest? Consider the underlying motivation for each value. Does it support what you really want? Are there any apparent or actual conflicts between your values? Is there any one value that on its own could prevent you having another at the same time?

So, if you have a value of success, are you prepared to achieve this at any price, such as damage to or inhibition of, personal relationships.

When you have identified a coherent, positive set of values for your life and work, check them against each other for possible conflict. If it is there, at the very least it may cause internal stress, or lead to misjudgments, as one value tries to override another.

Beliefs

Your belief set is almost equally important and part of your personal makeup. Are any of your beliefs in conflict with any of your values? If you had a value of Success, how could you achieve that if you also held a limiting belief in your ability to achieve success? (It may be that the success value was 'away from' failure. If your unconscious mind was preoccupied with failure, it might have used all its skills and capabilities to deliver that, in one form or another. When the last thing someone thinks about before hitting a golf ball is a fear about going out of bounds, should they be surprised if that is where it goes?)

Understand your values and beliefs and make them only positive. Use the section at the end of this chapter, now, to determine your belief set, as far as you are able, and your values set if not already done. You can also identify where any negative beliefs came from and, when you no longer need them, give them back to where they belong.

We may have personal and working beliefs. When they are set in our personality, they are ours and ours alone in respect of our actual, planned or consequential behaviours. A tobacco company's shares may be the most attractive investment in the stock market, at a given point in time, but if you have a value that ethically or morally goes against tobacco products, you may at least unconsciously find yourself experiencing conflict in considering the investment. This could affect your judgment and choices.

Some people have had limiting beliefs that have held them back in the past. Identify and remove your limiting beliefs and see your success improve. So, if you knew someone who had wanted desperately to succeed but had a limiting belief in their ability to do so (such as "I never have any luck"), they may have persistently inhibited their own potential, even if they rationally and consciously wanted to succeed. Once the limiting belief and its source was identified and removed, suddenly their performance and prospects for success are improved.

Most important, in your life in general, take on a belief of excellence. Have confidence (not arrogance) in your beliefs – or change them!

What are your expectations for yourself? Your beliefs will be fundamental to these. When you are totally in control of your self and your internal state, then you will dramatically increase your success ratio.

If you still have difficulty in replacing negative patterns with positive ones, look inside yourself and identify the stoppers to change, such as limiting beliefs, or negative value patterns, if they are present. Use one of the appropriate techniques later, to change or remove these.

What I am recommending in this book, is a mix of powerful, positive, NLP based and other techniques to improve your personal performance and deliver the success you have dreamed of.

We wish to avoid any possibility that a negative value or a limiting belief may override a rational strategy or decision, by creating a negative state, such as fear. In addition, we can all learn from past mistakes. I am not talking about an emotion driven error of judgment. You can obviate these, through all the personal change work discussed in this book.

From time to time, in the past, people have made simple, human errors. How did they occur? What was the set of circumstances? Was the person who made the error of judgment or commitment unresourceful at the time, e.g. due to tiredness, or domestic difficulties? With the benefit of hindsight and the raft of personal techniques written about here, how can we learn and avoid the possibility of error in the future.

It is also important to be realistic. Someone, who got an error out of proportion to the circumstances or consequences, may have been unnecessarily harsh on themselves, maybe leading to creation or exacerbation of an unresourceful, emotional state. Rationalization, pre and post (explaining away failure) may also be unproductive. If it led to self-deception, it could also exacerbate the prevailing condition. By balancing the rational and the emotional, the left and right brain we can enhance our prospects of success, having lost all thought of failure.

Meta Programs

Our meta programs are a set of filters, through which we receive, interpret and understand our experiences. Typical programs include whether we are introvert or extravert, thinker or feeler, largely towards or away from, etc. in a given set of circumstances. Recognize your own meta-programs, using the section at the back. Change them or make them work for you, as you think appropriate.

As you may have recognized from two of the examples given above, the MBTI™ (Myers-Briggs Type Indicators) profiles are part of our meta-programs. The other MBTI pairs are intuitor/sensor and judger/perceiver. These and some other psychometric assessment methodologies are based on the work of Karl Jung.

Meta program analysis can be carried out faster and can go much beyond MBTI and other psychometric profiling. Some NLP analysts have identified up to 60 different meta programs. We use much less than this number in the appendix, but sufficient for you to identify the major filter set, which with your values and beliefs can be used to understand, explain and also as the basis of modification for, your personality and thereby personal success. The most important thing is that any change you make should be an informed choice, recognizing the positive gains and new possibilities, which can flow from these.

As I will assert over and over, you are at cause not effect. You can be at cause in everything that you do. As you realize this, becoming calmer and with greater self-mastery, you can dramatically influence your success in life. As you go forward to a time when you have made your own choices and owned the consequences of your soundly based decisions, how many new possibilities for gain in all aspects of your life are you seeing?

In summary, identify your values and beliefs and recognize your meta programs. Change them if you want and/or make them work for you. By understanding them alongside your rational behaviours you can succeed and have fun doing it. What's more, don't be surprised if other people notice the positive changes that are taking place in your whole personality, and relationships with other people.

Capabilities – how and how well do I do things?

Behaviours – what do I do; how do I think/communicate?

Environment – what results do I get when I do all these things?

• **Capabilities**

The next logical level of change is Capabilities. This is about the skills you have in any aspect of your life, the level of skill and how well you use them.

Remember, the point about Logical Levels is that the higher the level at which you make lasting change, the more pervasive it will be.

Competencies, Strengths and Opportunities for Improvement

In a competitive world, many more organizations are doing an audit of competencies. Apart from helping to place round pegs in round holes, it more importantly identifies people with potential for growth. Both the organization and the individual need to continue to grow, adapt and evolve, in order to keep pace with the game.

As individuals, we have a set of competencies for every aspect of our lives. We can develop new ones as well as enhancing the existing. A presupposition of NLP is that if one person can do something excellently well, another can learn to do it. We all use similar combinations of thought and muscular movements. Even the ape has over 95% of the same genes as us humans.

When you can believe in your limitless potential and the ability to change and grow continuously, then life gives you the opportunity to see yourself as you can be. Every experience in life, is an opportunity to learn. What is the message inherent in the new or changed situation?

Some talk of strengths and weaknesses. I see what are described as weaknesses by some, as undeveloped opportunities. Among those we are now growing are insight and intuition. Insight is literally looking within to find an answer. When we restricted ourselves to conscious thought, we used only 5% of our mind's potential.

Through study of Eastern philosophy, many Westerners have sought the path to the higher self. Don Juan tried mind-altering drugs. Our minds are part of a greater consciousness. The paths we are beginning to tread are old paths that we lost thousands of years before.

Intuition lies within the unconscious. It literally means inner learning. This and the other specific traits to optimize your life are a function of your beliefs and your emotional state at the time. As you opened your mind to limitless possibilities and cleared the emotional blocks from the way, did you not begin to see the skills you already possessed? What is your desired trait-set, so that you are in control of your life and can be your very best? Having identified and closed the gaps, you can then see the whole. You can learn character traits or understand or change what's already within you.

A singular mindset could work against you. Stubbornness and single mindedness may have produced results for you in the past, and how many opportunities did you overlook in the process? Your unconscious mind records and remembers everything. Once you have found the way to tap into the void, where all understanding lies, then you can change anything that hasn't worked for you in the past.

Understand, for example, the source of your emotions, enhance the positives, change or remove the negatives, change or remove your limiting beliefs.

Representation systems

We all have a set of representation systems, which are part of our unique make-up. Each individual may have a primary or dominant representation system that biases the filtering process. The rep systems are: visual, auditory, kinesthetic (including physical and emotional feeling), olfactory and gustatory. Every experience you have, or memory you have stored uses one or more of these. The more we use to store a memory, the stronger it may be.

Use all your senses when you are assessing a situation or opportunity – look, see, hear, feel, smell and taste what is going on. I teach dyslexics how to read, spell, or write. Very often they were running an inefficient strategy, such as trying to spell through their feelings. A fifteen-year-old boy learned how to read and spell properly in just two hours. Can you imagine how many new choices open up for you when you have a similar experience?

Learn to do all that you can do by visualization, touch and intuition, as athletes and sports people do, finding their way into 'the zone', where they can be in 'flow'.

Insight has another connotation, for we can all make internal representations, especially pictures. When you have visualized a future memory, seen, felt and heard all that will happen, through your own eyes and internal senses, stepped out of the picture and put it out into your timeline, think of the limitless opportunities you can create. Look within yourself and see yourself as you really are, in your most positive light, or better still, as you really can be.

Nobody makes you do or feel anything. We do it ourselves. Understand that and change any unresourceful state to positive.

Some see life as a game of winners and losers. Winning and losing are an attitude created inside our own minds. Both are the consequences of our attitudes and beliefs and the steps we took. Remember the law of requisite variety – the person who is most capable of adapting to change will end up controlling the system, for themselves and in their own set of beliefs. When you have set out the goals, the rules, the strategy and the method; when you see yourself as you really are and see everything as an opportunity which only you can choose for yourself, then you will fulfill your potential. Start now...yes, right now!

Language & Behaviours

NLP is fundamentally about how we language and behave. When I was young, I thought I had discovered an original thought, when I postulated that everybody else might be the product of my imagination (or I theirs). Later I found many others had come to the same conclusion. It is part of awareness of self and beingness.

Rene Descartes said 'I think, therefore I am'. Chomsky invented *eprime*, the English language without any conjugation of the word 'to be'. Now, I realize that everything in the world is a product of my own mind. If anything doesn't happen as a representation inside me, then it doesn't happen for me.

When I do not believe in, or cannot create the state of losing in my mind, it does not happen for me. The mind is so clever and so powerful that we can create internal experiences so vivid that we cannot tell the difference between imagination and reality (hence 'mind-altering' drugs). When you have used the combination of techniques in this book to remove unresourceful behaviours and limiting beliefs, replacing them with limitless potential and positivity, there is no limit to what you can achieve.

Everything we do is represented in language and behaviours. Consciously or unconsciously we can represent and store every experience in models constructed in language. For example, the word sad, for me, conjures up a unique collection of memories and feelings, conscious and unconscious. Some people have worked on stripping away the structure of language from clients' experience and memory. Eventually they get to deep-seated emotions and 'prime concerns'.

NLP compares the surface structure of language and behaviour with the deep structure. 'The map is not the territory'. (The surface representation is not the whole person, we are always much more than that). However, in some senses the map is the territory. What the therapist, the client and each of us experience at the surface may often be the only clues to what is really going on deep inside. 'Where did that state come from'?

In NLP, Bandler and Grinder analyzed language and constructed the concept of 'Meta programs', which others have taken forward. There are many subdivisions of Meta programs, which can be discerned in the language patterns of the individual to give insights into the unique patterning of their deep structure. For example, some people are driven away from failure, while others drive themselves towards success. Offer the former a bonus or beat the latter with a stick and you may not get the response you expect, depending on your own patterning. The meta program questions later will help you discern some of your own and others most important patterns.

Based on their work primarily with Virginia Satir and Milton Erickson, they also constructed the 'Meta model', which 'chunks down' to precision and 'Milton model' which chunks up to more hypnotic language patterns.

We will also discuss MOPS and MONS and the possible positive changes you are already making. Many people have had an internal voice, or internal dialogue. This is called auditory digital and is catalogued alongside the other representation systems.

If you have ever had internal dialogue, how did it speak to you, or how did it behave? Did you ever come across someone who experienced the 'inner saboteur'? This was the voice that crept in to make someone irrationally frightened, guilty, jealous or whatever, when there was absolutely no need to be. It came from old patterns that were based on 'all good things must come to an end' and similar negative and self-destructive programs.

We shall come back to representation systems, when we have understood the power of submodalities to 'describe' our inner representations and especially as a medium for lasting change. In the meantime, understand the power of language.

As you visualize new opportunities and choices in your life, make them bigger, bolder, brighter and more powerful inside. Add in the infinite potential of empowering, positive language and you may already be noticing the many ways in which you are changing.

How do you describe yourself to yourself? "I am a great person/lover/athlete/mum/dad/etc., who uses a combination of great skill, and understanding, together with intuition, insight, vision and creativity to produce success beyond what I might once have believed possible..."

• *Behaviours*

These are about what you do, at any time, consciously or unconsciously. You do not need to be aware of these to have a possible impact on those around you. However, as you begin to be aware of and understand these better, noticing possible modifications or improvements, trying them out and noticing the benefits and effects, so you can move towards being your best.

Behaviours are also about how you think and how you communicate, consciously and unconsciously, verbally and non-verbally.

Many, if not most people, attempt to create lasting change at the behavioural level. We talk about behavioural psychology for example.

Take the example of someone who really wants to give up smoking. First, they try and just stop. If this works and lasts, all well and good. Stopping buying cigarettes is a behavioural change for example. Maybe this doesn't work. Then the smoker goes to the doctor or the chemist, to get chewing gum or patches. This is another behavioural change. This may work for some more people and for all these making change at this level, it can be an effort of willpower, until the new habits are installed.

How did the person start to smoke in the first place? I remember watching a biopic of Lauren Bacall. When she was young, she was much influenced by and modeled herself on Bette Davis, and started to smoke as a result.

For some people, the habit of smoking is anchored to their image (or identity) and for others to their values (e.g. my parent smoked so that's ok). In order to achieve lasting change in a behaviour, therefore, especially one that has become anchored at a higher level, it is ideal to effect the change at the highest level practicable. For example, by the time a smoker was forty or fifty, say, the effects of their smoking could have pervaded many aspects of their life and/or relationships.

• *Environment*

Every behaviour happens in an environment, including when the person is on their own. We shall spend more time on context and reframes later. Environment is about the results you get and the effect your behaviours have. Change the environment and you get different results.

In summary therefore, logical levels of change have a number of potential uses: they can be used to help you decide at what level the change needs to take place in order to have lasting results; they can also be used for planning and problem solving.

If you have a task to perform, a plan to make or a problem to solve, you could 'walk it through' the levels in a logical order, at each stage asking the appropriate questions as in the pyramid above.

Indeed, Dilts would suggest that you physically walk through the levels. My own preference is to start with mission, walk through to environment and then back up again. Through this approach you can gain many insights.

What are you really ASPIRING to?

So what do you really aspire to? What is your mission in life? Step outside of yourself and look at yourself and your life. Go forward to the end of your life. Look back with your own eyes and ask yourself "what have I achieved in my life that made a significant difference, or that people can remember me by"?

Have a mission, which is a clear, enduring, guiding light or beacon in your life...something you feel can be very much part of you...when you say it to yourself, it sounds right. Create an internal representation that seems to capture your mission in your life. Take it out into the future, to the end of that time, now. Let your unconscious mind decide. Leave it out there and come back to the now. Write it down and look at it every day.

Here's an example. My mission is to create an environment in which people's natural talents can flourish.

What is your mission in your work? In how many ways does this fit with your overall mission in life?

The 4Square exercise for NAVIGATING through life

Some years ago, I had lost my job and had no idea what I was going to do next. One day, I took a sheet of paper and divided it into four. In the first quadrant, I listed all the things I enjoyed doing. In the second, I wrote all the things I was good at. Then, I listed everything that I had the capability of doing which made money. Finally, I wrote down what was important to me in my life, in relation to my mission. I then crossed out everything that didn't appear on all four lists.

Practical exercise – making the most of your capabilities

- Take a sheet of A4 paper. Divide it into quarters.

- Head up the first box 'What do I enjoy doing?'

- Head up the second box 'What am I good at?'

- Head up the third box 'What makes money?'

- Head up the fourth box 'What fits with my mission?'

- Now, without editing, fill in each box.

When you have finished, cross out everything, which is not in all four boxes.

You will be left with a list of only those things, which fit with your mission, you enjoy doing, you are good at and can earn you money. Why would you want to do anything else? Open your mind for one more moment and see if there isn't anything else you feel would sound right in all four lists?

Life is a series of choices – for you.

Chapter 3

Why and where would you want to be your best?

In BUSINESS

WE LIVE IN a stressful age. It is often said that there are no longer jobs for life. In my time alone, the business of the Western economies has changed out of all recognition. The 'first' industrial revolution started in Europe and moved us from a farming to a manufacturing economy. The second industrial revolution could be said to be the arrival of the technological age. And where do we date that from? Punched cards for machine operation arrived between the two World Wars. I was studying computer programming on early 'analogue' computers in 1966. The PC was invented in the 1970s and the first commercial IBM PCs were on widespread sale in the early 1980s.

Which was more significant: the invention of 'management' (credited variously, but Deutsche Bank may have pioneered it on a large scale 80 or so years ago); the transformation to service economies (facilitated by machines, mainly from about 50 years ago); the two World Wars (which helped create massive manufacturing capabilities in the US, Europe and Japan); the Space Race and its effect on technology; etc?

Over 100 years ago, at the turn of the 19th century, 90% of people were self-employed. It is forecast that by 2050, 90% will be self-employed again (including short-term contracts).

Many people still have jobs. A growing proportion is self-employed or work from home. Whether we have realized it yet or not, we have much more choice than ever before – as well as much more challenge. We are also having to be more flexible and adaptable.

When I was a teenager, my Dad said "get yourself a professional qualification, it will be a meal ticket for life." It wasn't. I qualified as an Accountant, Banker, Stockbroker and Treasurer; had a pretty successful career, mainly in Financial Services for 15 years, was made redundant and had to reinvent myself, first as a HR and recruitment professional and now as a motivational speaker and performance coach.

Many of my peers have retired. For me it hasn't always been a bundle of fun, but now I'm having the best time of my life, especially doing the things that are in this book. For 15 years or more, I researched personal development methods both for myself and the organizations I worked in. Not only is there now more change and challenge than ever before, but there is now much more opportunity.

So, whether you are in business for yourself or for others, this is one domain of your life where you really want to be your best.

Take interviews. What is it and when does it happen that young people learn to fear interviews? Whether you are wanting a place at college or a job, isn't this one of those times when you really want to be your best?

Were you ever in a bar, a club or a pub as a young person? And what do you do in those places, other than have a drink, or dance? Socialize? What is socialize? How would you explain it to a Martian? Oh, you meet people and talk with them. Who are these people? Friends? So, were you ever out with friends and maybe a stranger joined the group...and is it possible that one time you met one of these strangers and by the end of the evening you were getting on really well with them?

So how did you do that? You talked to them...you listened to them and noticed what they did, consciously or unconsciously...you asked them questions...open questions...you created superb rapport between you, naturally and spontaneously...

So what is an interview? Who do you meet in an interview? A stranger? They want to meet your best self, not a bundle of nerves. They don't sit around all day waiting to meet no-hopers just to pass the time. By the time they meet you, they're sure you're the sort of person they want. And if you really, really want the job or the college place, don't you want to be your very best? And supposing you don't get the job or place and you were the best you could be? That's OK. There was someone more suitable and you wouldn't want to be a square peg in a round hole for three to five years, would you?

There are any number of situations in work or in business where you want to be your best. A growing proportion of our clients are people suffering from stress at work. The thing is that they are often suffering from stress in general. We can look to technology, the explosion of emails, fear of redundancy, etc as the reasons for stress and these are all triggers.

There are many good counselors and coaches skilled at handling clients with stress. The 'best of the best' of traditional approaches is based on a cognitive dissociative approach. The client is helped to discover the stress 'factors' in their lives and to make decisions to remove or better manage these. These are the 'demand' factors.

We use a different, NLP based approach. The sources of stress are what I call the 'supply' factors. These were largely laid down in childhood. What happens is that triggers in our life or work can stimulate the original pattern, causing stressful behaviour. When these supply factors are identified, they can be released or 'reframed' and suddenly the client can easily handle and cope with those formerly high stress triggers, if they are still there at all.

So what are the most important factors in Business and the circumstances when you would most like to be your best?

It starts with communication. Any relationship is based on communication. It starts with rapport. Did you know that you make a lasting impression on someone in the first four seconds after you meet them? And, for example, in an interview, after five minutes, even the best candidate will not change the interviewer's impression.

Successful businesses rely on sound communication. Miscommunication can lead to any number of problems from missed opportunities and misunderstandings to conflict and failure to deliver.

Everyone has choices. Communication is at an unconscious, as well as a conscious level. NLP is often thought to be mainly about Rapport and Communication. Certainly, by understanding all the patterns and processes, tools and techniques, you can learn how to create superb rapport with anyone, at business or at play.

The thing is, it's about understanding the other person's model of the world....and your own. Rapport and communication, are about engaging at an unconscious, as well as a conscious level. Some consultants and trainers train people how to consciously be aware of patterns of language and behaviour, to mirror and match, to create better rapport and communication.

So how does the superb communicator, or sales person do it? Many people would think these superstars were born communicators. NLP is about understanding and modeling excellent languaging and behaviour. At first you may do it consciously and deliberately and in due course, it becomes unconsciously programmed into your natural patterns.

We shall discuss later, the process by which we learn anything, from unconscious incompetence to unconscious competence.

Being your best in business involves being your best self whenever you choose to be and, in due course, without even thinking about it. This can be based on the tools and techniques of NLP and also an understanding of the components of Emotional Intelligence. By modeling and installing superb behaviour in yourself using NLP, do not be surprised when you can naturally and spontaneously create rapport, reproduce world class behaviours and demonstrate emotional intelligence.

The key areas we work on with clients, through *How to be Your Best* are also those aspects of business that you can most effectively influence in your own behaviours and practice of these things:

- Selling and Negotiation;
- Rapport and Communication;
- Meeting and interview skills;
- Leadership and People Management;
- Managing conflict;
- Managing stress.

EVERYWHERE else in your life

One of the things I constantly come across in both the workplace and in general, is a growing concern about 'work/life balance'.

I remember when I was at the HR and recruitment consultancy and was interviewing prospective partners for law firms. Two of the repeating patterns from men were: "I don't see my kids during the week, as I leave before they are up and arrive home after they are in bed"; and "I don't want to still be doing this when I am 45".

In the same vein, I was listening to a radio interview of two newly ordained priests: one Church of England; and one Catholic. What they had in common was that they were both in their late 40s and both had given up highly successful careers in business. The first had been a commercial lawyer and the second, Head of Marketing for Europe. The comment of the second was representative of both: "I was in a top hotel in Europe, reflecting on my success, how much I earned and the lifestyle I had, when I found myself saying 'Is this all there is to life?'"

Recently, many mainly men have taken early retirement, often as the result of 'downsizing' or 'rightsizing'. They are drawing an early pension and enjoying a comfortable lifestyle, with new choices. Many of these have not fully planned this next major phase of their lives. They may run out of things to do. One of the encouraging signs, however, is that as some of them look to fill the growing gap, they are turning to voluntary roles, working with charitable organizations and part-time posts in smaller and medium size enterprises that cannot afford a whole-time post in that aspect of the business (e.g. finance).

I was brought up with a 'three boxes' model for life: education; work; and retirement. Life is no longer in three boxes.

Governments are becoming increasingly concerned about the aging population and, while statutory retirement ages tended to come down towards the end of the last century, now they are more likely to go up. As well as which, people are living longer, remaining fitter longer and not necessarily wanting to stop work.

And the idea that people entered the world of work at 16, 18 or 21, depending on whether one stayed on in higher education, is being replaced by a model of 'lifetime learning'. Many organizations no longer see their employees remaining for their entire careers, or even long periods; they are also more reluctant to engage in a great deal of formal training. The preference is to pass the responsibility for personal development to the individual, sometimes supporting this with a cash contribution, a menu of training modules, a voucher system, or what have you.

So, NLP, an understanding of emotional intelligence and the other components of how to be your best are becoming more and more relevant in life in general. When you can improve your rapport and communication skills, your understanding of other people's models of the world, their patterns of language and behaviour and the many new choices you can have in creating new relationships or enhancing existing relationships, then your quality of life in general will surely grow. And then, there are all the many possibilities in relation to how you manage your own personal growth and development and your relationship with yourself...

With CHILDREN AND FAMILY

Life goes in cycles. While traditional family models and patterns of marriage appear to have broken down, at least for now, there is a growing undercurrent for us to return to more traditional values. Look at the growth of celibacy in, e.g. the US. Then you might have noticed the growing number of especially young people living on their own, the increasing suicide rate, especially in young males and the growing delinquency, disaffection and learning difficulties, also especially in young males.

There are many theories as to why these things are happening. My own view is that the configuration of the average male brain is changing. I don't know whether this is genetic or environmental, in the latter respect whether it is the product of changed hormone patterns in the diet or changing beliefs in society at large, which have meant that working women are now much more the norm, including a growing proportion in senior positions.

We could go on to observe the growth in single parent families, usually headed by a woman and a concern that many boys are missing a strong male influence in their lives. On the other hand, we might also momentarily reflect on the 'iceberg' of child and other abuse that has clearly been taking place for years and it is more often than not men that perpetrate this.

In relative terms the world is no more challenging for our children than it was for us at the same age. They were born into a highly technological environment, they are growing up with this as the norm and, if anything, it is their parents who are having more difficulty adapting. My reference earlier to the problem in being able to program the video is probably more pertinent to adults than young people, who seem to be incredibly flexible and adaptable (except where adults get in the way!)

In absolute terms, the world is becoming inexorably more complex. There is an exponential growth in data and facts to cope with. The wonder of the Internet brings with it a mountain of emails. There is more stress, whether imposed or self-imposed. How soon will the organism rebel?

So what can we do for our children and our families and how can NLP and these other skills help?

First, we can be more empowering. Let me be clear what I mean. Some parents think that children should be totally free to express themselves and discover boundaries for themselves. Research of older 'young people' in their twenties for example, consistently throws up the pattern that they wish their parents had been firmer, set and maintained stronger and consistently reinforced boundaries for behaviour.

My definition of empowerment in both business and personal life is 'creating the environment where people's natural talent can flourish'. In parenthood it would be proposing firm guidelines while leaving room for young people to learn from their mistakes and being there as appropriate for counsel and support afterwards. The single most important lesson I learned a long time ago is that the one thing that matters to young people above all is knowing with certainty that they are loved by someone they love and respect themselves.

Now, I am not advocating teaching children, family, relatives or friends the patterns of NLP unless they specifically ask. Instead, it is better to be a good role model and to promote and engage in discussion, so that people can apply their natural curiosity towards wanting to find out and know more. In this respect, my partner has adopted a sound approach to her own son. He has become more and more curious about the things she does, especially the NLP and other personal growth tools and patterns she uses. As a result, he has borrowed and bought books and courses, which he has integrated into his own study and relaxation time, gradually wanting to know and integrate these things into the positive patterns of his life.

The most important thing therefore is to be a sound role model. As you will learn, practice and become more curious about the patterns, processes, tools and techniques in this book, integrating them naturally and easily into your own lives, you can become a working role model for anyone who notices how you grow and change and wants to follow a similar path.

We can never give too much time and attention to our children and our families. By understanding and practicing the things in this book, you can change and improve your communication and the quality of relationships. You can become calmer and more resourceful in yourself, with inevitable consequential benefits for those around you.

And as you are being your very best, those that are around you can grow up being able to choose or be their best whenever they wish also.

In all your OTHER RELATIONSHIPS

When I'm doing *How to be Your Best* for 17 year olds, I often tease them with the possibility of practicing these techniques on their friends and especially prospective partners. "Whatever you do, I wouldn't want you to even think of trying these things out when you want to meet or engage with someone of the opposite sex, or a prospective love partner". (The unconscious mind cannot process a negative).

I am at great pains, as we shall cover later, to stress that we must always respect the other person's model of the world and, especially as we are trying out or using rapport and communication skills, it is even more important to notice and be aware of the effect you are having on the whole of the person's neuro-physiology, take account and modify your behaviours accordingly. Including 'backing off' if appropriate. If your practicing these skills becomes invasive to the person concerned, you may damage rather than enhance a relationship.

Nevertheless, to take just one example, did you ever hear someone relating that it had seemed like they had been 'talking at cross purposes' with another person. You will already have realized that NLP is as much about how we language and communicate as about other behaviours (including how we communicate with ourselves...). Through understanding all these things, you can not only improve the quality and 'receivability' of your communication in all your relationships, you can also dramatically improve what and how you receive the response you get back. Indeed, as you will have noticed, one of the presuppositions of NLP is that "the meaning of your communication is in the response you get."

In MEETINGS, INTERVIEWS, SELLING AND SOCIALIZING

We've mentioned meetings and interviews above and of course these aren't limited to our working situations. We are formally or informally meeting people every day. What's more, whether we intend to or not, we are implicitly 'selling' ourselves all the time, when we are in the company of, especially strangers and new acquaintances. We can call this socializing and wouldn't you want to improve the quality of your socializing? As implied above, quality time is increasingly being 'pinched' by work and other commitments. As well as which, we are spending a growing proportion of our time in the somewhat antisocial pursuit of watching television.

Whether we realize it or not, relationships are relatively of greater and greater importance. As we have less opportunity to form them, their success assumes greater significance also. There is enough conflict in the world already, without more misunderstandings taking place.

More and more communities are becoming more 'diverse', culturally and in other ways. The use of NLP and these other techniques gives us more opportunity to better relate to other people and enhance the quality of society in general.

In managing your EXPECTATIONS

• When things seem to go wrong

So what happens when things seem to go wrong? And in whose perception is that? "I can't seem to do anything right." Or "I never have any luck". So, what is it that you are projecting outside or inside yourself so that these results keep on fulfilling your unresourceful expectations of yourself.

As a NLP Practitioner, I am noticing more and more the immensely powerful negative patterns and language other people run. My golf partner hits a great drive on the first tee in our monthly medal. Then he duffs the second shot. "I told you I can never do well in medals...Look at that, I hit a brilliant drive and then I always mess up my 8 iron because I've got to get it on'the green..."

A business partner has interminable computer problems. "Everything I touch with computers seems to go wrong....I can never do anything on this computer without something happening". And another "why is it that I can never find anything when I need it?"

This reminds me of an interesting concept called the scotoma. As I understand it, when a baby is quite young, if you hold something up in front of them that they really want, they will reach out and try to grab it. And when you then put the thing under the table, it no longer exists for the baby because they have not yet learned the abstract skill of imagining where it can be.

So, was there ever I time when you couldn't see something or find something when it was there all the time. Your unconscious mind blocked it out temporarily, either for its own purpose that you hadn't understood yet, or because you were running a program that it elegantly fulfilled.

When I first met my partner she could never find anything when she needed it. She would rifle through her handbag several times and not find it. "Why isn't it here?" she would say. Then I would go through the bag and find it straight away. How was that? It was a scotoma and for whatever reason that only her unconscious knew, she was not able to perceive the object even when she was looking at it or had her fingers on it.

Another friend rang me in great distress. "I couldn't sleep last night because you hadn't rung me when we agreed". I apologized. Within minutes she was in tears down the phone because her son was very ill. Yet in bed the previous night she had not worried about him once. Her unconscious mind had elevated the importance of my missed call to give her a break from the personal fears and distress she had been feeling about her son.

So remember – what you expect might just be what you get.

• *When you want them to go right*

Ah, I hear you say, what about when I really want things to go right? Well I don't know because I'm not you and I don't know you that well. So let's try these.

Are you really and congruently ready in your life and your whole self for these things to happen yet? Or is your unconscious mind holding back until some other pattern or loose end has been resolved?

What was the very last thing that was in your mind before you wanted to get this thing or result? To take a golfing analogy again. When the golfer missed the putt, how and how much was this important to them? Was it just this putt? Was it just this round of golf? Was it something much more than that? And what was the last thought that went through their mind before they hit the putt? "I mustn't miss this putt..." Whoops, the unconscious mind deletes the negative and faithfully delivers.

So my golfing partner says yesterday "I bet I miss this putt." So what happened when he sank it? Well first of all he was close enough to have a reasonable probability of sinking it by accident. Second, all of the other patterns he shared with me (whether I wanted to hear them or not) were about failing. So maybe his unconscious mind delivered that pattern by proving to him that he could fail to miss the putt...

"Let me help you to help yourself" said Merlin.

He was wise from many hundreds of years of traveling between a multitude of different cultures. There was a softness and a gentleness in his voice.

"You see, as you've grown you've become so stiff in your sinews. In striving for the sky, you've temporarily forgotten what it was to be lithe and flexible, in your desperate battle to be as strong and tall as the rest. And the strength that lasts and lasts is one, which has a softness and a flexibility, which takes the nourishment that you draw from your roots, and mixes it with the warmth of the sun and the gentle rain from above. Learn to listen to the wind – not the moaning and groaning of a dark, dreary, rainy day, but the messages it bears from other parts of the forest and beyond."

The crack from the lightning had, fortunately done only temporary damage. In fact, no sooner had Merlin spoken these words than the healing process seemed to start from within. The electricity from the storm had stirred something deep within that had been forgotten until now. Suddenly the whole forest could be seen in a different light and the gentle whisperings that caressed the branches and leaves seemed to produce good feelings and many ideas that had not been noticed before.

The tree listened for many days to the wise counsel of the magician. It wasn't so much in the things that he said, or the answers he gave, it was much more to do with the growing flood of new thoughts and different ways of seeing things that seemed to be released from within. By the time the wound had been healed, new growth was sprouting all over and even the roots seemed able to tap into new and fresh sources of water."

Chapter 4

What can you already do (if only you knew)?

The limitless WISDOM of the mind

• Mind and Body, Intelligence and Emotions

One of the presuppositions of NLP is that the mind and body are part of the same system. There is daily growing evidence of the effect of positive beliefs on health and well being. Unfortunately, there is also worrying information about the effect of negative beliefs. On the plus side, the universal average for the 'placebo effect' is about 37%.

We may have conventionally believed that the mind was in, and associated with, the brain. Certainly there are elements of and processing centres for aspects of mind, in the brain. The mind is distributed throughout our physical whole, however. For example, every nerve cell has its own intelligence and, sufficiently nourished, could survive independently. If your body was dipped in a magic fluid, which could dissolve everything except your nerve cells, you would still be totally recognizable from the nerve cells alone. There are more nerve cells in the human body than there are stars in the visible sky.

This gives an insight into the phenomenal power of the mind. It has two major components – the conscious and unconscious mind. In addition, there is the higher self. In your lifetime, you may not use more than 5% of your brain. Einstein was found to have a much bigger brain than normal when he died. For a long time, it was thought that this was the reason for his 'super-intelligence'. Then it was realized that as he used it more, it grew more cells. In experiments, rats' brains have been halved, quartered, even shredded and they have still been able to run a maze they had learned.

The more we use our mind, the greater the number of connections made. When these unconscious connections are brought into consciousness, then we truly have limitless potential. You may use less than one third of your mind, which is distributed throughout you. As the mind needs new nerve cells and connections, it creates them. In one year's time, every nerve cell in you will have been renewed.

Our unconscious minds record and remember everything. Each thought, feeling or experience goes into the 'void' to be compared and processed against other thoughts, feelings and experiences. They are filtered by our meta-programs, values and beliefs, before influencing our memories, behaviours and states, as appropriate.

When we have found out who we are; accepted ourselves; changed as appropriate to completing the task in hand, or fulfilling our potential, then there is truly no limit to what we can achieve.

The mind is the domain of the emotions. It is the repository of emotional experiences and memories from the past, which have influenced our makeup during our formative years and our states, experiences and behaviours thereafter. Our philosophies are based on our values and beliefs, whether experienced or handed down. While we may be born with innate intelligence, our experiences and environment can enhance this. Similarly, experiences remain in memory and can influence our minds, manifesting themselves in states, language and behaviours.

Stress, where it occurs, may be the result of a triggered emotional experience from the past, a conflict between something, which is happening in the now, and is not in keeping with our values and beliefs, etc.

Psychological make-up is a major factor in life success. You may have an excellent life plan. If there were negative elements of your psychological makeup, which interfered with your rational decisions and particularly your self-confidence, and peace of mind, you may not have been able to fulfill your potential yet. Your intellect and intelligence are important, as is your philosophy of life, but for some, it is emotions and negative emotional experiences that have got in the way, unconsciously replaying unresourceful states or behaviours from the past.

Even intelligence is being re-appraised. As Goleman's work (ibid.) has recognized, 'emotional intelligence' may be at least as important as general intelligence in determining successful and appropriate behaviour. General intelligence reposes largely in the brain. Emotional intelligence is seated in the mind.

Much has been written about the different characteristics of the left and right hemispheres of the brain. The left is related to logic, language, rational thought and analysis, together with short-term memory. The right is related to creativity, people-centredness, long term memory, etc. The ideal is to have both working in harmony. Have you ever played Trivial PursuitTM, been asked a question, had the answer pop into your head and dismissed it in favour of a logical answer, or even a wild guess? Then you found that your first thought had been the right answer?

The right brain is intuitive and inspired, the left brain's logic may have sometimes overridden the best solution or the right path. We can be at our best when left and right brains, conscious and unconscious mind are in harmony. In the program there are some exercises to improve the left/right brain partnership.

Women tend to engage both sides of the brain most of the time. This is because the 'corpus callosum', which connects the two, is far thicker in women than in men. Men are perfectly capable of using either or both hemispheres, but condition and biological makeup has tended in the past to lead to engaging one or other (often the left).

We have nerve cells throughout our brain and, of course our whole body. Each has its own intelligence. The mind cells carry emotional intelligence, experiences and memories. I have heard it said "give me a manager with back pain and I'll show you a manager under stress". It is true that back pain can result from physical injury. The unconscious mind is very clever and in the past, even though the original injury may have healed, the mind may have hooked emotionally painful memories to the muscular seat of the original pain. Then, when internal conflict produced stress, the back pain may have returned, in the guise of muscular tension.

I had back trouble for 10 years. Since experiencing NLP Practitioner and Master Practitioner techniques and NLP based therapies, I have had no recurrence and expect to have a healthy back for the rest of my life. At my most stressful times in the past, I have occasionally been bent double with pain, or muscular seizure. Now I play golf with mental and physical freedom.

If you have an apparent physical infirmity, which may have appeared to manifest itself at times of stress, ask yourself "when did I decide to have this physical difficulty? What was happening in my life in general at that time?" When you have identified the source, you may decide to make some positive changes in your values or beliefs, releasing negative memories or experiences, having preserved the positive learnings. As you think of a time in the future, when you are benefiting from these positive changes, notice how, having experienced the new choices things somehow seem different now....

Freud talked of the ego, id and superego. In NLP, we talk of the conscious mind, the unconscious mind and the higher self. These are the three levels of consciousness. In meditation, you may go from the alpha (or waking) state, to the beta or deeper states. When the unconscious mind is in harmony with the conscious, we have progressed to a deeper state of consciousness, where more learning or understandings may be found.

Hypnosis is trance under another name. Trance is the ideal learning state. Some sports people talk of being in 'the zone' or in 'flow'. These are trance states, where the conscious and unconscious minds can be in harmony. Zen Buddhism, relaxation methods and other trance inducing behaviours may help us to engage the more resourceful sources of our mind, leading to calmer, more centred, more positive behaviours. People may talk of 'being in control'. The paradox is that to be in control we should learn how to let go. Trance is one way to let go.

Some people talk of opportunities and threats, others of opportunities and challenges. Every experience in life produces learning. When you see these in a positive light, you can change and grow. Think of the possibilities and the positives, not the impossibles. Newtonian logic may suggest that there is only black or white for each situation we find ourselves in. Wouldn't life be boring if there weren't shades in between.

If you are sat in a chair, what is 'not chair' – everything else. If the book you are holding looking at and reading to yourself represents success, then what is not success? Everything else. Failure is only one of an infinite number of possibilities, which exist outside of total success. Who defines success and failure for you? – You do. Using Cartesian logic (after Rene Descartes), ask yourself the following questions.

"When I have determined a mission, goals and a strategy for my life, together with making the positive changes in my values and beliefs to produce the possibility of great success, what will I get as a result?

What will I not get, as a result of these positive changes?

What would I have got if I had left things as they were?

What would I not have got if I had left things as they were?"

And notice the changes and new possibilities that are already opening up before you.

Sometimes, we may choose to go inside, to come outside. For some people, there has been noise inside, which got in the way of clear understanding and positive expectation. For me, one of the greatest gains from using all the tools and techniques in this book has been the end of the ceaseless internal dialogue and rehearsal, including running negative programs and possibilities, fears and anxieties.

Do you, like many people, have an internal dialogue. Did that inner voice ever speak to you harshly when things appeared to go wrong? Think of someone from your present or past, who you know loves you or cares about you deeply. Imagine if they spoke to you in the way that internal voice may have spoken to you in the past. How would you feel?

So, why on earth would you ever have wanted to speak to yourself in the same way? What highest positive purpose could that have served? So...frame it in the positive...

"What in particular worked well in the exercise or activity I have been engaged in?

What positive opportunities are there for me to learn, improve and grow?

Overall, how well did I do?"

When my son was very small, my wife and I separated. He was the innocent victim of the unhappiness at the time. After things had settled down and I saw him every weekend, I invented a game that we played every night that I saw him, for eight years. You could play it with yourself each night, before you sleep:

"Tell me something good that happened to you today?

Tell me something good about yourself?

Tell me something you are looking forward to doing tomorrow?"

Louise Hay has a further suggestion. Each day, find time, on your own, to look in a mirror and say "I love myself and everything about me."

We have discussed perceptual positions elsewhere. Take yourself outside yourself and see who you really are and redefine the possible. The unconscious mind is a reservoir for resourcefulness: mental, emotional, mind/body, spiritual, meditation, self-mastery, awareness, etc. Even physical (diet, sleep, exercise) resourcefulness results directly from *positive* thoughts, beliefs and expectations.

Create an internal representation of yourself with the physique and weight you want to be. Step into that internal experience, see and feel it through your own eyes. Now let your conscious or unconscious mind choose a time in your future when you want to be this person. Step outside of the internal representation so that you can see yourself, with the physique and weight you will be, and put that vision out into that future time. Relax and let your unconscious mind create that future certainty. It is so powerful that it is impossible to tell the difference between a vivid internal imagined experience and an external real one.

So, create the representation and feeling of what it will be like to be a success in your life in general and do the same for this, putting this future certainty out into your timeline. Do the other things in this book in your now and start noticing the immediate changes now.

The power of the unconscious mind can be observed in everyday life. One example is 'organ language'. Have you noticed how often people use descriptive language for states or behaviours and somehow that may be related to a physical aspect of their life? For example, "I must try and get my head round this... I don't mind... That was a mindless thing to do... She gets my back up... He's a pain in the butt, etc." Did you ever notice someone who had had physical symptoms in that part of the body or organ which they referred to in their language construction?"

• *The Brain, the Mind and the computer analogy*

Many people talk of the mind and brain synonymously. A growing number recognize not only the difference, but also the 'mind-body' connection. Much research is still based on the comparison between the brain and the computer. Let's be clear. The brain has a computing function, but no computer has its own feelings or discreet choice (especially irrational), separate from whoever originally programmed it.

NLP has been around for nearly 10 years longer than the PC. The latter has become central to our lives and yet, it merely automates processes that we have the brain capacity to do ourselves. The PC represents the consummation of the 'left-brained' world we have created for ourselves. Yet, while computers can process our consumer decisions, they cannot make them without knowing our instructions or priorities. Furthermore, they cannot anticipate our feelings or emotions, whether things are going well or ill.

Feelings are in the mind. They are born of emotional experiences in the past. Where these were 'significant' (in their context at the time), they may have laid down patterns of behaviour which seem to run themselves. When you feel yourself suddenly moved by an experience, where does that feeling come from? If you have ever felt fear, especially of failure or rejection, where did that originate? We could spend ages philosophizing over inherited traits and environment. As a reader of this book, you want to resolve the negative patterns, reinforce or install new positive patterns, so as to maximize your chances of success.

• *The untapped power of your brain*

We may not even use much of our brain capacity in our lives. Thinking patterns may be related to the brain or the mind. If I asked you what two and two made, you would probably answer four. Sometimes, language or experience can trigger an emotional memory or state, often unconsciously, on its way through processing. This is because everything passes through our filters. Someone who had experienced the break-up of a lifetime relationship in unhappy circumstances, when asked what one and one made, might not automatically have answered two. Indeed, in relationships, sometimes it has made two (partnership), sometimes more than two (synergy), sometimes less (conflict).

People also tend to associate the brain with memory. How many times have you heard someone say "I have a poor memory", or "my memory is fading as I get older". These are, of course, limiting beliefs. Nobody need have a poor or declining memory. The unconscious records and remembers everything. In a recent experiment, a probe was inserted into a woman's brain and she recalled in perfect detail, the occasion of her birthday when she was very young, even down to the feel of her party frock.

The skill we are needing is recall. This is simply a learned and mastered set of skills. First, there is the way we record the memory in the first place. The best technique is association. The more connections the brain can hook up to some information, the better it records it, especially by the use of pictures. Improving recall, is a matter of understanding and learning the most productive strategy. Elsewhere we have considered eye patterns. If you want to recall a memory with a visual component, look up and to your left. That will connect your thoughts to the visual centres of the brain.

In conclusion, through understanding something of how your mind, body and brain can work in harmony, you may understand that all problems you may have perceived for yourself in your life are actually in yourself. Otherwise they would not be a problem for you. When you looked for problems, you may have found you got them. If you ever programmed yourself for less than the best, you may have got exactly that. If a particular experience upset you, or caused you stress, what were the emotional triggers from the past which, when they were removed, left you only with the positive lessons to be learned?

• Creativity and Innovation

Many people may have feared change. To the onlooker, their lives may have seemed like ordered chaos. Change and apparent chaos can bring huge opportunity for you, now that you are seeing things differently. If it is true that change threatens other people, that already gives you an edge. Your new skills make change work for you. As for chaos, the world is in chaos.

Of course, if the present state is exactly determinable, then the future is predictable. The world is the product of innumerable systems and processes and the patterns and programs of about 6 billion individuals; most are subject to changing environmental conditions, directly or indirectly. They are in chaos.

When you can find any order here, you have an advantage over anyone else who sees simply chaos. You can bring your own order to life by understanding your own patterns and programs, which you know will work for you, because in results terms, only you matter. You determine the measures of success; you enjoy that success; you review and improve that success.

You must be able to think independently and creatively, if necessary in a contrary way, but not just for the sake of it. You are just as creative as the next person, in your own terms. You are an independent spirit and being, having an impact on your immediate environment, and able to choose and control the way you perceive and manage that environment. In this book, you have all the tools and skills to augment your existing talents and capabilities; to review, remove or change your beliefs; to change your values to wholly positive; to set your own mission and goals and, in visualizing the successful outcome, to create and program your own future.

In life, change is the only constant. In your positive frame of mind, change brings increasing options. We discussed at the start of this book, the levels of change – the levels at which you perceive change and at which it happens, for you.

One of my skills is lateral thinking. I don't know how I got it, or how I do it, without thinking. I can tell you how to create lateral thought for yourself, however. In the life that is happening around you, your ability to think laterally will make creative difference in your success.

• *Chunking and lateral thinking*

Think, for a moment, of your favourite food. What is this an example of? You might say nourishment. What is nourishment an example of? You might say health. What is health an example of?...You can keep on chunking up towards more and more abstract levels.

Now go back to that food. What is a component of that food? You may say tomato sauce. What is a component of tomato sauce? Water. What is a component of water? Oxygen. What is a component of oxygen? An atom...etc. This is chunking down.

Sometimes, in your life, you may need inspiration. Find it in yourself, by using your natural skills to create a lateral thought. The process is, to take the existing subject, chunk up, move to a parallel channel and chunk down.

In the film *Working Girl* Emily Griffith sees a market where the focus is on TV and telecommunications. She has a hunch about radio. She sells it to the client and it wins. To achieve that thought, she could have looked at TV. Then she could ask what TV was an example of? (Chunk up). Communications. What is another example of communications? (Chunk down). Radio. That is how you create lateral thought. That is also how you may be able to resolve negotiations or disagreement.

• *Introducing submodalities, the essence of NLP*

We all create internal representations. Each of us has their own process. Every internal representation is made up of aspects or components which Bandler and Grinder called submodalities.

For example, as you think of a vivid memory of when you felt you could do anything, was the picture colour or black and white? Was it moving or still? You can go through the entire list of 'submodalities', including the components of any sounds or feelings that may have been there.

Now, take a situation where you need to be resourceful, or where you may have been unresourceful in the past. Elicit and compare the submodalities of each. Determine the key difference or differences. Now take the component which has the strongest impact on the representation of your good or successful experiences and make a parallel change in your unresourceful situation. What now appears different to you. Now do you have the insight you need?

Changes in your behaviours can dramatically affect performance. Now add the change in your own personal perceptions and see what happens. Continue to observe, review and adjust until the new behaviours are comfortable for you. Before putting it into practice, you can also visualize your successful outcome, 'dry run' the movie of the upcoming situation (a 'dress-rehearsal') and then watch how you succeed and how did that feel?

Creating and using good HABITS

Your unconscious mind has many inherent skills and programs. Whether instinctive or learned, once the mind has understood what behaviour to use in a given set of circumstances, it can repeat that pattern at will, without you even consciously thinking about it.

Take typing. I have never been trained as a typist and, when I'm not dictating my books, I use the proverbial two fingers. I once started a typing course and got bored after two lessons. There was a test at the end of each one to see what my speed was. I decided to go and do the last test, to see how my two finger efforts would compare with the targeted whole hand approach. I finished the test, with 97% accuracy at 25 words a minute, which was average. So now, my fingers are skipping across the keyboard without thinking. If I stop to wonder how I do this, the mistakes start to flow. Try it yourself...

And talking about flow, no matter how hard you practice a newly learned skill, you will never achieve your full mastery until you can learn to let go and trust your unconscious mind. Of course you want to be focused on the job at hand and you can go way beyond what you dreamed possible when your conscious and unconscious mind are in rapport.

• *Unconscious learning – walking and speaking*

Addictions are a learned behaviour. Take any skill that you have acquired during your life. How many times did you have to practice it and perfect it for it to become a routine – a habit. So, the baseball player doesn't have the remotest chance of hitting the ball if they rely on their conscious mind. The ball is past before you could work out its trajectory and speed. Of course, some people were born with the appropriate instincts, including maybe hand-eye co-ordination. Most of us had to learn these, if at all, by starting early enough, or through years of hard graft.

So the baseball hitter has practiced for years, to perfect the 'habit' of precisely timing the strike to hit the home run. Even then, performance of the best is much less than perfect and any time out of the game means more practice to restore the good habits.

So with smoking, drinking or drug dependency. When those people started, it was such a nasty experience. The taste was bitter or unpleasant (have you ever tried inhaling a bonfire in the garden, drinking methylated spirits or snorting wheat flour up your nose). Whatever the drive behind it, those people had to stick at it and practice really hard to acquire the habit. How do I know?

Well, take walking or speaking. Presumably your parents sent you to walking classes when you were very young, so you could learn how to do it? Naw don't be stupid!

Yes but surely you went to speaking classes? Naw!

So how did you do that? Do you know how many muscles you use when you are walking briskly? Hundreds. Do you know it is completely unnatural for humans to walk? Once we were quadrupeds and once we had learned how to lift our knuckles off the ground and our physiology had adapted appropriately, we gained a whole new perspective on the world. But we still carry remnants of the old structure, which is why our spine has a curve and we sometimes get a sore back from standing so long. Also, do you know how much your head weighs and you have to balance it precariously on that flexible neck. No wonder we have to lie down at night to give the old body a rest.

And then there is the process of moving all those muscles in precise co-ordination, so we don't get out of balance. You can't do that consciously. Raise your arm NOW! Do you know how many muscles you have to co-ordinate to do that? Do you think you could organize over 160 in less than the blinking of an eyelid?

Watch a baby learning to walk. How many times do they tumble over before they get the knack. And all this is when they are only 9-18 months old. They have most of their intelligence potential at that age, but they haven't a conscious clue how to use one jot of it. It's all unconscious. So when did we learn the limiting behaviour of thinking everything through consciously and rationally before we do it? Time to rediscover the magic innocence and curiosity of the child.

And what about those things you learned when you were older. Riding a bike, or driving a car? How many times did you have to fall off your bike to learn all that co-ordination. And if you were to go for a ride now, some of you might get a bit nervous at first because you haven't ridden in such a long time, but here we go and pretty soon we're bowling along at 10, 15 or even 20 miles an hour, without even thinking about it.

Applying ACUITY – six senses and beyond?

Most of us would now be open to the possibility that we have six senses and maybe even more. My own theory is that once upon a time, we had much more than we have now and we have temporarily forgotten how to access or use them.

Remember, primitive people had an emotional brain. They lived by the sort of instinct that we find harder to set free. It was instinct that fired up the adrenaline for fight or flight. When we study ancient tribes and shamanic communities, whose history may be traced back 50,000 years or more, there are far more instinctive behaviours than we have. Think of the warrior who can smell an animal coming, or hear a stampede long before it arrives, or sense the impending danger. Think also of when the hairs stand up on the back of your neck when you sense that somebody is there, long before you see them...

Let's start with the standard five senses. Again, my feeling is that we are too passive in their use. While this means that some experiences can surprise us, in the meantime, our faculties are getting lazy or blurred.

We smoke, put too much salt on our food, smother it with ketchup, cook it to perdition and worse still fill it with artificial flavourings such as monosodium glutamate. Result, we often don't notice or discern what much of our food really tastes like. Many years ago, I stopped adding salt to vegetables. The tastes are much clearer but the downside is that overcooked food tastes awful or not at all in comparison.

Our eyes are becoming lazier as a human race. Do you see any cave paintings of prehistoric people with glasses? No seriously. We spend so much of our time with a fixed gaze, especially at the TV or the computer monitor, that the muscles get lazy. That's often why people need glasses. Neither my wife nor I have ever had glasses of any sort and we are in our fifties. How do we do that? We simply roll them round and change the focus from long to short and back again from time to time to keep them fit.

Hearing is deteriorating. It's all that noise. Do the speakers really have to be that loud in the club to hear the music? Oh I know all about feeling the beat and that – I still listen to heavy metal, as well as classical and a multitude of other tastes, but surely, the louder the volume is, especially on the earpieces, the duller the senses get? It's just like oversalting your food.

And so on for the rest of your senses.

Now here's the thing. We've discussed the structure of experience elsewhere and the 'building blocks' that Bandler and Grinder called 'submodalities'. Our mind and our memory especially work best when we can associate as many senses as possible to 'fix' the experience. So, it goes without saying that the sharper the acuity of your senses and the more you exercise and use them, the more powerful your mind, your memory and your experiences will be.

And when it comes to excellence and being your best, the greater your sensory acuity, or sharpness, the better you can be, especially when you are seeking to understand and model excellence in others. Without this sensory sharpness, you may be missing such a lot that can be of use to you now.

Ironically, one of the ways to enhance your sensory acuteness is to practice peripheral vision.

Try this. Are you sitting comfortably? Find a spot on the opposite wall. Any spot. Now, focus all your conscious attention on it. Now, as you relax more and more, notice how much more you can see, hear and feel outside of that spot. Notice how, without moving your eyes, your 'peripheral' vision can expand outwards. As I'm typing these words, for example, I can see each letter in clear focus and also see the sides of the chair, which are actually behind 180°, as well as most of the rest of the room and much of the garden, without lifting my eyes.

Incidentally, if you want to know how to go into 'the zone', practice peripheral vision. I use this with my golf, as I'm walking between shots and it gets me and keeps me in the zone.

So, it is possible to be completely focused on the task in hand and in the zone, at one and the same time.

They are not mutually exclusive. Focus occupies the conscious mind, while the unconscious mind is in the zone, or 'the void' as some people call it, where all possibilities reside and which is connected to the limitless universe.

Try it when you want to stop that incessant voice inside you. Go into peripheral vision. Clear the mind. If the voice or anything else, like a tune comes in, just tell it to shut up and go away.

You see peripheral vision is like meditation. With the latter, you use a mantra or sound or something similar to enter a meditative state. It occupies the mind, just like the spot on the wall, so that the power of your unconscious mind can have free rein.

TRANSFERRING EXCELLENCE

So now you're accepting and beginning to realize your limitless potential and certainly much more than you may have tapped into before. And maybe you've already started to notice the sometimes-routine daily habits that you have achieved excellence in...such as walking, talking, driving, etc.

And you surely will have noticed excellence in others, so how can you achieve this and move towards your untapped potential?

• Bridging your skills

Take something you know you are excellent at – anything – even if it's just the things I mentioned above. As you will discover later, as you are understanding, acquiring, practicing and perfecting the tools and techniques to move towards excellence, every skill can be broken down into its component parts. And now you realize it's not just the moves and practical, technical patterns we are talking about. It is especially what's happening inside your unconscious mind that creates the excellence. The unconsciously perfected strategies. The building blocks of experience.

The sensory awareness. The verbal and non-verbal communication patterns, especially with yourself.

So, by bringing together the appropriate techniques in this book, you can analyze, synthesize, improve, understand and transfer the elements of experience that make you excellent in one skill or habit and transfer these into the new skill that you wish to perfect.

• Modeling others

And this is especially true for modeling others. This was the true origin of NLP. Bandler and Grinder unpacked the building blocks and other elements of the total conscious/unconscious patterns of behaviour and experience from four people of renowned excellence in their own chosen fields and from that started the process of coding the whole of human language and behaviour. The result is that you now have the possibility to understand and improve everything you do and understand and acquire the excellence that other people do, that you wish for yourself now.

Once upon a time, it was truly believed that only a handful of people on the planet could ski excellently well...

• And what had you already noticed...

In My Voice Will Go With You, David Rosen recounts many stories about the work of Milton Erickson. For 30 years, Milton's primary therapeutic medium was the metaphor. He tells the story of Arthur, one of Milton's best students...

It was coming towards the end of the year and Arthur met his professor in the corridor. "How will you do in your degree exams Arthur?"

"Oh that's alright professor, you're going to ask ten questions and they're"...and he proceeded to reel off all the questions.

"What!" exclaimed the professor. "You've cheated. The only way you could know those questions is by breaking into my office and copying the paper. I'm going to take you to the Dean's office."

So he took him to the Dean's office and the Dean said "Arthur, is this true, did you know the questions on the paper?"

"Of course I did Dean. I've attended all the lectures this year..."

"I'm sorry, that's not good enough. You must have cheated. You will not be able to take the exam at the year-end, nor to graduate. You will be expelled as a disgrace to this college".

"But Dean!" cried Arthur "if you send to my room and get my notebooks, I can prove to you that I didn't cheat......"

Part 2

CREATING YOUR SUCCESS

The Power of Ten^{10} Steps to Your Best

• I can be what I'm best able....

We've talked about many things and now we've reached the ten simple steps which you can take towards self-mastery and being your best...whenever you choose... Here is the what, how and why...

What

Realize your limitless potential in life, in work and indeed in any of the domains of your existence now.

Understand all the things you are already doing, often unconsciously.

Use the power of your imagination.

Use the power of your mind. Learn how you can learn – best.

Understand the power of your beliefs. Create new positives and remove the negative or limiting beliefs.

Learn how to be your best and excel in any situation.

How and Why

Model others' excellence to create lasting success.

Choose the goals that will represent your success.

Visualize the outcomes.

Create a powerful motivation and drive.

Determine sound strategies.

Be in rapport, including with yourself.

STOP...or change your internal dialogue.

See, hear, do and have fun in life and in general.

Learn to love yourself, remove the negative self-talk, listen well and notice how well liked you can become.

Reframe the negatives and anchor the positives.

All the while learning and growing...

So that with all these things you can have more choices....

Where and When

...in every aspect of your life and love, work and play.

Whenever you choose...for yourself.

...and then go beyond...to achieve self-mastery

Use all these things to better understand yourself.

Review all the exercises, techniques and practical suggestions in this book.

Listen more, talk less.

Reflect on how your intelligence and your emotions can work positively in harmony.

Become open to your internal feelings.

Be aware of the effects on your behaviours and the attitudes of those around you.

Put yourself at cause in everything – yes, everything - you do. Life is a series of choices.

...to Be the Best...

'To be your best, you need a dream...a vision of what you want to be, what you want to achieve. You will also want good self-confidence and self-esteem, powerful belief in yourself and strong motivation to achieve your success.

In applying all the things we will have discussed in the ten steps to be your best, it will be highly beneficial to know where you are starting from. There is a model learned from business:

- Where are you now?

- Where do you want to get to?

- How are you going to get there?

Where are you now is based on the structure of experience. You set your mission and goals, plan your outcomes and the route map to get there and fundamental to all this is an understanding of where you are starting from.

It begins with believing in your limitless potential. It goes on to having a plan. It needs an understanding of the resources and capabilities and an awareness of your current patterns of behaviour. It may be that you need to vary or reprogram some of these, so that they facilitate your journey and especially that none of them get in the way of your ultimate achievement.

Everything you are is based on where you have come from on your journey so far. We are not entering into the debate of genetic or environmental. Sufficient to say that for our purposes, you emerged into the world like a clean, blank, white sheet of paper. Your genetic makeup may well have influenced some of your behaviours, especially the survival instinct, and everything else has been based on your experience during and since birth.

• The Structure of Experience

The makeup of who and how you are now, we can call the structure of experience. So what are the significant elements: memories (facts and experiences); language and behaviour patterns? Everything you experience goes through a set of filters, based on your experiences to date. The conscious mind only has a limited processing power, so the unconscious mind has to sort, filter and store 'events' as appropriate, based on the programs that have gone before.

Nothing in the world happens for you unless it happens inside you. Everything has to be processed through your internal filters, in order to be discarded as irrelevant, or processed to be understood or integrated. Many of these external experiences will access filters and/or memories with emotions attached. They trigger a state, whether we are consciously or unconsciously aware of it. It shows in our communication, wittingly or unwittingly, consciously or unconsciously, psychologically or physiologically.

Let's say something happens outside you that you experience. There may be sounds that you have to interpret, in order to recognize them, ignore them (e.g. background noise); decode them, especially when they are language. There may be sights, which are composed of a complex mass of elements. There may be physical sensations, i.e. touch or feel, taste and smell. All of these elements comprise each event and of course they are also the building blocks of memory, together with one highly important other – emotions.

The 'event' happens. Your unconscious mind 'decodes', filters, recognizes, understands, compares with existing patterns and memories, sometimes triggering a spontaneous reaction and presenting awareness for the conscious mind. This does not always happen. If I ask you to become aware now of the feeling of your body sitting on the chair, you may well not have been thinking about this until my communication triggered this into your consciousness.

So a fundamental consequence of the structure of your experience is a 'state'. Not all memories have an emotional component and when an external stimulus accesses a memory with an emotion attached to it, you will experience a state, whether conscious or unconscious.

Think of hate. You may immediately be presented with some conscious memories, experiences or feelings. As well as this, some of the feelings you have may not present conscious memories of thoughts beyond a feeling of unease, say. This is because the word has also triggered some deeper memories or patterns with uneasy associations. If you and I worked together, we may be able to elicit or discover the root cause of that unease, including the originating experience or memory. For now it may remain concealed and nevertheless you may have found yourself in an inexplicable state...or not.

During especially the first 5-7 years of our lives, we learned to do lots of things, especially speaking, walking, feeding ourselves and other fundamental movements. We also acquired most of our values and beliefs and many of our attitudes. Every one of these has emotions attached to it. When, for example, you may have found yourself in conflict with someone, this is because something they said or did triggered one or more of your values and/or beliefs.

Do you know why this is? As mentioned elsewhere, primitive people's brains were emotional. The rational, logical part evolved on top of the original 'amygdala'. The result is the 'fight or flight' response. It is why our values and beliefs are all programmed towards pleasure or away from pain.

'I want to be happy' is a value. Where someone had a largely happy childhood, the value may be 'towards'. For others, it may represent a wish to leave behind unhappiness.

So, in order to be your best and move towards your limitless potential, you will want to manage your state. There are a number of ways to do this: first, you can increase your total awareness of what is happening to you at any one time. You do this, by improving the rapport between your conscious and your unconscious mind, so that the latter learns to alert you, resourcefully, where there is something to be aware of and especially something to learn.

You can do this by understanding and practicing the patterns in this book, becoming more aware of yourself and the patterns and programs you run, removing, modifying or improving them as appropriate. You see, many people passively live their lives a great deal of the time, allowing their neurophysiology to respond to what is going on around them and then consciously or unconsciously reacting to the triggers, experiencing a series of states. When I was most desperate to lose 45 years of anger, it was because the anger was doing me, rather than me doing the anger.

You may already be understanding the link to emotional intelligence. People who are passively experiencing their lives, are not aware of, modifying and improving their patterns and programs to move towards excellence, probably also blissfully unaware of, or not caring about the effect they have on others. 'Take me or leave me, I ain't going to change'. If you always do what you always did, you'll always get what you always got.

I believe I have limitless potential. I also believe you have. This is a powerful positive, towards pattern. "I'd like to believe you, if only I could stop...." is based on a limiting belief that the person would like to move away from and haven't yet found the way.

During the day, we have billions of conscious and unconscious experiences, most of which we are unaware of. As our conscious mind can process only 7±2 at any one moment and the unconscious can process 2.8 million, it spends all day comparing events with past experience, deleting the irrelevant, distorting others to seem like something familiar, so that they can be deleted also or generalized for the purposes of experience and memory. Not everything fits.

At night we sleep – and we dream. The body needs an average of 8 hours or so to recharge the physical batteries. The mind only needs 20-30 minutes in total. In that time, it sorts all the day's experiences that haven't been rationalized, re-experiences, re-interprets and restores or rejects as appropriate the modified experiences and memories.

A new hierarchy for success

What we are doing in this book, is giving you a simple, better understanding of you, how you experience, how you process, how you understand, how you learn and change and especially how you can grow towards your limitless potential.

The approach is based around a number of simple models, straightforward exercises and standard NLP techniques. The appendix gives you more specific detail and the chance to learn and practice these techniques and behaviours and then integrate them, at first consciously and then unconsciously, into your everyday life as you move inexorably forwards. This can work so well that you may eventually forget the value of this book and it will have done its job when you are doing all these things naturally and spontaneously, living and experiencing the life you can have.

Frequently in this book, I refer to my own personal experiences. This is because I am making the same journey. Already I have reached the stage where the goals and dreams I programmed are becoming self-fulfilling. The best result is that I sometimes feel the wish to apologize that I truly am as positive as I seem. (The British culture is unnecessarily negative and critical, so many people find all this positivity uncomfortable. We're changing, learning and growing...)

I started by trying on the belief that I had truly limitless potential. Although not yet in a general state to move forward, I readily recognized that I had seen glimpses before. The point was, how to get there and how to get rid of the negative and limiting patterns along the way.

For me, it became as though I had a huge piece of elastic tied to my back and I was running as hard as I could to break it. If only it could be cut, I could zoom forward towards a powerful, positive destiny. So, having found the way to believe in, plan and program a positive future, I had to unlearn old patterns and habits that had got in the way or let me down and remove the limiting or negative beliefs that had held me back. As I am removing or changing more and more of those patterns, so I am able to add more and more motivation, self-confidence, self-esteem and self-belief.

As each day goes by, there are more opportunities to learn and grow, more techniques to learn and integrate and more lasting change.

So here is the first simple model:

• *How to Be Your Best*

- Believe in your limitless potential;

- Understand yourself better and how your patterns, processes and programs work;

- Discover and understand excellence, in yourself and others and model it;

- Remove the negative or limiting patterns or beliefs that once got in the way;

- Add plenty of motivation and self-belief as the fuel; and

- Create a lasting momentum towards a powerful, positive destiny.

(Oh and by the way, remember you're human; settle for less than perfection; receive any less than your desired behaviours as feedback and opportunities to learn and grow; always be open to change; reinforce the positives; remove the negatives, starting with the way you communicate with yourself...)

In order to create this lasting change, let's understand the elements of what I call your **hierarchy for success**:

• *Identity and personal Brand*

It starts with how you see, feel and think about yourself. Ask yourself the question 'Who am I?'

Write down a series of statements that capture who and what you are. Now take all the positives and, using the techniques in this book, reinforce these at every opportunity; Take the less than optimum or negative ones and reframe them (see appendix) or use other techniques to modify or remove them.

Now go forward to a time in the distant future and visualize yourself as you really, really want to be. Using the submodality analysis from the appendix, find out the most powerful way for you to represent this vision of yourself. Step into it and see, hear and feel what that will really be like. Then step out of it and leave it out there in the future. Revisit this vision every day and whenever you remember. Use the limitless power of your imagination to create a compelling future image of yourself.

• *Mission*

What is your mission in life. Have you allowed this to be passive so far. We're not talking about being mission*ary* here (although that's ok if it is what you passionately and congruently want to be. Just remember to understand and respect other people's models of the world).

Do the 4square exercise we discussed in Chapter 2. Keep it under review and revisit it, if appropriate, every year when you redo your long term goals.

• *Vision and planning*

What is your vision for what you can achieve? Have you introduced any planning or process into this? Your imagination can create experiences so powerful that they seem or feel more real than real. When you get to setting your goals, turn the culmination into a powerful, positive picture of yourself having achieved these goals. What does it look, sound, feel and seem like?

We have mentioned goals in passing and we shall also consider strategies. The mind has limitless creative potential and also likes to be given lots and lots of tasks to do. You can create a simple plan of action, with daily, weekly, monthly steps to effect, review and integrate into your growing, positive way of life.

• Values, Beliefs and Culture

Fundamental to who we are and what we do are our values and beliefs. Beliefs tend to change from time to time. Values remain largely unchanged, having been set during our younger lives. However, they will change to be even more positive as a result of you implementing the things in this book.

Values are at the root of conflict and emotional response also. Especially when you react strongly, unconsciously to some stimulus or situation, it is either because it has triggered an emotionally charged experience from the past, or because it goes to the root of or challenges your values. The causes and ideals that we are prepared to fight most passionately for are based on our values and most strongly held beliefs.

Cultural backgrounds also have an important bearing as they are reflected in many of these strongly held beliefs.

• Goals

In order to change and become what you most want to be, it is fundamental to set and program goals for the short, medium and longer term. By reviewing and resetting these goals over time, they will become second nature to you, integrated into your internal 'circuitry' and you may even find yourself pleasantly surprised as you effortlessly and easily achieve and even exceed these goals.

Several friends of mine review and reset their goals annually, especially with their partners. Without exception they report that the stretching targets they set at the start of the year, which seemed beyond achievement, are achieved and even surpassed, together with other successes they had not even contemplated. One of my friends cannot stop chuckling at all the positive things that seem inexorably to happen to him.

• Strategies

Having set and programmed your goals, you will want to take powerful, positive, practical steps towards their achievement. Strategies are not just about these things, they are also about the unconscious strategies you are using all the time, in your everyday life, how you can understand, modify and improve these to enhance the quality of your experience and reinforce your progress towards excellence and success.

• Resources and capabilities

What can you already do that you could do even better? What have you already got that you can create more of and use even more effectively? What are your skills, abilities and competencies. How can you grow and add to these, especially by trying new, varied and different experiences? By stretching yourself?

Take wealth for example. You might have said that you did not have enough money, or capital, to do what you want to do. So what about your human personal capital? What could you do that can create or overcome the need for money? Use your imagination or your wits. Take some calculated risks and there is also no substitute for working hard.

As someone once said, the way to become a millionaire is to develop more knowledge about a particular subject or skill than anyone else. Someone else said that many of the most successful entrepreneurs went bust at least twice to become successful. This isn't failure, it is the opportunity to learn. We all have choices.

• Implementation and Actions

Having decided what you want to be, what you want to do and how you are going to do it, get up and go and do it – and keep on doing it (always making time for review of course). It may seem a glib cliché to some people, but if you're not getting what you want, get up now and do something about it. And if you're doing something you don't want to do, stop it right now. Remove the pattern, interrupt the pattern, stop the pattern, modify the pattern, reframe the pattern to a positive, whatever. Just get on and do it! If you still have something inside getting in the way, it's probably a limiting belief, so remove or change that too.

• Environment

Now of course, we all live and work in environments. There are people and things in your environment. Some of these will help you towards and support you in your stretching goals. Others are neutral and some of them could damage, stop or get in the way of you achievement. So, change your environment. Move away from it, modify it or modify the way you see and experience it, so that it increasingly supports the delivery of your limitless potential.

One client I worked with was claustrophobic in the Tube train. They lived and worked in London. Getting around was becoming an increasing problem. When we worked together we started with three choices: move to a City with no Tube; remove the phobia; get to the root cause of these patterns of behaviour. The first would have involved moving to a different environment where the opportunity to exploit their talents was nowhere near as good. The second would dramatically improve their quality of life. We worked on the third and not only found an unexpected basis to the pattern laid down in early life, but also when this was re-experienced, the emotions were released, the learnings were understood and retained, the positive change had powerful, pervasive benefits across the whole of their work, life and relationships.

• Feedback and learning

People who are oblivious of their effect on other people may never fulfill their potential, displaying poor emotional intelligence. Those who receive and ignore the feedback they get from their results and their interactions with other people are missing opportunities to learn and grow in their own excellence and quality of relationships. People who are frightened of failure or, more puzzlingly success, may not get the rewarding experiences of rationally comparing actual with planned performance to learn and grow, instead being swamped with the deflating, demotivating, reassuring perception of their own limitations and boundaries.

There is no failure, only feedback. What was there to learn and how can you change your behaviours to get even better results towards an inexorable pattern of powerful, positive growth?

• *Learning and growth*

Look around you. In every experience, every event and every interaction, there are opportunities to understand better, improve the patterns and programs and grow. After all, this is the way your unconscious mind works, so how long will it be before you can have realized the power of rapport between your conscious and unconscious mind?

Using the techniques in this book, you can tune this capability. Are there any negative programs you are running and maybe ignoring or doing nothing about at the moment? The power of the unconscious mind can make these work better and better, so remove them or modify them so that they work for you, not against the realization of your potential.

• *A new direction*

For some, this whole prospect may be daunting. They may need to shake themselves out of their comfort zone. They may have been overlooking or not noticing different possibilities, opportunities or choices. They may not yet have found the belief and resource to make the fundamental, lasting change.

In my own case, I was twenty years in finance and financial services. Although I was very successful, I ended up redundant and for some time had, without realizing it consciously, been enjoying my life and work less and less. My unconscious had been trying to communicate the need to change for some time, in stronger and more urgent tones. Eventually, it stopped me by collapsing my immune system. I had to sit up and listen. I made a completely new set of choices and I have never been happier or more fulfilled...and I've hardly started...

The DRIMI model for Change

So I offer you a simple model for change. It is based on questions, questions and more questions. Start now and learn the habit of asking positive, objective questions and continue this throughout the rest of your life. The person who thinks they know everything knows little or nothing, because their mind is closed to new learnings, possibilities and personal growth.

What do you want to do?

You start by asking yourself what you want to do. What is your mission? What is your purpose in life? What are your goals? What are your plans?

What do you need to do it?

What resources, skills, capabilities and personal characteristics do you need to achieve this wonderful dream. Inventory these. Keep them constantly under review. Understand what you already have and what you are? Become aware of your growth and constantly review the resources and capabilities you need and are growing and acquiring as you move forward positively with success. Take time also to review, learn and understand what there is to know along the way.

How are you going to do it?

What are the plans, processes, programs and strategies that are going to get you there. I spend 10-15% of my time reading and researching, to constantly discover, enrich and renew the 'best of the best' of lasting positive personal change methods and techniques.

Take action and keep on taking action. In the last hour I have written 4,000 words, my arms hurt, I need a break and the ideas and thoughts keep bursting out of me, so I'm driving myself on...

How are you doing?

'What gets measured gets done." For whatever you set out to achieve, you need targets and goals, benchmarks that will let you know how well you are doing and how you have succeeded.

How can you improve?

Make time for review. Open yourself to the possibility of internal and external feedback. Every behaviour has a positive intent. Understand these and integrate the learnings into your personal growth strategy. You can follow a structured plan if you wish. You can learn, understand, introduce and integrate new patterns and techniques and all the while it is best when you remain open to the conscious and unconscious learnings.

Use the NLP feedback model:

- What particularly was good or useful about what you did?

- Where, how and in what ways could you improve and perform even better? and

- How well did you do overall?

Step 1

THE POWER OF YOUR IMAGINATION
– creating new reality

The first step on the way to being your best is to realize the power of your imagination and the ability to create a new reality and a limitless future...

Imagine for a moment, a sandy beach on a hot summer's day, where the sun is setting over the water. You're stood at the water's edge, in cool, loose clothing that feels soft and light against your body. You look out across the ocean, to where the sun is moving down towards the horizon. It seems so much bigger than normal. It warms you through and the sky around it is red and yellow and orange.

As you look across the gently lapping sea, your eyes drift up into the sky, where the colours are getting darker. From the reds, it moves through that turquoise sort of colour until you are looking overhead, where it is deep, dark blue. The first stars are starting to twinkle in the sky and, as you are looking up, you also notice some birds that you hadn't noticed before. They're making bird like noises as they wheel around in the darkening sky.

As your head is back and you're looking up, you feel the warm, gentle breeze, brushing your cheeks, drifting through your clothes and rustling your hair. You hear its gentle breathing and you are aware of the gentle beating of your heart and the slight tingling inside you. It seems to move in time to the sounds of the gently lapping waves as you hear the sea softly swish in and out.

As you hear those gentle waves, you become aware of the cool wetness of your bare feet, as they sink slightly into the wet sand at the water's edge. You look down to see the water lapping over your toes and your eyes are drawn out across the rippling waves to the far horizon, where the sun is now a giant golden ball that seems to be melting slowly into the sea.

You turn and walk back up the darkening beach, to your room. Opening the fridge, you feel the resistance of the handle as you pull it towards you. Reaching inside, the cool air floods out, brushing your face as it passes. Your hand finds a cold bottle of sparkling water. You're so thirsty....

Fetching a tall glass, you put it on the table beside the bottle. You return to the fridge for the ice tray and the metal dish sticks to your fingers with its momentary chill. The blocks chink into the glass and you turn to the fruit bowl for a lemon, feeling its waxy smoothness between your fingers. Taking a sharp knife, you slice through the lemon, releasing the zest and the spurting juice. Some of it trickles stickily onto your fingers. You lick it off absent mindedly, tasting the sharp bitterness.

Another slice with the knife and you can put a piece of lemon into the glass, its bright shining yellowness sliding over the melting ice. Picking up the bottle, the condensation on the outside runs over your hand, cold to the touch. Turning the cap, the pressure is released with a swisssh. With the bottle tipped up, the water sparkles and gurgles, fizzing over the ice and fruit, filling the glass.

Putting the bottle down, you pick up the glass and momentarily stroke its cool wetness across your warm brow. Putting it to your lips, you feel the hardness of the glass touch your lips and tap your teeth as the sparkling, cool liquid tingles over your tongue and pricks at your throat as you swallow. The coldness slides all the way down to your stomach. Another thirsty draft and you feel cooler, refreshed and at ease with the world.

Turning towards the wall, you catch sight of your reflection in the mirror. Take a long, hard look and....are you there.....

This is the power of your unconscious mind and, with your own imagination and language patterns you can make this more real than reality, because you can do anything to and put anything into this imagined memory.

There is a beautiful passage in *'Oscar and Lucinda'* by Peter Carey, where he is describing a Victorian garden. Carey had been compared to Dickens in writing this book and as I read the chapter in question, the power of his descriptive writing, no less than Dickens himself, or the grand master, William Shakespeare, transported me away from reality.

Recognize and harness the limitless power of your imagination and start to move towards your new, powerful destiny. To be your best, practice and grow the power of your unconscious mind to create and enhance new perceptions, especially the ability to visualize and make pictures.

Perception is reality

Have you ever stopped to think how powerful your imagination can be? Just reflect for a moment on your worst fears. What is the worst that can possibly happen to you? Just put the book aside for a moment, slump your whole body posture, lower your eyes and your head and really, really think about the worst thing that could possibly happen to you. What is your greatest single fear?

And as you have that image in your mind, make the picture really vivid; notice all that you see, hear and feel and momentarily step into yourself in that imaginary experience, just long enough to sense or feel how bad that could be.

Now, snap out of it, sit up straight, look up, breathe deeply and if necessary get up and walk around briskly. Sit back down, with that upright posture. Think or reflect for a moment on the challenges or problems you may have had in your life before you started reading this section. How do they feel or seem now in comparison to what you just experienced momentarily inside yourself?

Your imagination is so powerful, that it can create imaginary experiences so vivid that they can seem more real than real. Those imaginary experiences are composed of the same building blocks as real experiences. Recall for a moment the last time you were really upset by someone. What do you see, hear or feel inside yourself as you recall that time now? What was it that upset you, if you were to know? Was it something they said or did or didn't say or do? Was it a look, or just a sense or a feeling – a mind read? Or was it something that you couldn't put your finger on or specifically identify?

Whenever you find yourself in a state, it is because a stimulus has triggered a programmed response from the past in you. Fear is a future emotion. Therefore, you create fear, because before you get it, you didn't have it and the experience hasn't happened yet, if at all. What's more, if it were to happen, the realization of the fear would only happen if you consciously or unconsciously allowed the experience to trigger those programmed or preplanned responses or to go through the same pathways. You create fear. You control fear. You can stop fear. So, for what positive purpose for yourself would you ever want to experience fear, in the future or now?

Everything that happens, whether real or imaginary, only happens if it happens inside you. If you don't give it an existence in the first place, or if it happens externally and you either don't notice it, or block it out, or change the patterns so that you experience it in a different and much more resourceful way, it never happened, did it?

Everything that happens, whether real outside, or imagined, only happens for you if it travels through your perceptions, patterns and programs. Change the perception or the programs and it doesn't happen any more or it happens in a different, more positive or more resourceful way.

Take reframes, for example. The experience is the same and you recode it, in context or in time and it takes on a completely different, positive meaning. It travels through your filters in a different way. And you know who does that, who is really in control – you!

So, reality is always your perception and the powerful consequence of this is that when you change your perception, your expectations, your interpretation, your patterns and programs, to be totally positive, you change your reality. Let's consider the awesome consequences of this.

Create your own reality

There are three very powerful ways you can create a new reality for yourself and they are so simple:

- Change your perception of the past. You cannot change the facts of the past, but you can change the way you perceive those facts and memories. Indeed, you can obliterate a past memory completely (I suggest you store the positive learnings somewhere first). You can also modify a memory, by changing the structure (using submodalities changes), remove the emotion, distort or damage the memory so that it is either harder or even impossible to remember as it was, or even at all. You now have a new reality of the past, because when your mind goes to recover that memory, it isn't the same and therefore you have a different perception. Best of all, you can change the patterns and programs through which you experience such memories.

- Change your perception of the present. You will encounter a multitude of tools and choices with which you can change your present reality, either by the way you experience it, by what your programs notice and what they delete. To give an example, as you sit there, there is constant background noise that you hadn't noticed before I mentioned it. In the same way that your unconscious mind has learned to blot out or not hear the 'white noise' that you don't need, to do what you're doing, so it can also be programmed to not notice other aspects of present experience, remembering that all such present experience is processed through patterns and programs laid down in the past. To change the present, simply change your past...

- Finally, you can change your perception of the future. Need I say more?

And this is the most important thing. Did you ever worry about doing something, determine not to make that mistake and then go ahead and make it? Where did that come from? It came from your unconscious mind. First, it deletes the negative.

Try this. Whatever you do, don't think of a blue elephant...ok, one last chance, don't even dream of thinking about a yellow palm tree. Why does that happen? You never saw a blue elephant or yellow palm tree before, so your unconscious mind has to imagine what it would be like, in order to not think about it. Everything has to have a context and the context for not thinking about a blue elephant is...blue elephant...

The second thing is that your unconscious mind is a faithful servant and delivers efficiently what it believes you want it to do. So, it deletes the negative from "Don't slip on the floor", becomes preoccupied with slipping on the floor, tenses up all the muscles that might be involved in slipping and...whoops! (They don't put those signs up in factories any more, because the accident rate increased in the vicinity of the signs...)

Programming a successful future

So, now that we know that you can create your own reality, in vivid and exact detail, that means that you can program your future. Elsewhere in this book, we are going to prepare your vision, mission, goals, planned outcomes, etc.

All you need to do is preoccupy yourself with your powerful, positive future; get rid of the old limiting or negative patterns that might once have got in the way; visualize your success in achieving this; experience it in all its vivid rich detail in all your senses; and keep on thinking only about these future achievements, all the while taking practical steps towards fulfillment and your unconscious mind will deliver that reality. If it doesn't, then either you have still got limiting patterns to get out of the way and make sure that your achievement doesn't overly depend on the deliberate or serendipitous acts of someone else.

Oh, by the way, the 'inner saboteur'. Some people have experienced a powerful program that seems to intervene to try and destroy or inhibit positive achievement and fulfilling relationships. Get rid of it.

Deprogram it (it's a strategy, if you want to check later in the book); stop it; tell it to get the hell out of it; change its 'submodalities' to make it ridiculous; etc. Running the inner saboteur is self-indulgent. Find out for what reason on earth you might once have wanted to damage your own success or happiness and, keeping the learnings, change or remove the program so that everything is working resourcefully towards your pre-determined goals and dreams.

Dreaming

We all dream, passively. It just happens. It is a process that helps the unconscious mind to sort out, understand, reinterpret, integrate or reject the experiences of the day.

You may already know that more and more people are managing their dreams, so that they are dreaming more actively. Dreaming is a resource of limitless power for you. Make it work for you, actively. Plan your dreams, keep a notebook by your bedside and write down what you remember, when you remember it. Use them towards creating your limitless new reality.

Asking the unconscious

One way to do this is to ask your unconscious mind a question. Towards bedtime, or last thing at night, set it a task to be working on while you are asleep. Your unconscious mind notices and remembers everything. It is all there to be accessed – and much more than you ever thought possible and immeasurably more than you thought you noticed consciously.

That is why the process of hypnosis can be so powerful, for example with the witness to a crime or accident. The memory is there in vivid detail and just like your right brain when it tries to give you the correct answer to the trivial pursuit question that you override with your left brain logic, it gives the accurate picture, not an interpreted one.

Did you ever come across someone who was always looking for problems? Did you notice that somehow they seemed to keep on finding them? Ask, instruct or program your unconscious mind to find solutions and it is just like the 'Find File' macro on your computer. It will examine every memory until it finds what it is looking for, or what is there. Now the thing is, that if in the past we attached unresourceful emotions to the memory they might get in the way of, distort or blur the true events. So, we can clear the emotions out of the way and keep the learnings in a safe place for all time.

So, ask your unconscious mind a question; set it a task; and then leave it to work things out and find the answer in the way it knows best. Our daily thought processes have come to rely too much on rational, logical thinking (especially for men). Organizations are now seeking to recruit lateral thinking people or teach their people to do that (it's easy actually and you don't need an Edward de Bono course to learn it, in just a few minutes).

Your unconscious mind, whether in day or night dreaming engages both sides of the brain in the search, in the way that women are programmed to be and also in the way that creates long term memory efficiently.

(In my experience of working especially with educational or learning difficulties, or in life in general, the person with the poor memory is often someone who is trying to do everything in the left brain, rationally and logically. This hemisphere is most closely connected with the conscious mind and we have learned elsewhere how limited it is. The result is that it gets 'stuffed' and data starts to spill out. Engaging both sides in the process is commensurate with the process that creates long term memory, primarily through pictures and emotions, which are the product of the right brain).

So, start to dream. Your unconscious mind is more closely associated with the right brain, as it engages both. What you dream can be what you get, as the faithful servant delivers.

There is a well-known story about a basketball team that was divided into two halves. One half was told to stay on the court for two hours, practicing shooting baskets. The other was taken away out of the hall and sat comfortably, creating vivid mental images of shooting baskets successfully. After two hours, the two sides were brought together again.

The half that had spent the whole time visualizing, was at least twice as effective as the half that had diligently practiced.

Whatever it is you want to do or achieve, understand, learn and practice the power of your imagination, especially creating powerful images, rich in their elements of what you can imagine seeing, hearing or feeling. Use the incredible creative and processing power of your mind to create a new reality so vivid in your imagination that you cannot distinguish it from a real experience, or even better. Then be delighted as your dreams become a reality in the now...

Exercise - Using your creativity and imagination

Everybody can make pictures. Think of your car, or your house, now. The quality of the pictures varies from person to person, and all that matters is that as you practice making pictures more and more, the quality and aspects will improve.

Look up and to your right now and create a picture of something imaginary. Listen to someone's voice on the telephone, look up and right and make a picture of them speaking at the other end.

You can also recall pictures, by looking up and to the left.

You recall earlier we discussed 'chunking'. By chunking up and down on different subjects and in different situations, you can improve your chunking skills. As you listen to others, you can understand where they are chunking and move your own internal chunk size up and down until it matches theirs.

We have also learned about 'submodalities'. Use your skills now, first to analyze the submodalities of something you are seeing, hearing or feeling...first, outside yourself and then inside. Recall memories and run through the submodalities. The examples I have given earlier are only some. You can analyze any experience into your own list of submodalities. The more you use, the more vivid the representation, especially as you build, expand, enhance them more.

The purpose of this exercise is to practice your visualizing, chunking and submodalities skills, using and enhancing your creativity and imagination to see and modify your perception of the world in any way that works for you to make your world better. Having done these, bring them together and use your creativity to imagine all the ways you can use these same skills to enhance your understanding, decision making and implementation.

Step 2

THE POWER OF YOUR MIND
– learning the best way

The second step on the way to being your best is to realize the limitless power of your mind and how you can learn best...

Was there ever a time, when you were quite young maybe, and it was Christmas, or a birthday and there was a special present that you were hoping for. Or maybe you were just curious...So you looked at the presents, one by one, to see if you could make out what the shape was...maybe you picked one up and looked at it, because you were curious...or you could have shaken it, to see if it made a noise...or even have scrunched it and felt for the texture and feel...because you were curious...to find out...

The limitless power of the unconscious mind

We have already seen the power of the unconscious mind in so many ways. Your unconscious mind is made up of all the nerve cells in your body. If we dipped you in a substance that removed everything except your nerve cells, we would still be able to recognize exactly who you are. There are more nerve cells in your body than there are stars in the visible sky (10 to the power of 10 to the power of 11, to be precise). Each one has its own intelligence. Each one is capable of existing on its own in the universe as long as it has nourishment.

Our nerve cells, i.e. our mind, are the seat of our emotions. Mind and body are part of the same system, as we now know. And every memory that has any significance for us, has emotion as its foundation.

Remember, your conscious mind processes 7 ± 2 bits of information every moment and your unconscious can process 2.8 million bits in the same time. So why on earth do we spend so much time in our conscious mind?

Your beliefs influence your performance. In this book, you are finding new, powerful, positive possibilities to move towards your limitless potential. In the practical exercises and with some of the specifics we are covering, you can be finding the power that once you preoccupy your unconscious mind with a positive outcome, it will tap into that limitless potential to find ways to deliver it. If your part of the partnership is to take the practical steps and actions towards the goal, your unconscious mind will prompt you from time to time with measures of your progress and hints to keep moving forward. Be open to the messages.

We did an exercise at the start of this book, which gave you an insight into 'whatever you think you are, you are always much more than that'.

Walt Disney talks about the 'plausible impossible'. Supposing I was standing in front of you now, with a container of white-hot molten lead. If I plunged my finger into it, how long would it be before I was screaming with pain? A nanosecond, an instant, a microsecond, you might say. And yet, if we did not meet again for ten years, you would instantly recall me burning my finger. I would certainly recall it and here's the thing...you would recall everything we did or said that time, what I wore, what you wore, everything that you had done that day, eaten, drank, etc....because that's how fast the unconscious mind works...and it never forgets anything...

Let me show you. What would you score your memory skills out of 10? Most people score themselves between 2 and 7. Lots of older people tell me that memory deteriorates with age. Apart from showing them how they also have a 10 memory, I remind them that they are using less than 5% of their brain power anyway, so no matter how fast their brain cells die off, there will always be plenty of room. And that's without mentioning that if you need more brainpower, you simply grow it, unconsciously...

Take Einstein. Did you know that he was dyslexic and that he failed his college exams. Did you also know that he dreamed one day that he was sliding down a light beam and that's how he came up with the theory of relativity ($E=mc^2$). He is generally credited with being one of the cleverest men that ever lived. When he died, they found he had a much bigger brain than anyone else they had ever encountered. "That's why he was so clever" they said. For 35 years, this was the prevailing wisdom until one day it was realized that he had a bigger brain because he used it much more.

And then there is the mind...One of the things that makes a genius like Einstein is the ability to engage both hemispheres of the brain. This creates better memory, integrates the power of your imagination with the ability to make sense of anything and makes real or imagined experiences more real.

The mind stores everything with an emotional component and it stores it anywhere in the body that it thinks fit. I was working with a young man who had just started asthma. Previously he had suffered from hay fever for 18 years, which seemed much more than that, because he was forever sneezing, especially around animals.

Doctors will tell you that asthma and hay fever are connected allergies and did you notice that growth in the incidence of allergies has not only occurred at the same time as the growth in pollution, but also the growth in stress, especially the stress of relationships, including marital and similar breakdown.

On questioning further, I found that his worst asthma attack had occurred on the morning of an important exam. Also, that his sneezing and apparent allergy to animals had originated when he was three or four years old and the breakdown of his parents' marriage was taking place. By releasing the emotional linkages there was the possibility to release the asthma...

Learning how to learn

How did you learn how to drive? How did you learn how to ride a bicycle, or even to walk? How did you learn to read, write, or even speak?

By now, you will be having many insights.

When you were born, you weren't even thinking about riding a bike. You were *unconsciously incompetent* to ride a bike.

When you first sat on a bike, with the intention to learn to ride, what were the thoughts flooding your mind. Distilling them, you may have realized *consciously* that you were *incompetent* yet to ride a bike.

After many attempts you were able to ride without falling off or anyone holding the seat. You may have been a little wobbly or uncertain, but you had made it. You were *consciously competent* to ride a bike.

Later, you were very much more confident, so that you could leap on the bike and ride off with your friends, without so much as a thought of whether you might fall off. You had become *unconsciously competent* to ride a bike.

This is the process we go through in acquiring any skill. You may be very aware now of the many ways in which you are seeing change and opportunity in your life. You may be realizing that you have reached conscious competence as you have tried and practiced these skills and techniques. You may even have noticed that you, or other people, were already doing these things, out of conscious awareness. Now that you understand there are so many choices to improve still further.

Take some time to choose and practice the areas of competence, which seem right for you, to practice until they have been reinstalled now.

We learn best in trance. Meditation is a good way. Going out into a peripheral state can enhance learning. You may be seeing or feeling many other ways or times in which you know you are in trance. Rapture, ecstasy and even boredom are trance states. As you go deeper, reading this book, you are understanding and learning so much now...didn't you?

So, someone mentions memory. "I have a hopeless memory" (limiting belief). The unconscious mind records and remembers everything. Dreaming is a process for analyzing, sorting, connecting, deleting...What you need is recall. Here's how.

How to remember...anything

So, how would you score your memory skills out of 10? OK, this is what we'll do. I'm going to give you a list of over 30 unconnected things that I want you to scan for thirty seconds. Then I want you to turn the book over and recall as many of these things as you can, starting from the beginning of the list, *in the right order.*

Inn
Change
Aspirin
Navel
Bus
Everywhere
Children
Otters
Meat
Eggs
Wisdom
Habit
Acupuncture
Transfusion
Imagination
Mind
Belly
Explosion
Sucking
Tractor
Action Man
Bee
Love Heart

Eggs
Arch
Net
Desperate Dan
Ten dollar note
Hairnet
Exercise Bike
Nerve
Gripping
Octopus
Best
Emperor
Yawn
Opium
Nuts
Dessert

Did you do that? That's OK, that you may have tried to prove the limitations of your mind.

The way to remember anything is to make pictures and to associate into a memory as many different aspects and things as you can, using as many of your senses as possible. After all that's how your mind works when you're not even thinking about it.

Tony Buzan is credited with inventing the 'Mind Map'. The best ones use different colours and pictures. I created one to design the structure of this book.

Did I hear someone say that seems very complicated and must use a lot of memory? First, the most important thing is that when you structure your memories in this way, they will be in the form that your mind would have used anyhow. It likes associations – as many as possible, it loves pictures and symbols (which is why mnemonics work so well). Second, you have far more mind and brainpower than you are using. Imagine for a moment that your brain stores all the facts and your mind stores anything that has an emotional connection or association. They work best together when you associate the right brain creative, emotional skills with the left brain logic and language skills.

And if you were to run out of brain or mind space, your unconscious mind would simply create more and you already have more power than the entire computing capability on the planet. After all, how many computers do you know that can process 2.8 million bits of information every moment in background, while processing between 5 and 9 bits in the foreground?

And the core skill is making pictures and associations. So let's return to that list. In order to store pictures, move your eyes up in your head while remaining comfortable. For most people it works best if you move them up and to the left, because that is where your eyes access the visual recall part of your cortex. (See eye patterns in the appendix).

So in a moment I am going to tell you a story and as I do, turn it into a series of pictures, ideally a movie. You might want to get someone else to play with you and you can both practice proving to yourselves how good your memory really is.

So...

It's a nice sunny day and you're out for a walk. You come across an **Inn** and you go inside to get some **Change**. You buy an **Aspirin** and stick it in your **Navel**.

When you get outside, there's a **Bus**, with a sign that says it goes to **Everywhere**. It's full of **Children**, with pet **Otters**, which are guzzling **Meat** and **Eggs**.

Driving the bus is an old time comedian called **Norman Wisdom**. He's wearing a **Nun's Habit**. There's a hole in his arm like **Acupuncture**, but he tells you it's from a blood **Transfusion**

You wander off into your **Imagination**, making pictures in your **Mind**.

Suddenly, from inside your **Belly** there's a sort of **Explosion**. It's from **Sucking** the aspirin and just then a **Tractor** comes along.

Action Man is driving it and there's a **Bee** buzzing round him because he's eating **Love Hearts** and chocolate **Eggs**.

He drives through an **Arch** and suddenly he's caught by a huge **Net**, which is held by **Desperate Dan**.

He wants to borrow a **Ten**-dollar note, to get himself a **Hair** net. He throws an **Exercise** bike, which hits Action Man on a **Nerve**, just as he's **Gripping** an **Octopus**.

Watching all this is George **Best**. Beside him is the **Emperor** of China, who lets out a huge **Yawn**, because he's smoking **Opium**, chewing **Nuts** and eating Chocolate **Dessert**.

Repeat this story a few times, using the power of your imagination and noticing particularly the words that begin in bold.

Now put the book aside and run the story, all the while looking up and to your left and replaying all the pictures, or better still the movie. The more you do this exercise, the easier you can remember the story and will it be then or now when you will have realized that the key words spell out the mnemonic from the start of the book. The letters stand for the key words in the contents page of this book and also spell out the key elements of 'How to Be Your Best', the course we run. You may also notice that the key words start similarly to the key elements in Be Your Best. That way you can carry all these learnings with you forever.

> I CAN BECOME
> WHAT I'M BEST ABLE
> AND THEN GO BEYOND

Remembering names

We run this powerful routine every time we do *How to be Your Best* and invariably the question of remembering people's names comes up. It was Dale Carnegie who once said "the most important thing to a person is their name". I never forgot that. So why is it that people believe they can't remember them?

First of all, how important is that person to you? Really how important? If you only had one holiday a year and this year you were going to Hawaii on 31 December, you'd easily remember that, because it's important to you. And when you first met someone you really cared about, did you keep getting their name wrong every time you spoke to them?

It seems that lots of other people are more concerned with what they can get out of life than what they put into it. More people live on their own or lead quite solitary existences and stress may or may not be a factor. Would there be such a concern with emotional intelligence if one of its prime elements – empathy – wasn't too often notable for its absence. Empathy is an awareness outside of ourselves, of other people and their needs.

When you watch other people, either at work or at play, how often does it look or seem like everybody wants to have their say and most are 'queuing up' for their turn to say what they want to say. And then how well do they listen to others?

The best way to learn is by asking 'open' questions and then listening to the answers. The best way I know to make a favourable impression on someone, if that is what you want, is to take a genuine interest in them and their needs, wishes, likes and interests. We can do that by asking open, interested questions, engaging our whole selves in listening to, responding to and playing back or otherwise appropriately replying to them.

So what is the key to remembering people's names? When you meet someone for the first time, especially in business, what do we often do? That's right, we shake their hands.

When you walk into a shop that offers excellent customer service or as you leave the supermarket checkout, what does the checkout operator do? That's right, they engage you with their eyes and a smile.

So, the next time you meet someone, offer them your hand, introduce yourself, and ask them their name. And as you do that, repeating their name back to them carefully, all the while looking at their face and noticing what you notice. A good trick is to check the spelling of their name. Even with a simple name like Smith, there are alternate spellings: Smith; Smyth; Smythe. And the Christian name also.

So you might say " hello my name is Terry Carroll, what's your name?" "Ruth Hepworth" "Oh, Ruth Hepworth? Are you related to the Hepworths in Ilkley?" "No, I don't think so." "Ah, Ruth Hepworth, can I just check the spelling of your name?" "H E P W O R T H" "Thank you, Ruth Hepworth"

Now all the while you will be smiling and engaging her with your eyes. Meanwhile, you can allow your unconscious mind to suggest associations with the name, Ruth Hepworth. You might think of Babe Ruth, the baseball player and have an imaginary picture of him stood beside Ruth. Build into the picture as many associations as you can. You could also put into the picture a card that Ruth can be holding with her name written in block capitals. You know, rather like a convict in a crime photograph.

The key is in making as many associations into the picture as you can, especially as you repeat her name. Most of all, take a genuine interèst in the person as they answer your open questions, playing back their answers and subtly slipping their name into the conversation from time to time, all the while engaging them with your eyes.

Some people feel a little uncomfortable looking into someone's eyes for such a long time and find it easier to look at an imaginary spot just above the eyes on the forehead. (Incidentally, this is often the position also of what is known as the 'window into the soul'.)

As you have already discovered with the story at the start of this section, remembering facts and details is also best done by associating as many of your senses or other relevant things into the memory, especially pictures.

Exams, what have you...

I work a lot with young people, especially college students. Naturally, they are invariably interested in how they can best study for exams. So I tell them the story of when my stepson came to live with us.

At that time, he was studying hard for exams and like many other young people became more concerned as the events approached. " How can I learn all this stuff?" he asked.

The first step is to create the right environment. Music really helps. There is a huge amount of evidence, for example, that baroque music can improve productivity by up to 200 per cent. He didn't know what baroque music was but within a few days he was regularly playing Vivaldi while he studied.

When it came to revising for the exams, I suggested that he might like to read his notes onto tape and then play the tape back as he reviewed the material. Writing out your notes or a summary of them also works well, especially if you read them out loud as you write. Writing on a piece of paper is making pictures. The pen is in your hand, which uses your kinesthetic sense, that is your sense of touch or feeling. As you read the notes out loud, you are also accessing your auditory sense.

I further suggested that he might like to go to the pharmacy and buy himself an aftershave that he liked but had never used before. He could put it on himself in the morning when he started to study. He might also get himself some extra strong mints and suck these while he studied. In these ways, he would associate the learnings with the smell of the after shave and the taste of the mints.

On the day of his exam, he could make sure he wore the same after shave and sucked the same mints, so that as he started to write on the paper, the pictures, feel, voice in his mind, after shave and taste could associate him back into the learning state, from which he could readily recall all that he needed to know.

So these are just some ideas and you can have fun playing with your own variations for the challenges and opportunities that present themselves in your life.

The learning state

The best state for learning is a state of light trance. So anything that you can do to associate yourself into such a state, together with those things that stimulate your senses appropriately and make you feel good, can dramatically enhance your learning.

As we have already found, as far as memory is concerned there need be no problem. The unconscious mind remembers everything. It's not about memory, it's about recall. Your mind is like a highly sophisticated recorder that keeps everything you ever experienced in memories constructed by associating as many sensory experiences as possible. One step forward is to improve the efficiency of your recall process. When you add to that an efficient process of recording a memory in the first place, especially using techniques such as the Mind Map, you can be surprised how much more effective your memory is now.

When you reflect on how narrow the gate is through the conscious mind and how huge the processing capacity of your unconscious mind, then there is every incentive to open your mind to new possibilities as often as you can. When Tommy is looking out of the window, in a dream state, he may be thinking of doing other things, thereby engaging his conscious mind, all the while his unconscious mind is open to everything that is going on in the classroom. The skill is for Tommy to find the way to recover what is there.

When I'm running *How to be your Best*, I set out to deliberately distract the conscious mind so that the unconscious mind is open to the huge amount of learnings that are available during the session.

When the teacher asks Tommy a question and he looks up to the ceiling, did the teacher ever say "You won't find the answer on the ceiling." By now you may already have realized that while the answer isn't on the ceiling, Tommy is highly visual and is searching in the visual part of his brain to recall the memory.

When I am working with dyslexics or anyone else with a spelling difficulty, I only ever teach them how to spell backwards because the only way you can spell backwards is by recalling a picture of the word. I don't even need to tell the student to use the same trick for spelling forwards, because the unconscious mind learns very fast and once you can spell backwards, spelling forwards is a cinch.

So, whenever you wish to learn something, make a picture. Look up and to your left as you do this (this stores the memory in visual recall). Associate into the picture anything, which seems to you to be appropriate. This works very well for remembering peoples' names. Now, when you want to recall a memory, look up and to the left and see what pops in...

The RAS and Filters

We have talked a great deal about the power of the unconscious mind. We could write a book on that alone. Before moving on let us consider the importance of the Reticular Activating System (RAS) and the filters through which you process the world. Leaving aside the extraordinary power of your unconscious mind in being able to rapidly and efficiently process the phenomenal amount of data with which you are constantly being bombarded, we need for a moment to consider the filtering systems through which the data travels.

Everybody has a RAS, which is a cluster of brain cells that acts as a filter to your perceptions. It filters information in the context of your beliefs and what you consciously and unconsciously set out to achieve or expect. It filters out the bulk of irrelevant information and prevents us from being overwhelmed.

We discussed the primary filters earlier and here is a list of the filter categories through which information and experience passes:

- Values, beliefs and attitudes;
- Memories;
- Decisions;
- Language;
- Meta programs;
- Time, space, matter and energy.

Once it has passed through these filters, the input is compared with existing memories in order to interpret, reinterpret, understand and create an internal representation. Where the unconscious mind associates the input with a previous emotionally based memory, this may trigger a state which is displayed in the person's physiology, together with an associated behaviour. Very often this will happen without the person being consciously aware immediately, and sometimes not understanding where the state has come from or why it has appeared.

In this book you are already learning the so much about how you can understand the old patterns, programs and behaviours you may have run in the past. Also, how you can choose to change, modify or even remove those that no longer serve you in your journey towards your limitless potential. Part of this process is learning how to become aware of your unconscious patterns and programmes, create rapport between your conscious and unconscious mind, determine new choices and make the appropriate change. As you move forward these new and better patterns and programmes will become unconsciously installed to serve you in the future.

Understanding your filters

Take the time to complete the questionnaire in the appendix. Let your unconscious mind intuitively or logically represent the answers and the interpretations. Understanding the key filters through which you process all experience, you could choose to change them or share them with someone special so that they understand you even better. Use that understanding to enhance your growing success.

Try on the other patterns, which do not currently represent you, just to see how the rest of the world feels. What are the messages that come to you inside about the new vista of opportunities opening before you?

Step 3

THE POWER OF BELIEF – realizing your limitless potential

"Beliefs represent one of the larger frameworks for behaviour. When you really believe something, you will behave congruently with that belief." *Beliefs* (Robert Dilts, Tim Hallbom & Suzi Smith)

What are Beliefs?

"Beliefs are the presuppositions we have about certain things that either create or deny personal power for us. At this level beliefs are essentially our on/off switches for our ability to do anything in the world, because if you don't believe you can do something, you probably won't have the opportunity to find out." (Tad James, Wyatt Woodsmall, *Time Line Therapy and the Basis of Personality*).

We mentioned earlier the 'Logical Levels of Change':
- Spiritual
- Identity
- Beliefs & Values
- Capabilities
- Behaviour
- Environment

In the past, 'blockages' may have arisen in any one of these, creating opposite or limiting beliefs to those that a person may wish to move forward on. Together with values, beliefs can be pivotal to lasting change, whether by removing limiting or negative beliefs, or also by installing positive beliefs. We shall return to removing limiting beliefs later.

If you think about the logical levels now, and make statements at each level, which relate to or describe you, those statements are by definition beliefs. Beliefs are one of the fundamental filters through which we process our model of the world. We express our beliefs at the 'surface' through language and behaviour. At the depth of our minds, they are represented through the building blocks, or 'submodalities' covered in the appendix.

A belief is formed from individual thoughts. Once formed, other thoughts will attach themselves to one or more of the existing beliefs within the unconscious mind through the sorting process of generalization and serve to reinforce the existing belief.

Within the unconscious mind, a thought will never be free-floating on its own; it will always attach itself to another thought. The unconscious mind sifts and sorts through all the thoughts we have and then collects these in certain ways, often with one thought having more than one other thought connected to it. This has been compared to the London Underground system.

In the same way, every belief in our mind will always need to be connected to another belief.

"What exactly do we mean when we talk about beliefs? In NLP terms, they represent the assumptions we make about ourselves, about others in the world and about how we expect things to be. These assumptions determine the way we behave and shape our decision-making processes. They are often based on emotions rather than facts. We tend to notice 'facts' that reinforce beliefs. For example, if you believe that 'everyone is easy to get on with', you will only notice how well you interact with people. If, however, your belief is that 'you can't trust anyone', you will be suspicious and expect to be duped, and the chances are that others will sense this and be wary of you. Hence the term 'self-fulfilling prophecy': what you believe about yourself is what happens to you." (Mo Shapiro in *Understanding Neuro-Linguistic Programming in a Week*)

Why is an Understanding of Beliefs of Benefit?

"What are our beliefs designed for? They're the guiding force to tell us what will lead to pain and what will lead to pleasure. Whenever something happens in your life, your brain asks two questions:

1)   Will this mean pain or pleasure?

2)   What must I do now to avoid pain and/or gain pleasure? The answers to these two questions are based on our beliefs, and our beliefs are driven by our generalizations about what we've learned could lead to pain and pleasure. These generalizations guide all of our actions and thus the direction and quality of our lives." (Anthony Robbins, *Awaken the Giant Within*, Fireside, 1992.)

And here's the thing...the stronger the emotional basis for a belief, the greater the motivation and the stronger the belief.

"You see, it's never the environment; it's never the event of our lives, but the meaning we attach to the events – how we interpret them- that shapes who we are today and who we'll become tomorrow. Beliefs are what make the difference between a lifetime of joyous contribution and one of misery and devastation. " (Robbins, ibid.)

An understanding of beliefs, how they are formed and sustained and therefore how they can be changed, is fundamental to positive personal development and how to facilitate an environment of change.

A friend who uses NLP in counseling and therapy was once asked if he had ever had any failures. "I don't believe so, or at least no-one has told me. You see, I believe that everyone has truly limitless potential and by the time they have chosen to work with me to create lasting positive change in their lives, they already believe that what we will do will succeed...and that's most of the reason why it does. People choose their own journey. Lasting change is belief change, anything else doesn't last, as the old belief structures re-establish themselves."

So, an understanding of beliefs, how they are formed and structured, can be the basis for lasting change. By understanding and using the detailed structure of beliefs you can change anything from a belief to a habit, a phobia or a compulsion.

With an understanding of beliefs, you will be better able to understand and take account of some of the patterns of expression and behaviour of others. They may not fit with your own; indeed, some of them may 'jar' or even seem incomprehensible.

How are Beliefs Formed?

During early childhood years, you often accepted certain ways of thinking or behaving as absolute and correct, especially from your significant others, or other 'role models'. This fundamentally affected your development as you grew up, collecting and sifting information at an enormous rate. At birth, there were very few, if any, 'reference points' within your mind. For some time, through curiosity and fascination, you will have accepted most of what you saw, felt, heard, smelled or tasted absolutely and without any questioning whatsoever.

Accepting everything without question, however received, whether positive or negative, you were not at first asking "Is this right?", "Is this true?", "Is this fair?" Think of some of the beliefs you had as a child: Santa Claus; the tooth fairy; etc.

In this early stage of development, we all have many things suggested to us. Each message, suggestion, imagined response and comment becomes connected to other, previously accepted memories and stored away in the unconscious mind.

A useful analogy could be where a father gave his son a CD-ROM, with programs to use on his computer. Dad may have had that disk for some time. He may have got it or copied it from someone else. He will only have used it for his own purposes and in his own way, if at all. The son takes it and runs it on his own computer, not realizing whether it will work in his own, more recent and personalized, operating environment, nor whether it has a virus on it, or even if the software has become corrupted in some way.

Did you ever receive an email from a friend or acquaintance who had forwarded it on? Perhaps it had a pleasant thought, or a good idea? Perhaps it was a charity letter, or a pyramid scheme of some sort. If you had or knew of this experience, did it ever contain a virus? Had it been forwarded to you in good faith? Maybe the person who sent it had virus protection software and, unquestioningly forwarded it, not knowing whether it had been corrupted. Maybe you also had virus protection and innocently forwarded it to someone else? All of these assumptions were based on good beliefs.

"Within the unconscious mind there exists an operating system which governs how every one of our thoughts and situations is collated and combined with those already present. This law is known as *The Law of Belief*...(it) is a natural law which states that whatever (you) believe (your) mind always achieves for (you) either in reality or with (your) imagination as fantasy." (George Phillips & Lyn Buncher, *Gold Counseling*).

How beliefs are organized within the mind

Thoughts, ideas and images come into our minds from a myriad of sources and in a number of ways. We receive them through our representation systems (auditory, kinesthetic, visual, primarily) and translate them through our own unique set of filters, comparing and contrasting with previously stored information, thoughts, ideas, images and beliefs. Once this process is complete and any original or modified inputs have been accepted into our unconscious mind, it simplifies them by a process similar to that by which a summary or synopsis is produced. Fundamental to this is the RAS mentioned earlier.

Each thought is processed and once the summary has been created, it is automatically and in an instant connected to other thoughts related to similar subjects (generalization). It is from this framework of combined thoughts that beliefs are formed. By simplifying everything, rather than having to re-evaluate every situation to understand what it means, the unconscious mind is able to file every experience it ever received, assuming that it means the same now as it did in the past. In other words, it will interpret every related experience in the context of an existing belief, reinforcing that belief, or distorting to fit with it.

Following the acceptance of a belief, the unconscious mind will use the belief structure to assist in assimilating any further information it receives. Furthermore, once this belief structure is in place, the unconscious mind will do all it can to keep it there, since to change it could mean a drastic re-interpretation of many previous memories. While this process tends to perpetuate itself, it can also be used against itself by the powerful NLP based coaching methodologies and 'therapies' such as Timeline or Visual Squash. Once the unconscious mind has been persuaded to change a belief, it can then rapidly change all other parts of the belief structure, including whole collections of memories, beliefs, emotions and behaviours.

Once a belief structure has been created within the mind, it will seek out and attach itself to other beliefs, with which it can have some affinity or similarity. Once this happens, belief structures can join together to form belief complexes which will in turn seek other beliefs to bond with, all designed as part of the process whereby the unconscious mind can readily process and interpret a multitude of inputs from a complex world.

Through these processes, the unconscious mind is constantly seeking to sort out and simplify itself and its surroundings to reduce the number of processes it needs to carry out, e.g. by taking 'the path of least resistance'. It further simplifies these procedures by sorting into Primary and Secondary Beliefs. Primary Beliefs are the main beliefs that underpin the whole belief structure. These are commonly the memories with the greatest emotional weight and often the oldest beliefs.

Governing all of these processes is a belief strategy. Remember that you have a strategy for everything. Belief strategies are the ways in which we maintain and hold our beliefs. Every strategy starts with motivation. Our unconscious mind is motivated to maintain a belief strategy in order to keep things simple. A belief strategy is different than a reality strategy in that it cannot be tested with a sensory based check. For example, we know that an onion is an onion, by look, feel, taste and smell. If the tears flow while we are watching a film, we may not know in that instance whether this is happiness or sadness or whatever, because the response is based on a belief or beliefs seated in the deep structure of our mind.

Belief strategies are a set of evidence procedures that you use to decide whether something is believable or not. This kind of evidence is usually in the form of submodalities – the qualities of the modalities, i.e. pictures, sounds and feelings (and tastes and smells).

A friend lived next door to a good and kind family. The parents and the two boys had sound values, were engaging, had strong positive values and worked hard. One Saturday, the friend saw the younger son, A, next door working in the garden. They had a warm conversation, reinforcing the inner beliefs the friend had about both A and his family.

The next day, the friend was woken early by a knock on the door. Opening it, he was confronted by two grey-looking people who seemed to have shrunk from the warm, outgoing couple he knew as his neighbours. "What on earth is the matter?" he asked. "A is dead!" "But he can't be, I only saw him and spoke to him yesterday!" was the friend's instant, unthinking response, based on the belief that A was still as well and healthy as the day before. "He's dead, he's dead" was the mother's shrieked retort.

The shocked friend's state changed immediately as his unconscious mind connected death, love and friendship, caring, concern, etc. and asked the neighbours in. The belief of A's existence changed in an instance, while a new lasting belief in lifelong friendship with the couple was created in that same shocked moment of trust and need.

Beliefs in business

"The level of belief systems and values contains statements about yourself, other people and situations that you hold to be true. They are emotionally held views not based on fact:

'I believe that people in general can be trusted.'
'I believe that I can learn from any experience I have.'
'I believe that the customer's needs are the heart of business success.'

For a company these would be the beliefs on which the company and the way it goes about its business are founded. They only function as beliefs if the everyday behaviour of the management and the employees are an expression of these beliefs. For this to be the case the beliefs need to be ones that are drawn from the organization's actual employees. Ones picked from a textbook on management because they sound, look or feel good won't work and are more likely to lead to increased dissatisfaction if the everyday behaviour contradicts the published beliefs. However, where they do match, the result can be a major contributory factor to the cohesion and congruence of the organization." (Sue Knight, *NLP at Work*).

There is a very real and meaningful correlation between the role and meaning of values and beliefs for the individual and the organization, especially the critical importance of convergence.

Beliefs and creating lasting change

- Our RAS has been shaped/influenced by beliefs. It filters our perception to influence our behaviour.
- It also affects our feelings, perceptions and self-talk.
- Beliefs can be changed, whether over time or by coaching intervention. Limiting beliefs can be readily and effectively removed or positively modified.
- Positive self-talk creates and reinforces confidence.
- Our comfort zones are founded on emotions and often strongly held beliefs, which is why they may have been difficult to shift.
- Problems involving or based on self-talk, comfort zones and limiting beliefs need new positive pathways.
- Our beliefs influence our thoughts and behaviours.

Some of the NLP Presuppositions (beliefs) are of value here.

- Every person is unique;

- Everyone makes the best choices available to them at the time;
- There is no failure, only feedback;
- Behind every behaviour is a positive intention;
- The meaning of your communication is the response you get;
- The person with the most flexibility in thinking and behaviour has the best chance of succeeding;
- The mind and body are part of the same system.

And as you progress elegantly and expertly through your own journey, having unconsciously absorbed the above beliefs, you will have been seeing, hearing and feeling all the wonderful new opportunities and ways of perceiving things that can have opened up for you now.

In early life you may well have been exposed to 'old wives tales', old sayings or saws, religious teachings, etc. which somehow seem to have become part of the fabric of human beliefs, e.g.:

- 'I want doesn't get';
- 'Ask and it shall be given':
- 'What goes around comes around';
- 'Children should be seen and not heard';
- 'In this world you only get what you work for'; etc.

Other people may have experienced such as:

- 'You're lazy';
- 'You're stupid';
- 'You're the ugly duckling of the family';
- 'You'll be bald before you're 40, because I was and your grandfather was';
- 'You're fat';
- 'Bad luck runs in this family';
- 'All the men in this family dies of a heart attack';
- 'Alzheimer's runs in this family'; etc.

You, however, may have taken on unquestioning beliefs, such as:

- The sun sets in the evening and rises in the morning;
- The sun rises in the East and sets in the West;

- The only certainties in life are birth, death and taxes;
- Every four years is a leap year and we have February 29th;
- 'I was born on xxx (your birthday);
- The moon revolves around the sun;
- Gravity prevents us falling off the earth.

A practical exercise

Here is a suggested set of processes that can be used to dramatically influence your beliefs and facilitate the possibility of new choices and resourceful behaviours:

- Discover, collect and understand your most significant beliefs
- Use **reframes** to loosen limiting beliefs
- Understand what positive beliefs are present and **bridge across** the patterns to modify limiting beliefs
- Use positive thinking and self-talk to modify or create new positive beliefs.
- Use **anchors** to reinforce positive beliefs (including new or modified beliefs)
- Use **visualization** to facilitate new choices and planned positive outcomes
- Test the new beliefs and planned outcomes by imaging past or future situations which are relevant

Bridging Across for Changing Beliefs

Visualize two situations, maybe one where you want to behave differently and one in which you behaved in the way that you want to behave. Compare the differences between the submodalities of these two pictures. You can change the negative picture into a positive one by changing the submodalities so that they match the submodalities of the positive picture. For example, the negative picture may be dim and the positive one could be bright. In this case, make the negative picture brighter to change it to a positive one.

Understanding your beliefs

So what are your core beliefs, for yourself, about your life, work, relationships, etc.? How do you believe now that you are successful? Go out into the future, to a time when you have been successful and what do you feel are the positives as you are feeling good about that now?

Write down your positive and enhancing beliefs. Look at them. For each, write down at least three ways in which that belief can make you the person you plan to become now.

If you wish, make an internal representation of each belief. Take it forward to a time where it seems most appropriate to be in relation to your growing success. Step outside the belief in your mind and leave it in that future space. Come back to the now.

Removing a limiting decision or belief

For some, the odd negative or limiting belief may have popped in. Change those now at your choice.

Just go inside now and get a sense or a feeling of where any negative belief may have come from. Become aware of the person from your childhood who may have represented that belief or otherwise presented it to you. It was never your belief, it was always their belief and you took it on at that time when you were young, because it was in your awareness at the time and in some way it may have seemed right.

Sometime, it became a limitation. Its purpose was to carry forward a positive learning that was there for you. You no longer need it.

Close your eyes and create a representation, which is right for you, of that belief. Make it no bigger than a box you could carry. Now, inside yourself, use the limitless power of your imagination to create vividly beautiful wrapping paper, ribbons and whatever. Wrap the representation with all your loving care, in the beautiful paper.

In your mind, give the beautiful wrapped present to the person from whom the belief came originally, with all your love and tender care. It was never your belief, it was theirs. Indeed, it may not have been theirs originally, it may have come from their past...So give that belief back right now, as you no longer need it, now you have stored the positive learnings in that special place.

And finally.....

"*What we hold as true or not true* powerfully determines our behaviour. Indeed, our beliefs present a major driving force of our lives. If you believe you can accomplish something, you probably will. If you believe you cannot accomplish a particular task, the odds pile up against you that you won't.

A belief involves a generalization about experiences, about relationships between experiences, and about the meaning of experiences....Our brain knows what we believe, what we doubt and what we don't believe by the structure of our internal representation – and this sometimes involves submodality differences." (*The User's Manual for the Brain*, Bodenhammer & Hall).

Roger Bannister believed the four-minute barrier could be broken for the mile. In the year that followed, dozens of runners changed their beliefs and followed suit. It was once believed that no-one could travel faster than the speed of sound and any plane trying it would be destroyed in the process.

Cliff Young was a 61-year-old sheep farmer from the Australian outback, who entered and won the Melbourne to Sydney long distance race. Others had beliefs that: you ran 18 hours and slept for 6; you needed special equipment and training. Cliff 's only practice was running around his sheep station doing his job. He shuffled along in overalls and working boots without sleeping, winning by *one and a half days*.

Step 4

THE POWER OF EXCELLENCE

– modeling the very best

Modeling

Once upon a time, there was a conventional belief about skiing. Now anyone can learn to ski. In the origins of NLP, Bandler and Grinder set out to understand what makes people excellent. They were able to codify all the patterns of human language and behaviour, including especially non-verbal communication.

They found that no external event will be experienced without going through an individual's filters. Some of these were quite near the surface. We could equate these to some degree with the left brain conscious processing that we have learned to rely on too easily. Other filters were more deeply seated and were connected with longer-term memory, experience and emotions. These would be more closely associated with the right hemisphere and the unconscious mind.

They found that experience and memory had a structure, which was comprised of the primary representation systems (or modalities) through which we process the world (Visual, Auditory, Kinesthetic, Olfactory or smell, Gustatory or taste). These in turn were comprised of a multitude of submodalities. Not only could all experience and memory be reconstructed using this code, but also the unconscious strategies we run to do anything in our day to day lives could similarly be analyzed through these structures.

So excellence in an individual has a structure and while each person has their own minutely specific way of doing excellence, it is possible to 'elicit' or analyze the overall structure, thereby giving us insights into how we can learn excellence for ourselves. The process of understanding the structure of excellence and then replicating it has become known as modeling.

Now, one of the interesting things is that we can learn to trust our unconscious mind more as we go forward and it can intuitively understand how to be excellent. So for example there is a game called 'walking in someone's shoes'.

Get together with another person. One of you thinks of an event or activity they are going to. They walk round an open space with the other person walking one pace behind. The lead person thinks of nothing else other than where they are going. The follower clears their mind of everything else and opens it to all possibilities in the mind of the person in front. After two minutes, the two of you stop and the follower suggests where the leader is going.

Played with superb rapport you can achieve an extraordinarily high success rate in communicating unconsciously this way.

Finding a Role Model

My partner had three role models: Tina Turner; Richard Branson; and Naseem Hamed.

Tina Turner was a singer with and married to husband Ike. It was an abusive relationship. Eventually she found the personal courage and strength to escape. As a solo artist she became arguably one of the greatest rock icons of all time, still performing and looking years younger than her age into her sixties.

Richard Branson left school at 16 with a qualification in Art. His head teacher wrote, "Branson won't amount to much." In 1999 his wealth was estimated at $3.5 billion, making him one of the richest people in the UK. What is amazing has been his business success despite his lack of qualifications and also despite being dyslexic. He has pursued one death defying challenge after another, creating in the process a global brand name for his Virgin business.

'Prince' Naseem Hamed was diminutive when he was noticed as a schoolboy by Brendan Ingle, his former trainer. He modeled himself on Muhammad Ali and Sugar Ray Leonard, two of the most outrageously talented boxers of all time. His flamboyance does not appeal to everyone but his showmanship and boxing skills made him one of the greatest British boxers of all time.

And you in your life can find role models of excellence for any or all of the areas of your life that you can move forward in. In the end of the book, you will find a detailed explanation of strategies and yet you may not ever have the chance to sit down with your role model and elicit what makes them excellent.

You can, however, watch them on TV or video, listen to what they say and how they say it and even analyze what they write. In all these things, together with what you pick up by opening your mind to the intuitive messages that are there, you can find enough to model and move you forward towards your own personal excellence.

As a motivational speaker, I am modeling Anthony Robins, Jim Rohn, Martin Luther King, Nelson Mandela, Jack Black, Russell Webster, Billy Connolly and a number of other brilliant performers who I may never meet.

Ski boards are an excellent example of how quickly people can learn something that had previously been completely new. Ski boards were only invented recently. These new techniques had to be specially evolved, through balance and synchronized movement. Now thousands of people are spectacularly successful in using them. How quickly did you learn to walk? Were you instructed, bit by bit, exactly how to configure and move all the hundreds of individual muscles you use? Or did you observe and model other humans around you?

NLP has shown us how, through modeling, we have already observed and acquired the skills and strategies we have understood. If you wish, you can consciously unpack, understand and apply the skills and strategies you see in others. Better still, to 'stand in their shoes'.

I watched Nick Faldo, over and over, not to learn his golf techniques and mechanical movements, but to get a sense or a feeling of what it was like to be him as he played a great golf shot. This is insight and intuition. If I could have met him personally, I might have asked him to go minutely through his motivation, decision, convincer and reassurance strategies for hitting the great shot. All the while, I could watch his eye movements and listen to his predicates, to get an understanding of everything that was happening for him inside and out. I could then exactly model these.

Modeling is a skill we all have. Most things we learned as young children were unconsciously modeled from those around us. Our skills and our strategies. Being required to watch and listen, when adults were around, we not only learned the skills we saw, but also learned how adults unconsciously modeled other adults and the results they got. We took inside what worked and didn't work.

Much of what we do in our lives is in an unstructured environment. You can put your own structure on it and one that is right and works for you and you alone. You can take any aspect of a skill you wish to acquire: the strategy; style; methodology; mentality; etc. and add to that the models you have seen to be highly successful around you. How much better can you be now that you can listen to, watch and get a feel for, model and apply the internal strategies of someone who you regard as excellent.

Strategies

We shall be covering strategies in more detail in Step 7. And now that you have realized you can develop your own strategies and methodologies, you need to be sure that your style and implementation are all your own. It is fundamental that your personal implementation strategy fits with your personality and that your chosen strategy for a particular skill fits your everyday strategy for things in general.

Exercise - Modeling the best

Today, think of someone in life and/or in business, whose skills and ability you wish to model. Use your perceptual position skills (see appendix I) and your peripheral awareness to have a sense or a feeling of what it is like being that person being the best they can be, in business, life or both.

If you can, elicit their strategies to be and do what they do best. Watch their eye patterns, mirror and match to enhance the sense or feeling. Understand their style and methodology. Use it, improve it, or modify your own as you see or feel to be appropriate to enhance your success.

Drawing on all the appropriate skills covered earlier, practice modeling that person inside yourself and also in whatever movements or mannerisms seem acceptable to you. When I model Nick Faldo, I even copy the bum club wiggle he does as he settles down in his set-up routine. As I hit that ball, I am as near to Nick Faldo's swing and strategies inside myself as I can be. (By the way, it hasn't mattered to me that he has had a period of less success, because I am modeling him at his very best, such as when he hit the 2 iron into the green to beat Greg Norman in the US Masters).

Step 5

THE POWER OF SUCCESS – Visualizing your achievement

The Formula for Success.

The six most important principles for ultimate success are:

• To know and be able to visualize your outcome	*Sally Gunnell*
• To be highly motivated to achieve	*Dean Macey*
• To take massive action	*Nick Faldo*
• Have sensory awareness of what is happening around you and how well you are doing	*Michael Johnson*
• Have behavioural flexibility in all that you do	*Tiger Woods*
• Operate from a physiology and psychology of excellence	*Denise Lewis*

Knowing and visualizing your outcome

Now that you understand that you can create your own reality, the single most important factor in creating the basis for ultimate success is being able to clearly define and visualize the outcome that will verify your achievement. In moving towards your limitless potential, we have already discussed the importance of having clearly defined short to medium and longer-term goals. Whether in general terms, therefore, or for specific achievements, you can program your future success by visualizing the outcome in every clear and vivid detail.

Although the concept of submodalities may at first have been a little difficult to grasp, now that you understand the critical significance of these 'building blocks' of experience, that means that you will have realized how they can be incorporated into the future vision of your success.

Someone who demonstrated this eloquently, was Sally Gunnell in the 1992 Olympics. In her early career, Sally was an average 400m runner. With her coach, she decided to step up to the new event for women of the 400m hurdles. The culmination of her athletics career was in winning a gold medal in Barcelona.

Coming round the final bend, Sally was not winning - in fact she was second or third and yet she came through strongly to win the gold medal. Afterwards when interviewed, she was asked whether she was worried coming round the final bend. " No, because last night I ran the movie of the race. I knew some of the other girls were stronger than me and that I might not be leading coming to the last 100m. In the movie, I saw myself coming through to win the gold medal."

So Sally Gunnell was very clear in her goal and had visualized the outcome in detail. She got the result she wanted.

Motivation to succeed

It goes without saying that to achieve the success that you will have visualized, you will also want to be highly motivated. We have discussed motivation earlier.

Dean Macey was only 20 when he entered the decathlon in the Sydney Olympics. He had originally been inspired as a young boy while watching Daley Thompson, one of the greatest athletes Britain has ever produced. Going into the last event, Macey was lying in the silver medal position. Unfortunately, he ended up in the fourth position missing out on any medal at all.

Interviewed afterwards, he confessed to feeling 'gutted', adding "I have learned so much and next time I shall win the gold medal." Macey has huge motivation. In the 2001 world championships he was leading at the end of the first day. Carrying painful injuries to his thigh and right arm, he still had another five events to do on the second day. Gutsily refusing to acknowledge the pain, he completed the event and won a bronze medal, beating the winner at Sydney.

Once again, he admitted his disappointment and continued to reflect on his progress towards what he regarded as an inevitable gold medal in due course.

Take massive action

No athlete has to train harder than men in the decathlon and women in the heptathlon. It means work in all seasons and weathers, year after year. What drives these people other than the incredible motivation?

Now that you understand that you can be excellent in any way that you choose, it makes sense that to be world class you would have to invest as much time and effort as the best in the world. So how important to you is it to be your best self in life and in general?

Nick Faldo was an average British PGA golf professional. He decided he wanted to be the best in the world. He was recommended to David Leadbetter, at that time the best golf coach in the world. He was told he would need to completely remodel his swing. Was he prepared to do what it takes?

For 20 months, Faldo worked ceaselessly towards his goal. At times he hit up to 2,000 golf balls a day, occasionally making his hands bleed. Not long afterwards, he achieved his goal of becoming world number one, where he remained for a couple of years. Arguably the greatest British golfer that ever lived, he even inspired his team to more than one Ryder Cup victory.

Have sensory awareness

While you are progressing towards your chosen goal and ultimate success, it is important to be aware consciously and unconsciously of anything relevant that is going on around you that can enhance your potential and give you feedback as to how well you are doing.

Michael Johnson is in many people's book the greatest athlete who ever lived. He was certainly the best 400-metre runner. In the Sydney Olympics, barring injury, disqualification or some other shock, there was no question as to whether he would win, only by how much and whether he would beat the world record.

As I watched the replay of his inevitable victory, I was struck by something astonishing. The camera that had tracked him all the way round showed him looking up at the screen as he ran. Now he had no reason to fear any other runner in the field, so what was he looking at? Eventually it dawned on me. He was looking at himself as he ran. Inside himself he was able to feel and hear how it felt and to notice with his peripheral vision all that was going on around him. By watching the screen, he was able to add the picture to integrate the whole experience.

We now live in an age where the video camera is pervasive so you can do the same in whatever you choose to be excellent at, whether golf, public speaking or whatever...

Have behavioural flexibility

There is an old saying "if it ain't broke don't fix it". The new one I like is "if it ain't working try something else, try anything else."

As we considered earlier, the person or part of a system or process with the greatest flexibility will end up controlling the system. And so with Tiger Woods, still only a young man and to many people already the greatest golfer who ever lived.

It was fascinating watching the President's Cup in 2000. This is an event like the Ryder Cup, played between the US and the rest of the world outside Europe. As I watched Tiger finishing one of his matches, it was obvious how many of his teammates were there to support him. But what else was happening? As he hit one great shot after another, you could almost hear the inner groans as these world class golfers realized that he is in a class of his own.

It can be argued that he has single handedly taken golf to another level. It is more popular at all ages. The prize money has more than doubled. For a while, Tiger was seemingly invincible. Then a number of golfers like Phil Mickelson decided that they could not beat Tiger by being defensive and changed to a more aggressive strategy, taking more risks. Mickelson soon became world number two.

So what is it about Tiger's behavioural flexibility? He may be winning a competition by several shots. He comes off the golf course having had a fine round. Where does he go? Straight to the practice ground. And when he comes in on the morning of the final day, a comfortable leader, he goes to the self-same place. There is always something he can do to improve.

A physiology and psychology of excellence

Added to that, Tiger works out for a couple of hours a day and is probably the fittest golfer around. So how excellent do you plan to be? If you are single minded in your goals and determined to achieve the success you have dreamed about, you will do anything to create the fitness of mind, body and for that matter spirit to achieve.

Look at Anthony Robbins. A dumpy big kid at college, he is now as fit as anyone around. Not only does he apply his outstanding NLP based motivational skills to himself, he also has a demanding physical and dietary regime.

Denise Lewis was an Olympic debutante in Sydney, in the equally demanding women's heptathlon. After she had won the gold medal, she also was interviewed. She was an absolute vision of fitness and health, but what is more, her internal spirit and captivating personality shone out of her. As also when collecting her women's sports personality of the year award at Xmas that year, she was charming and gracious. No more so in congratulating Steve Redgrave who pipped her for the overall award and a world class paraplegic athlete who had won her own class.

If she chose, Lewis could have a career in media or politics because she was the personification of physical and psychological excellence.

Putting it all together

So how do I do that, some might say? The answer lies within and without, using the many tools and techniques described in this book, you may try in vain to recover any of those old patterns that you once ran, which used to hold you back.

It is true that to fulfill our limitless potential we can choose to unlearn any negative patterns of thought that we once had. These patterns had an emotional component. This component served to remind us from time to time that there had been an issue unresolved from our younger years. If we had ever gone into an unresourceful state, such as fear or panic, what was the origin of that behaviour?

There was a positive lesson to be learned from that old memory. Our unconscious reminded us that the lesson had not been perceived or understood. Once we learned it, we could let go of the emotion and move forward in any aspect of our life that might previously have been affected.

In order to be as resourceful as we wish to be, we had to unlearn any negative patterns of behaviour. It was never necessary to be driven by fear, when we can choose instead to be driven towards success. That way we can use our unconscious programs to motivate our desire to succeed.

For every goal, use the process of visualizing outcomes to unconsciously program your success. If, for any reason it is overtaken by circumstance, you can, in a wholly constructive and positive frame of mind, make a rational judgment that the game has changed and you will vary your strategy. When you do this through the process of self-mastery, your conscious and unconscious mind work in harmony to optimize your overall success.

Living and working, making money and enjoying your leisure, success and not success, for the time being, are all part of the rich pattern of life. Remember, you are just one component of your world as you perceive it. And how soon will you have perceived that success is only defined and achieved by you on your own terms. Nobody else can define failure for you if you refuse to accept that and instead recognize a God given opportunity to learn and grow.

Frustration in life may in the past have occurred through not knowing, not being in control, rather than failure or disappointment. It can be one aspect of human nature to seek resolution. Life creates more questions than answers. It's when you think that you have all the answers that you can realize you need more questions.

NLP based therapies produce lasting, fundamental resolution and success. A trainer was once asked "you have been using these techniques for ten years – you must have resolved every problem you ever had?" The reply was "life can be like a road...you go down a road to the end...and there's another opportunity".

Life is like golf. If you cheat, you are cheating yourself. When, on the other hand, you are being the best you can be...or better, you set the rules for your own success. Nothing else matters. You are at cause in your world and in your life as you perceive it. It cannot make you do anything you do not choose to do.

More on success factors

"We all have purposes that drive us...wherever we see people succeeding, the same factors seem to appear time and time again... We always find, for instance, a drive, enthusiasm or passion... We find strong beliefs...beliefs about yourself, what you are capable of doing... And linked with these, there is usually a strong system of values... We also notice that successful people, as well as knowing where they want to be, usually seem to follow some plan or strategy... They seem organized in their thinking and the way they marshal internal and external resources... They also seem to have a certain energy – not just physical strength and fitness, but an inner energy that keeps them going against all the odds when ordinary people would have given up." (*NLP*, Dr Harry Alder).

The above book was one of the earliest on NLP to be published in the UK. In it, Dr Alder identifies four steps to success in any situation: know what you want (know your outcome); take action; learn to notice the results of what you do; be prepared to change your behaviour until you get the result you are after.

Whether reading Sun Tzu's thoughts on the art of war, Zen Buddhism or chaos theory, you may come to the same conclusion on the value of counter-logic and the value of following your own intuition and instinct, rather than the herd.

From quantum physics, we understand that a particle moves as a result of being observed. Schrodinger's puzzle is whether a cat put into a box with a radioactive isotope has died. If we open the box some time after, finding the cat dead, how do we know when it died, or whether indeed it was us opening the box and observing it that caused it to die.

If we keep looking out for a possible negative outcome, how do we know if it occurs whether it was a result of our act of observation. My wife visualizes car-parking spaces in a busy town and they persistently appear. Ever since I set my mission and goals and visualized the outcomes, my 'luck' has changed dramatically, with wonderful consequences...

In his wonderful books 'Creating Affluence' and 'The Seven Spiritual Laws of Success', Deepak Chopra also writes of limitless potential:

"Inherent in every intention and desire is the mechanics for its fulfillment...intention and desire in the field of pure potentiality have infinite organizing power. And when we introduce an intention in the fertile ground of pure potentiality, we put this infinite organizing power to work for us."

And...

"Therefore you have the ability to acquire anything that falls within the realm of your imagination, and even those things that are currently outside the limits of your imagination. The more you acquire, the more your imagination will expand. What is unimaginable today might become imaginable tomorrow."

In life in general, we are on a road of continuous learning, improvement, personal growth and self-discovery. It does not take much to become an expert in a particular field. As someone once said, all you need to do to become a millionaire is to know a bit more than anyone else about one subject.

Learn speed-reading and read as much as possible. Lateral thinking comes from the integration of right and left brain processes. Intuition also comes from the right brain. For too long we may have let left brain thinking dominate our daily activities. By all means use logical and rational thought. Where do inspiration and insight spring from – inside? If you want average performance, settle for average thinking. It is the extraordinary thought that comes from intuition partnered with judgment, which can inspire your success.

Goals and Outcomes

You are not alone in desperately wanting to succeed, so what will set you apart? Going back to levels of change, how do you see yourself? What is important in your life, its purpose and mission? Are your values and beliefs all positive and supportive of the success you want to achieve? Do you have a plan? What long term and intermediate goals have you set yourself? In this section we also talk about setting and visualizing outcomes.

What capabilities do you have for being successful in whatever you choose and how can you enhance these, both in brain and mind? What purposeful behaviours are you displaying? What language patterns are you using, including internal? Are they positive? How do you perceive the environment in which you exist and work? What changes can you make in that environment and especially the way you perceive it, that will help to optimize your performance?

As I am writing this book, I have broken it down into 'bite-size chunks'. That way, I can write up to 8,000 words in a day. I set myself mini-targets during the day, like stepping-stones across the river. As I achieve each of these, I reward myself in some small way – chocolate biscuits with my tea, etc. Also, as I write each idea, all the time I am working towards an ultimate goal, which I have visualized.

As I write, I am also visualizing many of the situations I am writing about. My environment is warm, conducive and relaxed. Baroque music is playing (it creates the right brain waves for productivity) and I am relaxed, purposeful and happy.

Having a goal or goals to work towards enhances any major project or process. These may be long, medium or short term – whatever works for you. A friend of mine sits down with his wife every New Year's Day and they work out joint goals together. As they review them, they may wonder if they will achieve them all in one year. Each year, they marvel as they achieve and surpass them.

There is a well-known story about the group of Yale students, to whom it was suggested they might wish to do a life plan. Many years later, they were followed up. Only 3% had set a plan. Every one was emotionally and financially secure. Their total income exceeded the total income of the 97% who had not set a plan. Give the unconscious mind a clear set of goals to work towards, turn them into a vivid internal representation, see yourself in the picture, put it out in your future timeline and watch your unconscious mind deliver!

Goal setting is a traditional process for many companies. I used to think the majority would do strategic planning before I became a management consultant. In practice I found only 5% or so carried out a meaningful exercise that they reviewed and renewed annually, monitoring progress in between.

Any individual can decide on an overall goal, purpose or mission. You can then set the intermediate goals, decide on and implement your overall strategy and the elements of your 'business plan', reviewing the opportunities to learn, change and grow on the way.

What are your beliefs and wishes, aspirations and goals in life? Turn your planned and actual experiences into pictures, or even vivid internal representations, through which you experience in your imagination what you will see, hear and feel when you have achieved your inevitable success.

In setting your goals, you may choose to optimize, rather than maximize your goals. Rewards involve some risk. The optimization process in for example wealth creation involves optimizing the gains in the context of a chosen or managed level of risk. You could choose what risk you are prepared to accept before you begin. Through self-control, you can then optimize your performance in the context of that chosen limitation.

The intermediate goals we set should be in keeping with the longer-term goals. They should be developmental or progressive. Sometimes, in achieving intermediate goals, we may go through a period where we may question everything that is happening and its possible effect on ultimate success.

Through this book we may understand more about other people, as well as ourselves. It is often said that success at poker is based on psychology as much as probability. If we understand motivations and behaviours, we can take account of these.

Nevertheless, sometimes, things may not have gone according to plan. A major setback might have caused us to review or even abandon a strategy for the time being. Console yourself that you can learn even more from mistakes or misjudgments on the road to inevitable success.

There is the true story of the Executive who made a mistake costing his company $1 million. Summoned to the Chief Executive's office, he took and offered his resignation. "That won't be necessary" was the response. "The way I look at it I have just invested $1 million in your personal development. Go away and prove me right."

Setting, changing and accepting goals and objectives for your ultimate success involves parking your ego, making sound decisions, understanding and managing your behaviours and your self, achieving self-mastery.

Success in any aspect of your life can have such a meaningful impact on so many aspects of your life, that it is a good idea to cross check all your goals to make sure they integrate with your interim life goals. Be relaxed and comfortable in yourself in the sure knowledge no part will conflict with any other aspect of your life. You are at cause in everything and making objective choices in everything you do.

Setting and Visualizing Outcomes

This process is described in the Appendix M. Once you have set your medium term goal, determine some event or outcome that will demonstrate to you beyond doubt that you have achieved this goal. Check the well formedness of the outcome, visualize it and put it out into your future. Determine and stick to your chosen strategy and entrust your future success to your unconscious mind. Be unsurprised when you may find yourself resetting your intermediate and longer-term goals even higher, as your success outstrips your previous expectations.

In summary, when you will have determined your goals, written them down and kept them under regular review, for continuous improvement, you may be delighted at the growing success you are achieving?

Everything is an aspect of life – make it work for you

Do you want to accept any of those old emotions of fear, loss, pain, guilt (and self-recrimination), anger, frustration, loneliness that you may have had as normal for yourself, or do you want to make them work for you? Are you bound up in emotions that sometimes lead to errors of judgment, errors, wrong or hasty decisions, or can you choose to think, believe and behave in different ways?

Do you want to change your negative beliefs and scripts – creating the desired states for success as appropriate, so that your appropriate strategies can be perpetually played? People may sometimes have blocks that inhibit them from being their magnificent selves and achieving their goals and everything is an opportunity to learn and grow.

If you can identify some aspect or memory from your life, where you were successful and fulfilled, what is it that inhibits you from transferring the same skills to every other aspect, especially your chosen goals? Let me repeat. We all have truly magnificent potential, especially in the things we choose to do.

So what has prevented us from fulfilling that potential? It was only blocks in our mind from our formative years. Patterns which were laid down at unresourceful times in our childhood. These might seem insignificant to an adult, but they were meaningful to the child at the time.

As we went through life, the unconscious mind may have skillfully attached later, relevant experiences to those original significant emotional experiences, until a 'gestalt' (after Fritz Perls) of fear, anger, fear of failure, etc was created. Each time we faced a new relevant situation, those old limiting beliefs and behaviours may have resurfaced and even when rationally there was no reason to believe we could not go forward and achieve, those limiting emotions got in the way.

When you will have applied the techniques of NLP to release those old, redundant emotions, won't that have left you feeling you can do anything? Just one shot of self-confidence and there is no limit to what you can be, or do.

How can we discover and resolve the blocks that may once have been created? The keys are in our language. "I can't do this because....Why do I keep repeating the same unresourceful patterns of behaviour..." If you find yourself in an unresourceful state, for whatever reason, listen to your language. Go inside and ask yourself "where did that come from?" "For what purpose for myself would I think those thoughts, or feel those feelings?"

Elsewhere we have considered your competencies, strengths and weaknesses and having done so, you can be better able to manage yourself, positively and thereby be more resourceful. Part of this is in managing your ego. Self-esteem is a priceless commodity. When ego is overinflated or misplaced, it can work against everything that you desire. Rational, calm, silent, honest appraisal of your self is different.

Losing any over-inflated ego does not obviate rational self-esteem. In order to succeed, you must lose that ego and replace it with sound, self-awareness. Arrogance can be a prelude to disaster. Many captains of industry, political leaders and achievers in other walks of life behaved as if they could walk on water. We need look no further than some 20th century Presidents in the US and politicians in the UK. British industry is littered with people who became a 'legend in their own lunch hour' believing their own self-publicity. They foundered.

Ego involvement means emotional attachment. Let it go and learn how to plan and program your success. Put this out into the future and let your unconscious mind look after it, while the conscious mind sorts out the day to day details against the predetermined criteria. We are not talking about sloth or procrastination. Professionalism and diligence in your work, for example, is a fundamental prerequisite of success. Meanwhile the unconscious mind creates the 'x-factor' of differentiated success. The conscious mind assembles the data, the unconscious mind notices the patterns, makes the connections and guides you towards your goals.

We are all one with the universe. Preoccupation with self takes from the rest. "True self-interest teaches selflessness. Heaven and earth endure because they are not simply selfish but exist in behalf of all creation. The wise leader, knowing this, keeps egocentricity in check and by doing so becomes even more effective." (John Heider, *The Tao of Leadership*).

You can be a leader in every aspect of your life. The calm, quiet leader is best, always believing that there is more to learn, more to know. For the now, all that matters is the now. Visualize and program your future and your unconscious mind will sort that out. The past can't be changed and the future is unknowable. You can only do and be the best you can be.

"Prosperity is not defined by money alone; it encompasses time, love, success, joy, comfort, beauty and wisdom... Know what your beliefs are, they can be changed in *this* moment. The power that created you has given *you* the power to create your own experiences. You can change!" (Louise Hay, *Love Yourself, Heal Your Life*).

Louise Hay also says that the power of the future is in this moment. Fear, of failure, rejection, or whatever, is a future emotion. It may be based on emotional experiences from the past and you may feel the emotion in the present. It is an emotion about something that has not happened yet, and may not. So why worry? Live your life in the present moment and start to visualize your inevitable success and, having done so, enjoy the pleasure of anticipation as you diligently build that success right now.

Setting your goals

Sit down now, with three pieces of paper. On the first, write down your long-term goals. What you will achieve for yourself. Now, on the second, write the goals you will have for the next year. On the third set down your goals for the next three months. For each goal, make an internal picture and, as before, put it out into your future. Review these goals every day.

Visualizing your outcome

Take an outcome, which for you seems to most powerfully represent your most important goal. One which, in achieving it, you will realize how much you have changed. Now, make sure it is only for you (although others may benefit through you), that it is ethical, decent and generally sound.

Create a representation for yourself as if you have that outcome now. What is the last thing that needs to happen for you to know that you have that outcome? That's right. See it through your own eyes. Now, take that outcome to a future time in which your unconscious mind suggests it is most appropriate to be set. Step out of the picture and entrust the outcome to your unconscious mind at the time that is right. Come back to the now.

Use this as many times and as often as you wish.

Determining your plan

In how many ways you are already realizing the power of your unconscious mind. And as your conscious mind becomes aware of the ways in which you are changing now, use the partnership of your conscious and unconscious mind to create a plan that looks, seems, sounds and feels right for you.

The elements are: the medium and longer-term goals; the strategy you will use to achieve these; the resources you will need to implement the strategy, knowing that this book is already framing your mentality, style, attitude, beliefs and positive states.

Write down all these things and the practical steps you will take to implement your plan, understanding that, as you write it on paper, you are writing it into your unconscious mind also. The mind that never forgets anything and from which you can recall as you choose.

Write down and review the measures you will use to determine and observe your growing success now.

Schedule a time, at the end or beginning of any day or week, when you will review your progress and performance for that period and overall, so that you are learning and growing every day. Use these questions and any other question, which by asking it of yourself means that you recognize your growing and changing:

What specifically have I done well?

Where can I continue to improve?

Overall, how well am I doing?

Step 6

THE POWER OF TRACTION
– in achieving your goals

Motivation

What does it take to get you motivated? What does it take to get you up in the morning? What goes through your mind after the alarm has gone off? Do you want to change that?

Then there was the game with my son. You could do the same with yourself last thing at night. And if you can't find positives for yourself in any of these, you're either not being totally honest about yourself or you must have some powerful reason to feel bad about yourself.

If you do, then ask yourself this "What is the positive purpose of feeling this way about myself?" Now, before you throw the book through the TV, just check back. Your unconscious mind is totally motivated either away from pain or towards pleasure. There is no other way. And you may not have noticed yet. So, everything it does has a positive intention.

"But I'm feeling worried that my partner doesn't love me." For what purpose? "Because I don't want to lose them." So isn't it great that you can love someone that much. "But you don't understand, I'm really concerned that I might lose them." So why would you do that to yourself and what is your unconscious mind telling you that you need to change that maybe you hadn't noticed yet? And by the way, when are you going to make the changes big enough to love yourself totally as you are, so that you can allow yourself to be loved by someone else?

In Meridian therapy, as with Louise Hay, the first step on the road to your limitless potential is total acceptance of yourself as you are, including the things that you are currently denying. Then you can move forward. "But you don't understand, it's my Dad's fault that I'm so crusty with everyone, I learned it from him." So you accept that you're the one being crusty now. Look in the mirror, accept that this is a behaviour that you have taken on and make new choices.

So find the highest positive purpose. If it comes out as something that you don't want, then what is the opposite that you can move towards, now?

And while you're at it, check your goals out and wonder whether you have set those big enough now. If you set them much higher, you might find that you have to get off your 'butt' and take massive action towards that change.

Change has been one of the things that we may have found to be toughest in the past. Lou Tice used to talk about comfort zones. The little boy is going for his first day at school. He's excited as he gets in the car and chats away to his Mum or Dad as they are driving along. They get to the school. The lad is taken to his classroom, smiling, introduced to his teacher and then the parent who has been with him for most of the last four or five years turns and leaves him. After much screaming, the teacher is left clinging to the child and the parent escapes. When they get home, they find the child clinging onto the back bumper.

What happened? Unfortunately the parent hadn't considered the value of taking the lad to the school a few times before and staying awhile as he got used to his new surroundings and met some new playmates. I remember the first time we took my son on a plane, aged 20 months. Not knowing how he would react, I got loads of holiday brochures and together we found and cut out pictures of the Boeing 737 that I knew we were going to fly on. I told him all about Madeira, where we were going and showed him more pictures.

On the day we flew, I walked him up the steps of the plane and as he saw the stewardess he announced "this is a Boeing 737" with a broad grin on his face. I sat him in his seat and presented him with a new picture annual I had bought him. Thoroughly absorbed, he was still reading it when the plane had landed, oblivious as to what had happened. I shall never know what he thought when we stepped onto the tarmac, the temperature some 30° warmer and a completely different scene in front of him. He has loved flying ever since.

And comfort zones are pretty important to understand. I always knew I was better than a 25-handicap golfer. Sometimes I would be four shots or so over par after nine holes. During the second nine, my unconscious mind would make sure I was about 20 shots over, so that I could continue to live in my 25 comfort zone. Then one day I won a 36-hole tournament by 16 shots, with two rounds of 82. Now my handicap plummeted to 17 and I was a proud 17 handicapper. I proceeded to shoot round after round in the 80s and I still play off 19. This year's goal is to get down to single figures. I'm having a temporary difficulty....

As Anthony Robbins says "there are two things that motivate people to success: inspiration and desperation." In other words, moving towards pleasure or away from pain. And how desperate are you?

A famous UK NLP Master Trainer tells the story that a client came to him desperate to change. "How desperate are you?" he asked. "I'm desperate, I'm desperate, I tell you". "OK, get all your clothes off except your pants and go out into the street, lie on your back waving your arms and legs in the air and scream 'I'M DESPERATE' at the top of your voice." "Don't be so silly." "OK, come back to me when you're desperate..." Robbins himself acknowledges that he was driven to success by being so strongly motivated away from the relative poverty he found himself in after relative failure in sales.

So what does happen when you wake in the morning? Does it take fear of the consequences to get you out of bed, or do you leap out to experience the joys of a new day? And does this have anything to do with going to work in the first scenario and being on holiday with the second?

I'll bet you can be motivated to finish a task really quickly when you have something else exciting you want to do with your life, such as going out for the evening. And if there is nothing to look forward to and no time pressure, what gets done?

What are you best at? Starting, doing or stopping? And what are you worst at? Starting, doing or stopping?

So what is it that you want to have that you can't get yet? And what is it that you had previously overlooked that you were trying to avoid?

Towards pleasure or away from pain

Earlier we tried some questions to find out your major filters, including towards/away from. Although you will likely use either in at least some circumstances, you will also instinctively know what you are in general.

So let's suppose you are away from, in the main. There are a number of possible disadvantages to this pattern. First, it may take quite a lot of pain to get you going and of course once you start to move, you get further away from the potential or actual source of pain. The urgency starts to ease a bit and that might explain why you tend to 'blow hot and cold'.

Second, while you were moving away from all this pain, you might not have been looking where you were going. This could lead to 'running into' a different scenario that you don't want (out of the frying pan into the fire) or a vagueness and lack of general direction. If I asked you where you were going and you said "I'm getting as far away from New York as I can". You might either end up in the ocean or drift aimlessly from place to place never feeling at home.

Finally, if people rely totally on an away from motivation, they might find themselves going through an unnecessary amount of pain, distress or just stress in the process. There's more than enough stress around as it is.

The world is full of both types and, whether at work or at play, you could not only modify your own patterns so that you can choose each as appropriate, and also the way you communicate with other people, recognizing that they may have a different motivation direction to your own.

So, supposing you feel yourself to be primarily motivated towards. You're playing the stock market. If you didn't have a certain degree of away from, you might have racked up huge losses in technology stocks as the Nasdaq fell.

Motivation and goal setting

We can combine your understanding of goals, values and motivation now to supercharge your journey.

Take the goals that you wrote down earlier. Now take a separate sheet of paper for each. At the top, write down the goal. Then ask yourself 'what is important to me about this goal' and list all these aspects. Now, for each of these 'values' in relation to the goal, notice whether you are moving towards or away from that value. Ask also what you most treasure about this goal.

Now, for each goal, visualize an outcome that will mean that you have achieved that goal. As you see, hear, think and feel about that outcome, use the submodalities analysis in the Appendix B to analyze the future experience. Play around with these elements until you find the one(s) that have the greatest effect on how you perceive that outcome. Now you can make those goals really powerful and be strongly motivated to achieve, with your conscious mind and unconscious in superb rapport as you do so.

So in summary, you can identify whether you are motivated towards or away from; discover your most important values; supercharge your chosen goals; and change your overall motivation more and more towards.

Building Self-Esteem

Now some people are lucky enough to have very strong willpower that drives them forward. There is an even stronger power force and it is your self-esteem. When you are feeling really good about yourself, achieving your goals becomes a self-fulfilling prophecy. Next?

And yet you do not have to do anything outside yourself to build high self-esteem. So, you might say, if something really good happened to you, you might feel much better about yourself. The thing is, you were comparing that external experience with your existing expectations for yourself. Change the expectations even higher and reward yourself from within. Self-esteem is by definition not something someone else or something else, does to you or for you, it is how you esteem yourself.

The way to build it is first to identify inside yourself how you think about yourself. You may well get a series of images connected with these inner feelings. Play with the submodalities of each to tune down the negative or limiting patterns and build up the positive patterns. Building self-esteem is simply a matter of changing your internal representations about yourself. And then watch your motivation to do anything....So what are you waiting for...

Changing Limiting Beliefs & Negative Patterns

We shall cover changing limiting beliefs and negative patterns in more detail in Step 10. For now, you can recognize that it is about changing internal representations and the result is even more motivation. You see it was those old beliefs and patterns that had held you back and when they were shifted, suddenly you found the motivation you needed...

When and how are you at your best?

Try this. Discover for yourself a time when you were at your very best. Use this as one of the experiences to stack into your motivation anchor.

Now analyze the elements of that experience in terms of what did you see, hear, feel, etc. Create a powerful internal representation and anchor it (see Appendix K) to call on it any time. Notice also what are the main drivers and learn to bridge these across into other aspects where you want to be powerfully motivated towards.

Do the same for peak experiences. Think of the most powerful positive experiences of your life, especially where you were strongly motivated towards. Discover what was in those experiences that you can also utilize in your motivation, for example to get you started on a mundane task that must be done, or even to get up in the morning.

How you stand or sit is important. Your body language reflects your thoughts and emotions. Think of a time when you felt terrible about something. Now slump in your chair and look down and to your right. That's enough!

Now, sit up, look up, or even get up and walk around briskly. Smile. And as you are doing all these things, try in vain to feel as bad as you did a moment ago.

As well as your posture, your language influences your motivation. We mentioned elsewhere the use of negative self-talk and imperatives. Those old imperatives might well have worked when all you knew was how to drive yourself away from the pain or consequences of not doing. How much better can it work when you are getting to Yes...YES...YESSSS!

So when you change your language to positive, caring, encouraging, supporting, reinforcing, etc. you will have changed your internal state and your motivation. Do you have an internal voice that talks to you negatively or beats you up when things went less well than you hoped? So stop it now and if it reappears change it to Mickey Mouse or Popeye or something silly – maybe a high pitched squeak.

Listen to yourself and notice all the negative patterns you have been running. Stop them or reframe them into positives.

Exercise – focusing on your life values

Take a sheet of paper and write the following headings, evenly spaced, representing the important domains of your life:

- Career/Business/Professional

- Relationships and Social

- Home and Family

- Leisure

- Health and Fitness

- Spiritual

For each of these, quickly write down the four to eight most important things to you. Keep going and capture the spontaneous thoughts, as they occur.

Now look at each of these values and find the three that seem to be most in common across all lists. Denote them as A, B and C.

Ask yourself the following questions in order:

1) Would I need B in order to have A
2) Wuld I need C in order to have A
3) Would I need C in order to have B?

From these questions, you will be able to determine the order of importance of these values, which are common to most aspects of your life.

Sleep on these and let your unconscious mind go to work overnight.

And finally, procrastination...

So with all that you have learned and changed now, maybe there were one or two who had still found procrastination to be a problem. What could you do?

First, you could create vivid internal representations for each of 'being highly motivated' and procrastination. Notice the differences in the submodalities and make the desired change.

And, using the technique in the appendix of chaining anchors, you could find two logical steps in between procrastination and high motivation and then anchor these four states to your knuckles. Then by 'chaining the anchors' you have a means to readily change your state whenever you choose.

Step 7

THE POWER OF ACTION – doing whatever it takes

SO FAR, on the journey to be your best, we have discovered the limitless power of your imagination and creativity, based on the limitless potential of your unconscious mind. And if you hadn't got there already, you might have wanted to understand what your empowering beliefs are and how any negative or limiting beliefs might once have got in the way.

We are only interested in excellence here and once you have achieved excellence in anything or everything, you might wish to redefine excellence and reset your goals. Using the power of your unconscious you have challenging goals and using the power of your imagination, you can visualize the outcomes that mean you will have achieved those goals now...and then you can reset your goals higher...

To kick-start and fuel your success you have access to any amount of motivation and as you release any old patterns that you have moved away from, move forward towards that success now.

And having decided that these goals and this success are the things that you really, really want you would be prepared to take any action that was necessary to get to your new destiny. On the way, you may have checked to see that you have the right strategies and after this section you can have realized how you had made those even more efficient, in every aspect or domain of your life and being.

And being can be about being in the moment, when you can communicate elegantly and effortlessly with anyone, including yourself, when you will have learned how to create superb rapport with anyone on the planet....including...of course...your self, with your conscious and unconscious mind in harmony.

And you won't have been surprised, were you, when that rapport and harmony sometimes led to love, including the recognition that you can love yourself and that is the greatest love of all because in doing so you can be infinitely more aware of the patterns and needs of others, as you move effortlessly towards emotional intelligence.

And now that you have glimpsed your limitless potential and are set on your course, you can be constantly open to and aware of the changes and opportunities to learn that pervade your environment, so that you can go beyond what you once dreamed possible.

How much is enough?

In the 2001 World Athletics Championships, Maurice Green won the 100m gold medal, despite severe tendonitis and risking serious permanent damage to his leg as he ran the last 40m in intense pain. In Maurice Green's absence, John Drummond ran the second leg of the 4x100m relay, also in intense pain which was so debilitating that he could not run straight and wobbled out of his lane. This courage kept his team on course for the final, where they also won the gold medal. Every member of the team paid tribute to John, without whom they would not have achieved the dream of a lifetime.

So how much is enough and how desperate are you? You could read this book over and over and constantly find new ways and new choices to move forward. Whatever you most long for in your work, your relationships or your life in general is worth any amount of effort to achieve, isn't it?

The importance of strategies

So here's something else. As we found in the section on modeling. Much of what we do is based on an unconscious strategy. We already have our own strategies so we don't need to learn the whole of someone else's unless we have an outcome that depends on skills that we have never tried or applied. In the move towards excellence in anything else, we can observe, understand, or even unpack (with their permission) the strategy that someone of excellence runs, to gain insights into the changes we can make or the tweaks we can do to achieve our own excellence.

There are two fundamental structures to understand here: the TOTE model (which is a basis for learning anything); and the order of strategies that leads to excellence in our processes of achievement.

To take the latter first, everyone has a decision strategy for anything. It is preceded by a motivation strategy, and is followed by a convincer strategy and a reassurance strategy. Indeed, we have a strategy for everything from living and learning to loving. The unconscious strategy you use to select a partner may be broadly similar to that which you use to buy a car, clothes or any significant discrete purchase.

In order to understand how you can improve any strategy that you run, review the sections on representation systems and submodalities at the back of the book and try these...how did you know it was time to perform that activity in that way? Did you see something, hear something or feel something? Run the movie from start to finish, observing what is happening in your internal representations (what you see, hear or feel). Write down the apparent pattern. Does it seem logical? Is anything apparently missing, or out of order, such that you can improve this strategy?

Decision strategies are at the core of all of our actions. Some of us run what are called 'synesthesias'. The clues are often in the words, or the actions, e.g. 'it grabbed my eye' (KV, kinesthetic/visual synesthesia), or 'I saw it and bought it' (there is probably a K in between, because presumably we have a feeling about something just before we decide).

When we buy or sell something, or make any other decision which is significant for us in our lives, we may also run a strategy that is to do with being convinced that we did the right thing (a convincer strategy). So you bought the watch. How long was it before you were convinced it was the right decision? Did you know immediately? Did you need to ask some other people? Do you have to look at it every day to be sure?

How do you know someone is good at their job? Do you have to see, hear or feel something? How many times do you need this evidence before you are convinced, or do you need constant evidence? If the latter, will you ever be reassured? What would have happened if you had run a constant convincer strategy for choosing a partner? Might you have been in constant self-doubt about whether you had made the right decision? On the other hand, if you were automatically convinced, how many unsuitable choices might you have made? Maybe a little fundamental evidence to augment your decision would be a good thing.

So, having elicited your own strategy and checked it out for shopping, let's say, would it be good to put some constructive self-talk in there somewhere, to ask inside "is this the right decision?   What evidence is there to confirm my decision?" Only once may be enough, because this is confirmation and getting your conscious and unconscious mind working in harmony, until it becomes second nature.

When you bought something in the shops, did you ever find yourself taking it back? When you bought through the Internet, have you ever made a decision you regretted (buyer's remorse). What positive change could you make to any of your strategies that will improve your percentages in shopping, loving, life, for that matter?

Any successful strategy should be created, tested, constantly applied, and kept under objective review. Your learning strategy is pretty important to your work and life in general. How do you learn best and how can you ensure you go on learning? What check is built into your processing, which reviews your decisions, looking for ways to improve your performance?

So on the journey to our limitless potential, first we can understand and consider the strategies that we are running in general:

- How do we become motivated;
- How do we make decisions;
- How do we convince ourselves this is right for us; and
- How can we be reassured?

And if we still found that the action or decision were less than optimal:

- What are the characteristics of the strategies of the excellent individuals that we seek to model;
- What results do they get;
- What results did we get;
- What can we learn, change or tweak as a result;
- How many times did we run the new or modified strategy before it became installed and we are producing the excellent results we had visualized?

We have found that the key strategies as well as the above are: learning; and loving.

The TOTE Model that we all run

We have also considered the TOTE model in Appendix F. Derived from scientific thought, this is an exquisitely simple model of efficiency in testing any process or procedure. It is also the unconscious basis for a successful strategy. It is of particular significance when you want to install or modify a strategy towards your own excellence. It not only ensures optimum efficiency but also checks that you have considered every stage of the process.

Its simple elements are as follows:

	(T)est;	- how did you know it was time to run this strategy?
	(O)perate;	- how did you know there were alternative paths forward?
second	(T)est	- what has to be satisfied in order to complete the strategy?
	(E)xit	- how do you know that you have completed the strategy?

So, having been motivated to achieve the goals you have visualized, you will have wanted to check that you have been running the most efficient strategies to get there. Or to put it another way, you may have a Ferrari for a 1,000 mile journey but if you put diesel fuel in it or travel without a road map, food and drink, money and other necessities and without a clear overall plan, don't be surprised if you arrive late, if at all.

Because your goals are worth having and they are something you are strongly motivated to achieve on your path to excellence, and because the sun will rise tomorrow morning, that means that you will be prepared to take any amount of action in order to achieve it, all the while checking that this is congruent with all the other goals, values and positive beliefs in your environment.

Putting it together...

A friend rang me. "I've got a problem. Could you come round and help me?"

So I went round. "You see I've got all this stuff and I don't know what to do with it all."

I went round the house and especially upstairs and he had so much stuff. It was coming out of the cupboards. It was on the floor. It was blocking some of the entrances. In fact it was piled up most places.

"Let's sort it out and get rid of what you don't need." I said.

So we did that and there was still too much to fit in all the cupboards.

"What should I do now?" he asked.

"How about getting some more cupboards?" I suggested.

So we went to IKEA and got some of those 'flatpacks' – you know. We went back to his house and we carried them upstairs and put them down on the floor. I left him to it...

Step 8

THE POWER OF BEING –
communicating with others

SUCCESSFUL PEOPLE appear to have the power to influence others, consciously or unconsciously. We all have that power. We can all model our behaviours on excellent behaviours we see elsewhere. If at this stage anyone had a limiting belief pop into their mind, they already know how to have removed that by now.

Rapport is one of the 'buzzwords' of the 21st century. How do you create rapport easily and effortlessly with anyone you choose? How do you do it with yourself? Think back to that time when you felt so much in tune with someone else and consciously or unconsciously you could see how well you were getting on together. Did it feel as if you were in a bubble together, or as if time stood still, the rest of the world melted away… Did you have a feeling, maybe from your centre that you knew you were in what you now understand to be rapport?

How did you do that? Not by consciously thinking and planning. It came from inside, effortlessly and easily. As you go back to that time now, notice how good it felt and how easily you did it without trying. What do you see, hear and feel as you're in that time right now…

And was there ever a time when you felt you could do anything, even for a brief moment, a time when it felt so good… Then you were in rapport with yourself.

All of us have the talents to create rapport, to be powerfully persuasive with others and ourselves, to be in flow, or in the zone.

In the Appendix G, you will learn the specifics of eye patterns, mirroring and matching and the way to transform a situation you are in through perceptual positions and sensory acuity. These will allow you to create rapport with anyone, including yourself.

Research shows that we make a lasting impression on a stranger in the first four seconds of our meeting. Four seconds! It used to be 14 seconds. In recruitment, after the first five minutes, even the very best candidate would not change the interviewer's impression of them.

Now, you and I can choose to be different and understand much more about each other. And yet, how much of ourselves are we wearing 'outside ourselves' in our neurophysiology? In NLP Practitioner or Master Practitioner training, we have been trained above all to respect another person's model of the world. One of the earliest skills we learned was to calibrate someone's whole neurophysiology.

If we were conversing now, you would be deriving only about 7% of your own interpretation and understanding from the words themselves. 38% would come from the way I said the words (intonation, etc.) and 55% from non-verbal communication (similar to what Desmond Morris called body language).

So, what is it like for others to do what they do? We may never know, because we are not them, we did not have their upbringing, their genes, their environment. We may believe we have similar values, attitudes and beliefs and maybe that's how we seem to relate to them or like to be around them. We are all as unique as a snowflake and infinitely more complex. The cells that are in you did not just appear from nowhere. They were once in other living beings, plants, water, rock, the atmosphere, etc. We are all part of a connected universe and every one of us is different.

When we believe we understand someone else, we can only understand our own filtered version of someone else. Perception is projection and everything we recognize in someone else is a projection of something inside ourselves. Otherwise, how would we know how it looked, sounded or felt?

So realize that we are all different and all unique. Take account of that and use it to your limitless benefit in all aspects of your life. I'm not talking about taking the maverick view for the sake of it. We are understanding the importance of choice and owning the consequences.

Stephen Covey wrote about the Seven Habits of Highly Effective People. We are all highly effective at all we do, otherwise we wouldn't be able to do it. Someone tells me they are a failure. How long does it take to become an alcoholic? How hard did a person have to practice before they became world class at drinking? How often do they have to do it every day to 'keep their hand in'? So how long did it take for that other person to become a failure? And did you ever think that anything less than total failure is success at not failing?

By all means understand the habits and patterns of others who you regard as being highly successful. Then ask yourself how you know they are highly successful? Are you just convinced by the words of someone else, or what you see or do you have a feeling? Whichever way works for you, how do you know they are successful unless you know…and you do you know, you know… So when are you going to be as successful in your life in general as you are at breathing, or eating, or watching TV, or knowing that someone else is highly successful…

So watch and understand others' moves. Model the best and beat the rest. And you might add to that baseline tennis.

When Bjorn Borg won Wimbledon six times, he did it basically by standing on the baseline and knocking the ball back into the other guy's court. He waited, patiently for the opportunity to strike, for the other guy to make a mistake. Andre Agassi does a lot of the same thing, only he hits the ball harder and harder. No-one works harder round the court than Agassi. He has the shots, OK, and he also has the confidence, the self-belief, an eye for the narrow window of opportunity that wins point after point after point.

When you're with people and you are creating superb rapport, how do we communicate? How can you get people to tell you what you want to hear? First, you ask open questions (the ones that need more than a yes or no). Then, you listen, with your ears and all your senses, you pick up *all* the cues they are giving you. Did you ever see anyone who said yes, while their head shook from side to side. This was incongruent. Their neurophysiology was giving the real answer.

So in how many ways are you already seeing the possibilities for using these skills that you really knew you always had? And when you have unpacked them and polished and adjusted them and maybe practiced even more than you were already doing, and repacked them, what are the opportunities you can see or feel you have for yourself, what are you telling yourself you can do now, in your work and your life?

And when you're in the thick of things, at work or at play, immersed in the sights and sounds and thoughts and feelings, you can still find space for yourself, through the peripheral vision exercise, through meditation, and by going somewhere else, an environment which is very different, where your thoughts can happen naturally, where the helpful little voice can come up with its suggestions.

Wherever you go, you are always there, consciously and unconsciously and, now that you can create rapport with anyone, especially yourself, you can be an individual as part of the crowd that makes your life exciting.

Being yourself... being your best...

So who, and what, are you, and what do you do, and how do you do it, and how will it be when you will have learned, and tried, and integrated, all these other things to be your best?

The key is just being. In Zen, it is just being...in the moment...in what we might call 'flow' or 'the zone'. I like the description that someone else gave of 'the void'. Now we might think of the void as being emptiness. The Tao teaches us that 'everything is nothing and nothing is everything'. Stop for a moment and consider. When you did science, didn't you learn that the world is made up of molecules, made up of atoms, made up of particles, etc. And when you get it all right down to the basics, there is nothing in between the particles, that is about 99.9999% nothing...or more.

Hmmm. So my preference is to consider that in 'the void' are limitless connections with the universe and infinite possibilities. Remember, you have more nerve cells than there are stars in the visible sky and how much of that are you consciously using. And if you need more, you just make more. Like did you know that the human liver can reproduce itself? That certain lizards, if you cut off their leg they can grow it back. Like human beings grow from the union of two cells that carry the most sophisticated programming in the universe. Like there was this guy with an IQ of 120 and he had no brain...

So, the best way to communicate with yourself to be in touch with your limitless potential is to clear the mind completely...and just be...

And when you can create superb rapport with anyone else on the planet, then in that moment you can just be...at one...the two of you...together.

How we Communicate Best

NLP is about excellence, and is the codification of all human language and behaviour.

First we understand the importance of context. As Tad James says 'There is no content in content worth knowing. Do you know how they make dictionaries these days? They get a computer to read books and as it comes across a new word, it looks at the context. No word has meaning on its own. So, if I say blue, you might think of the colour of the sky and I might be reflecting on sadness.

So it's not about content, but context. It's not about meaning, it's about process and these are two of the most profound things in NLP and especially in this book.

Let's take the first. You can find out all that you want to about a person who you consider to be excellent and the only thing that matters is *how* they do what they do. What is the context of what they do? And here, we are talking about the internal context, or to be even more specific, the internal representation of the context.

Let's take tennis. You could read a book, work with a coach, practice for 10 hours a day and still not reach club standard. If you were able to meet and spend time with Pete Sampras, 'elicit', unpack and understand the internal strategies that he runs when he's being his excellent best self, then you can move to a new paradigm. It's like what does he say or do unconsciously in that instant before and during hitting the forehand pass.

It's like Timothy Gallwey said in *Inner Tennis* "bounce, hit" and you can practice that routine until you have it perfect, but the inspirational shots come from the void, the excellent unconscious strategies that even Pete Sampras doesn't know consciously until you unpack them.

And communicating superbly in rapport with another human being is about both verbal and nonverbal language and behaviour. In person, 55% of communication is non-verbal and 38% is tonal. Over the phone, only 14% is in the words. So why did we ever worry about what words to say. The student who frets over what to say after you say 'hello' is already speaking volumes with their non-verbal communication. "Hey, I'm really incredibly nervous about this and I'm probably stimulating an unconscious nervous state in you as well, so why the hell would you want to get to know me?"

You can start to create superb rapport with anyone on the planet by doing just four things. First, create a powerful, positive state inside yourself before you even meet the person. Second, engage them with the whole of your neurophysiology. Third, ask open questions and fourth, listen with your whole self...

And it starts and ends with the eyes. It's no coincidence that checkout operators are taught to smile and engage the customer with their eyes. And the other thing is that their eyes are not only the window to their soul, but also their innermost thoughts and, most important their strategies. As you will find in the section on eye patterns in the Appendix G. So what was it that lead us to doubt Bill Clinton's words in testimony...

And as well as their eyes, there is the whole of their physiology. Did you ever watch what someone's feet were doing in a meeting, like were they getting impatient, were they nervous as they spoke...Or the guy that brushes the imaginary piece of fluff off his trousers, who is bored...

The night before Glenn Hoddle was sacked as England football coach, I was watching Sky News. David Davies was caught outside the headquarters of the English FA. "Is Mr Hoddle going to be sacked?" asked a reporter. "We haven't made that decision yet" said Mr Davies, obviously oblivious of the fact that his head was nodding up and down as he said it.

And you know what? A week later, the day before Kevin Keegan was appointed coach, Mr Davies was also interviewed outside the FA. "Is Mr Keegan going to be the next England coach?" We haven't made that decision yet, he nodded....

Rapport & Communication

So the secret of being, is in rapport and communication with anyone you choose, especially yourself.

We shall consider the specific techniques in more detail in the Appendices G&H. For now you can understand that this is only about what you do already, unconsciously. So, because you want the very best for yourself, are you content to rely on the unthinking patterns that you currently run, that mean those conversations at cross purposes, the misunderstandings, the blank looks, the unwitting trampling on other people's feelings, the unrealized look that attracted someone to you, that you didn't necessarily want to meet...Or will you unpack and understand all these processes now, so that you can improve these towards excellence in being and communicating?

It's about **eye patterns**. When you were a tiny baby, you could only see a few inches. What was in that space? Probably your mother's face and the thing that was most captivating was her eyes. And as an adult, did you ever hear someone say 'why did you look at me like that?' Or 'you won't find the answer on the ceiling.' What about the person who when asked a question shifted their eyes rapidly from side to side faster than you could do it consciously and then stumbled or mumbled out an answer?

So, having asked an **open question**, you can watch the eye patterns and begin to understand consciously what you might previously have 'mind-read' unconsciously. Then, as you begin to relax, you can be **mirroring** what Desmond Morris called their 'body language' (Manwatching). You could then move on to **matching** their tonality, expressions, even their breathing pattern (that is the most powerful pattern I've come across). And we are not talking about mimicry here, we're talking about exquisite, elegant, excellence with **total respect for the other person's model of the world**...and maybe insights that you would never have dreamed about.

And another thing you can notice is their '**oral predicates**'. Specifically, whether they use lots of **visual, auditory or kinesthetic** words, that give an insight into the **primary representation system** that they use to process, interpret and communicate with the world.

Having asked an open question, you would want to '**actively listen**' to what their response is. By that I mean noticing all that there is to notice, engaging with your whole self and replaying the key things they say to validate their communication. Their verbal communication also tells you whether they tend to be towards or away from, an options person or like routine, introvert or extravert, internally approving or seeking external assurance and all the other '**meta programs**' that make up their **filters.**

Ask   them   the   question   'what's   important   to   you about?'....anything...and they will share with you their key **values**...about anything. And you could choose to incorporate these into how they respond.

And if for some reason you still can't seem to relate to their unique and special model of the world, which you can choose to totally respect because you want to create meaningful communication, then you could try out the different **perceptual positions** until you have the answer.

And above all, this is about unpacking, understanding, learning, **modeling** (at first consciously and then unconsciously) **so that you can be your very best**...at just being...in this moment and every moment. And why would you ever have wanted to have still lived in the past or continued to worry about the future?

Step 9

THE POWER OF LOVE –
being kind to yourself
and others

MOST PEOPLE have a gap in their self-esteem. For some it's a wee gap and for others it's as wide as an ocean. It's interesting to compare the different cultures of the US and the UK. The US is largely a positive, empowering, enterprise culture. (And in saying that I recognize that this is a simplification as there are disadvantaged individuals and groups in every society).

In the UK, we are so negative. I've stopped watching the news, because it's mainly bad news. A few years ago, I contemplated setting up a new newspaper, called 'And Now the Good News'. There doesn't seem to be much. We indulge ourselves in bad news in this country. If there's a really bad news story, the media can spin out the column inches and the broadcast hours for days.

And then there are our heroes. We don't allow ourselves many and when we have them, we allow the media to try and shoot them down. The tabloids particularly seek out the dirt on anyone famous.

There was the case of Laurence Dallaglio, England's talented rugby captain. Once someone found out he had tried drugs in his teens, that was him smashed off the pedestal the media had put him on in the first place. And God forbid that we should ever find out anything shady about Sir Steven Redgrave. I think I'd emigrate.

I was once told that by the time our kids leave school, they have had ten times as many negative patterns as positive. Don't do that...you can't do that...you'll never be able to do that...you're no good...are you stupid or something...you'll get cancer because my mother did and her mother did and...you'll be bald before your 40, because baldness runs in our family...etc.

And then there's fear. Oh, I don't mean the fear of ghosts or horror movies or what have you. I mean things like fear of failure and, most perversely, fear of success...

Did you know that if you drop a newborn baby into the deep end of a swimming pool, it spontaneously swims? And babies don't even know what a plane is, let alone have a phobia.

You see this is the whole point about modeling. Babies and young kids learn most of what they learn up to about age five, by listening to, watching and generally modeling their 'significant others'. So if they can do it, so can you, including unlearning all those negative and limiting patterns and modeling excellence.

And who beat, shouted, abused, frightened, browbeat, nagged or generally programmed their lack of self-esteem or self-confidence? And who (before they learned the patterns themselves), consciously or unconsciously reinforced all those negative patterns that went wrong until they became self-fulfilling and self-generating.

Once upon a time, you were like a blank sheet of paper and everything you learned (yes everything) can be unlearned, or better still erased. And in this book, there isn't even room to mention timelines...

Self-Confidence and Self-Esteem.

Be careful. Whatever you do, don't let that self-confidence and self-esteem build inside you. Promise me that you will keep on constant alert for that spark of confidence or that warm feeling, the positive voice inside you, which can catch you unawares if you are not vigilant. You must watch for it night and day, because I warn you, self-confidence and self-esteem are addictive. Once you have tried a bit, it will grow inside you like a thundercloud, building and spreading up and across the sky. Once you let it get hold of you, there will be no stopping it.

People talk about positive mental attitude. That is one of the fundamentals of NLP. Only, we are talking about more than PMA. There are many courses and books that tell of or teach PMA. If you adopt, repeat and reinforce a positive mental attitude to anything and everything in your life, you may already have found many of the ways you have changed for the better.

Using the techniques in this book, you can go several steps further. First, you may already have eliminated negative beliefs, patterns and programs that may in the past have held you back. You may have elicited and changed your values, to substantially positive. You may be using anchors and reframes to bring so much more positivity into your life and work. You may be meditating regularly, eating a balanced diet and drinking more water.

When you go inside, you may already find signs that all these many positive steps you have taken are growing day by day. We can institute a positive attitude and a positive set of beliefs and how much better is it being pervaded by positivity, having found the way to release old negative emotions which may have been holding you back, so that you can move forward in a positive frame of mind at will. Please try in vain, now, to not have all those positive feelings which are growing in you now.

Look out for negative thinkers and don't you wish that they could be as positive as you. By all means give them a fair hearing. Listen to their woeful tales and warnings and compare your own positive feelings. Smile down deep inside you from your head to your toes, letting the warmth of your good feelings about yourself pervade every cell in your self.

When you have seen negative feelings in the past, you may have asked yourself "where did that come from" and, having gone inside, you could have cleaned up with that internal cleansing spray that we all can find, leaving the sparkling glint of positivity shining from within.

Now you are moving forward in every aspect of your life, you may have learned the most effective techniques, you may be practicing with real skill and excellence each and every day. Remember, there are no systems and no technology in the world that can be as sophisticated as those that you already possess inside you.

How many muscles are there in your body? How many nerve cells throughout your body-mind? You are receiving up to 2.8 million bits of information at any one moment. Without your conscious thought, your unconscious is filtering, sorting, analyzing, comparing, processing, deleting, etc. all this information. Some people have become overwhelmed by the amount of information bombarding their conscious senses daily. And yet, your unconscious mind is processing more information in a day than the entire air traffic control systems of the world, often as you relax!.

How much can you do now that you realize the power of the partnership between your conscious and unconscious mind? Trusting your unconscious, are you going to wait till tomorrow to see the limitless positive effects this awesome power is having on every aspect of all these things you have limitless potential to do now?

By all means practice, review, learn from the past and improve, for there is no substitute for consistency of self-belief and being in flow. And, having put in train those practical, conscious initiatives, ask yourself who is driving your bus? The plain truth is, you are. The whole of you that you have begun to glimpse. For what highest positive purpose for yourself would you have wanted in any way to restrict this limitless potential by the relatively much slower processes of your conscious mind?

Self-confidence and self-belief are just that. Belief and confidence in your self. Think of the one person in the world in whom you have the greatest confidence. No more than 55% of you is appraising this person unconsciously. You are aware of yourself unconsciously, 100% of the time. Since you were born, life's experiences had put in your way the residue of some of the negative experiences you had had. Once you were whole and had none of that.

Think of a fence that faces a horse, galloping in the country. It was planted or erected by someone. The horse rarely refuses: it sails over it, or crashes through it and the might of its power continues across the landscape ahead. If you are the rider, preparing the course, in how many ways can you think of removing or avoiding the fence as any possible obstacle to your progress. This was a fence built by man or woman and in an instant in your mind it doesn't exist any more. And once it was open fields where you can ride and ride...

There never has been any bar or obstacle to your success other than one your unconscious erected at some time in the past. The builder of the arch knows exactly how to place the keystone such that it holds the entire structure. The maker of the chain instinctively knows the weakest link. The architect of the building knows the exact spot to place the charges so that the structure can fall safely in one go exactly where it was planned. Your unconscious mind knows all of these things and...knowing...you can be your best now...

Exercise - maximizing self-confidence and self-esteem

Sit quietly, in a chair, in a space of your choosing, in your own time. Have paper and a pen beside you. Fill yourself with all the positive feelings and many new insights, which are growing every day.

As you are filled with these pictures, sounds and feelings, do anything you wish to enhance this internal experience. Fill yourself with impressions of people who you know love, appreciate or respect you now. Bring to mind all the positive qualities you know or are discovering daily about yourself. That's right. You could refer inside your mind to the lists you have made consciously or unconsciously...

Now, as you look at the wall or window opposite you, fill yourself with an impression of someone who you know loves or appreciates the good things about you. Go to position 2 (see Perceptual Positions in the Appendix, I), such that you are on the other side, being in that person, looking back through the transparent partition at yourself. As you do, what are only the positive thoughts or feelings, which come into your mind as you look at yourself from another's perspective, maybe for the first time? Allow yourself only as much time as it takes for your mind to be flooded with these positive experiences.

Now, as you see yourself, through the eyes of another's perspective, have the experience of floating out of that second self, so that you are looking down at yourself in position 1 and position 2, from above. Look at the person in position 2, looking at that person in position 1, being in position 3, above and beyond the other two positions.

Now, be aware of all the thoughts and feelings that are in that person in position 2. Understand the positives that are flowing between position 1 and position 2.

With all these awarenesses, come back through position 2, into position 1 and write down absolutely everything that is positive that floods your mind now. Write until you have exhausted every thought or feeling. File these thoughts and return to them every day, such that they become a natural and spontaneous part of your being, in trading and in life, noticing all the while, how the positive impression of yourself has been steadily growing and changing...

Our beliefs and values are recognized in our internal dialogue, as well as our external language and behaviour. Is our self-talk positive, or negative? If it is negative, and especially critical, STOP IT NOW. How often do you use imperatives in your self-talk – "I must do this, I should do that, I've got to do this, I shouldn't have done that..."- as opposed to choices: "I can do this, I may do that, I would like to do this, I choose to do that..."

If someone, who you know loves you or cares about you, were to talk to you in the way you may have sometimes criticized or otherwise beaten yourself up, how would you feel? Start now to change your internal dialogue to loving and caring. See and feel the immediate and lasting changes in your outlook on life, your behaviours and attitudes to other people.

Language and internal dialogue

Did you ever know anyone who used to beat themselves up if things didn't work out? When they spoke of a new initiative, or were practically or implicitly challenged, was there negativity in their response, or their self-talk? We have covered limiting beliefs elsewhere, but your everyday language is not only important for your positive state of mind, it is also a window into your innermost feelings and the programs and patterns you run.

After I recovered from illness, I got up one morning and was planning my day. I heard myself say "Today I must do ...and I've got to do ...and yesterday I should have done ...so I'll have to do it today...". My language was full of imperatives. We call them modal operators of necessity (MONS). So I asked myself what I was going to do about it. Replace them with choices. So, I would like to do...and I could do...and I can do ...and I want to do ...and I will do ...These were modal operators of possibility (MOPS) for possibility, options and choices.

Use MOPS and MONS as you see or feel to be appropriate. You might decide to use MONS for method, strategy or implementation. Make it your own decision. If anyone else makes those decisions for you, be sure you understand it is your choice to implement them. If you have ever said to yourself "I cannot..." about anything, did you already understand that this is a MOP – I *can* do the process of not... So now are you seeing things with more possibilities?

How are you going to do it – positive language and behaviour

We have considered many things as you have moved forward with this book. It is a horizon of new choices. You may already have noticed the balance is changing, as the self-development aspects grow. Now that you are understanding so many positive and constructive things about yourself and as you try out all the fascinating tools and techniques, in how many ways is your life changing for the better. How many new opportunities are opening up for you? How many new insights do you have, including into other people?

Creating positive internal dialogue

Think of someone who you know loves you, or appreciates you and the positives about you. It could be someone from your present, or your past. It could even be a dream lover, who will love you without condition, as you are and for what you are. Imagine or recall the way that they speak to you, with love or appreciation...Why would you want to speak to yourself any other way?

Stephen Covey suggests that you repeat the affirmation "I like myself, I like myself..." every day. Louise Hay recommends that you look at yourself in the mirror, at least once a day and say to yourself "I love myself and everything about me".

As you try these ideas on, you may already be noticing the changes and the new possibilities opening up before you...

......I didn't hear anything for a few weeks, so I called my friend.

"How are you getting on?" I asked.

"You'd better come round," he said.

So I went round and he took me upstairs. There was still stuff all over the place and the flatpacks from IKEA were lying on the floor where we had left them.

"You don't seem to have done much?"

"I know," he said. "You see it says on the boxes 'Self-Assembly' but nothing has happened yet...."

Step 10

THE POWER OF EXCEEDING – going beyond by rewarding and improving

How can you improve – returning to DRIMI, the continuous cycle of success

What do you want to do?

Be your best

What do you need to do it?

Mission, vision, goals, values, strategies, patterns, programs and processes of conscious and unconscious language and behaviour. Motivation and self-belief.

How do you want to do it?

By understanding the patterns, programs and processes in yourself and that you can learn by modeling others, integrating and modifying to achieve the best of the best.

How will you know how you are doing?

Feedback, objective self-awareness, perceptual positions, achievement, milestones, reward, happiness...

| How can you improve? | By always believing there is something or someone new to understand, learn or model. By practicing and integrating these things, at first consciously and then unconsciously until they become second nature, like walking and talking to most of us. |

Review is a time to balance logic and intuition. What does your analysis tell you: about yourself; about your opportunities to learn and grow; about the trends, outcomes and opportunities? What does your instinct or 'feel' tell you? Most of all, how can you improve and grow the new, positive patterns of success in your own behaviours and their implementation in every domain of your life?

Success and Failure

Success and failure are attitudes or beliefs. They are based on patterns we learned in childhood. We are programmed to achieve. Otherwise, how do we stay alive? Do we have to ask all the organs and cells in our bodies to perform exactly as well as they do, or does the blueprint of perfect health in our higher self maintain everything in the good condition it is. Where you knew someone who became ill, how did they do that? Do you know what a miracle it is to be able to sustain a cold or flu for days on end, when you are programmed for cells in your body to strive for perfect health?

Now that we realize all the skills we have that do so much for us in every aspect of our daily lives, which run in our unconscious mind, how much more can we do? So, whether small or large, think of all the things you ever succeeded at in your life. Start with 'I succeeded in getting dressed on my own today'. Just try in vain to stop all those successful thoughts that are popping into your mind. No ifs, buts, explanations or justifications, just simple, raw, achievement and success. Now, as they keep on coming, try not to stop laughing inside yourself or outside yourself.

So what is it in success that we may have overlooked if we ever scored ourselves at less than that?

What is present in success that is not present at other times?

What is not present in success that is present at other times?

What is not present in those other times that is not present in success as well?

What is not present in success that is not present in success at other times either?

Finally, realizing that failure was never a choice that you wanted to make, in how many different ways can you represent success in your mind? What does it look, sound, feel, smell or taste like? Fill your senses with success now.

Elsewhere we have dealt with anchors and reframes. Whenever you have a powerful, positive feeling (and just for a moment try in vain to stop even one of those successful memories you just had from seeping back into your consciousness), anchor it. Decide the different categories of good and powerful feelings you can recall and anchor them wherever you feel they are most accessible when you want them.

Failure in one person's model of the world can be success in someone else's. Fran thought she had failed when she lost money on trading the stock market. Bill thought Fran must be incredibly successful to have the money to trade. James was in awe that Fran was successfully courageous in trading. Bob thought they were all incredibly successful to just get out of bed in the mornings. So ask yourself now, "will it be by the end of today or lunchtime tomorrow when I have realized in how many ways I can already be successful and the many opportunities there are to learn and grow"?

There have even been people who were frightened of success. This might have been just as limiting as fear of failure. Others might have lacked self-confidence and been easily persuaded or influenced away from a chosen path by friends, well-wishers, nay Sayers, enemies or those that resented others succeeding because they had such a low opinion of themselves.

Henry was a perfectionist. I asked him why? He said he was frightened of failure. I pointed out that anything less than total and utter failure in everything he did was not perfection. When he opened his mouth, the words would not come out, but he breathed as he gasped. Life goes on...

Fear and Motivation, Loss and Stress

I thought long and hard before putting anything with negative connotations in this book. Who could possibly be upset by all this positive thinking? Fear and motivation have been linked for some. We talked elsewhere of the 'meta programs'. When someone had a filter of being driven 'away from' failure, they might well have achieved. And how much more can they achieve now that they are driven towards success.

Negative motivation towards a goal was driven by patterns from the past. Once we have removed those old emotions, all the while keeping the learnings, we can have positive motivation.

It is said we live in a world of stress. I guess this is something many of us feel from time to time. Adrenaline can be a mixed blessing. It is, after all, the most powerful drug we know. If you choose to have stress, understand it and control it. Make it work for you.

So let's do this for a moment. Imagine you have bought some shares on the stock market and the price is going down steadily. How do you feel inside? Now imagine that you've just bought and the price is going up steadily. Now how do you feel?

Now imagine you just sold that stock and the price is going on up, even faster than before. How do you feel now? Or you just sold the stock and the price is going through the floor. How does that feel?

How did you do that? How did you manage to feel bad when the price was going down and going up! Context my friend. You can run all these feelings without even thinking about them. You can produce exactly the state you want, with the right trigger.

So change the script. Remember a time when you were feeling really great about an important decision you made. And see what you saw, hear what you heard and feel what you felt, inside yourself as you relive that moment right now. And make the picture as powerful as possible. Anchor it.

So now that you know how great that can feel, think of a time when you felt awful about a different decision you made. As you are in that moment, grab the feelings of that positive memory from your anchor and now see, hear and feel what happened to that old negative memory.

You can dry run everything you plan to do, a system or whatever. When you realize how well you can do it, then you are motivated. Ah, I heard someone say that it's not like the real thing.

So go to your favourite beach right now and imagine you can see the sun set over the sea. It's warm, as you know it and you can see all the sights, hear all the sounds and feel all you feel right now. Oh no, don't close your eyes and do it. What is that feeling of calmness that comes over you now...

Intensify any imagined experience and it can seem so real. Fear is an emotion of the future. If a wild animal had confronted you, the pattern might have been learned in the past, but the fear was what would happen next, or even the possibility of the worst.

So, if you had ever had any vivid experience of fear, how can you use those same skills of imagination to experience the thrill, pleasure, joy, warmth, etc of success?

You can make a feeling so real you can almost smell it.

Stress is a state created in ourselves. Resilience is a quality we have to have to have come so far. We are all mortal. This is the only certainty in life. While we are here this once, what are we going to do with life?

If you were world class at failing, you could do the throbbing temples, the hammering heart, the perspiring brow, the racing thoughts, the vivid images of disastrous outcomes, the sounds of other peoples' voices berating you and that deep feeling in your guts, at will. And if you imagined even one of those states as you read that, will it be tomorrow or next Monday when you have decided to start being totally wildly successful?

Luck, repeating mistakes, conflict, anguish, frustration are all states people have created inside themselves. One day, I had a terrible headache. I had no idea where it came from. Pills wouldn't touch it. I decided I was not going to do this.

I found a quiet spot, settled down, closed my eyes and went back to the last time I knew I had felt incredibly well. I filled myself with those well feelings and in my mind I created a glass ball. I poured the feelings into the glass ball and, in my mind, carefully transported the ball back to the now. Finally, when I knew I was in the now, carefully holding the glass ball, I poured those wonderful well feelings, in my mind's eye, down through the top of my head and through to all parts of me. Within an hour the headache had left me, never to return.

All the skills and all the feelings and all the successes you plan to have, or ever had, are in your mind now and forever. So, flood your senses with them and start to be the successful being you always dreamt you can be now that you are.

Anchors, reframes and much besides....

With all that you have seen, felt, internally processed and understood, from this short text, you now have more than enough to run one winning strategy after another in your life, work, relationships....

You are driving the bus. Success and failure are now concepts defined only by you – for you.

To enhance your performance and your positive states even more, you can change for the better every situation you find yourself in. By enhancing the positives of your state while you prepare, before you do, while you do and when you review, to improve, you can now create limitless positive frames of mind. The processes you will use include anchors and reframes.

Anchors

In the Appendix K are practical exercises for you to do to improve skills that you already have.

Did you ever hear someone say, "they're playing our tune"? The tune was an anchor. The unconscious mind latched onto a happy experience the music that was playing at the time, or which afterwards seemed appropriate. I cannot listen to Enigma without melting into the first few moments in which I met my life partner, Heather. The music is anchored to the memory.

And so it is with you, in a myriad of ways. And how will it be now you have perceived the possibilities to use anchors in your life? Before you commence any activity at which you want to be your best, you can anchor yourself into a positive frame of mind.

Before an interview or important meeting, for example, you could fire your anchor of calmness and observed detachment. When a decision point approaches, you could fire an optimal decision making anchor. As you review your decisions, you can be in a state recalled by an anchor of calm reflection and outstanding judgment. When you succeed at anything, you stack the euphoria of success to your existing success anchor. If things didn't work out, you fired another appropriate anchor that moved you into the frame for learning and growing. And on...

Think of, or let your unconscious mind spontaneously suggest to you, memories or times when you were at your best in the following:

A feeling or a belief, even for a moment, that you could do or be anything...

Loving...

Laughing so much you could almost fall down...

A time when you felt or knew you had almost limitless energy...

A time when your thinking, analyzing, decision making skills were at their best...

A time when you were your very best at being successful at anything...

A moment, even a single moment, when you were incredibly successful at something.

For each of the above, choose a part of your left hand or forearm (or your right hand if you are left-handed), onto which you will shortly anchor the relevant experience.

Now, inside yourself, go back to that time when you were at your best in one of the above. As you are in that time, now, seeing, feeling, hearing, smelling, tasting and being in that time now, notice all that you notice. Understand all the submodalities. Take all of these aspects of the memory and build them up as intensely as you can, take the tip of your index finger and press on the spot you have chosen for that particular anchor. Hold it on as the intensity builds and, just before the intensity peaks, release the anchor.

Break the state, by doing or thinking something ordinary or banal. Now, think of a situation in which you would like to be able to draw on the anchored experience. Fire the anchor and what do you notice...?

For each of the anchors above, stack them over and over in the same place, each time breaking state in between. After you have anchored a particular feeling in the same place four or five times, do the test again and then move on to anchor another feeling in a different place on the left hand or forearm.

Now, for each of these anchors, think of the sorts of situations in life, where you will be able to make most use of them. For each, imagine a real life situation, or even one that really happened. As you do, fire the relevant anchor and notice the changes in your perception.

When you set the anchor, your whole neurophysiology filled up with the intensity of the original experience. As you stacked it over and over, that anchor has become fixed in that place. Whenever you fire it, whether you are consciously or unconsciously aware, your mind will automatically recall every aspect of it and fill up your neurophysiology once more.

A word of warning...the more you use anchors, the stronger they get. When you have an experience that is akin to one of your anchored experiences, you can stack the intensity into the same place as the anchor. Then, when you fire the anchor in the next appropriate situation, the memory of that positive experience will be there also, improving your performance and feelings more and more...

Anchors work especially well in sport. I use three different anchors in my golf: one to put me 'in the zone'; one to re-experience how good I felt about myself the day I met my life partner; and a third to re-experience all the great golf shots I have made. I also have a precisely repeated 'set-up routine' which is an anchor in itself. I visualize the whole shot and as I hit it I am modeling Nick Faldo at his best. (So why aren't I on the PGA tour? It's not what I want to do and I still have some work to do on the mechanics of my swing. Meanwhile, my internal thoughts are totally positive).

Anchors are even better than s**. You can use them all day, every day. You can also anchor intimate experiences on yourself or someone else you care about very much. Have fun...

Reframes

Add to these the ability to reframe any context, behaviour or event.

Let's say one of your decisions didn't work out. You lost money, your job, triggered unhappy feelings in someone. Look around you at those who have lost more; at those with less. At those who don't have the insights, learnings, goals and motivation that you now have. Also, what can you learn from that unresourceful event or feeling that you can keep as a positive resource for other aspects of your life going forward?

On a day that didn't work out quite as expected, go home to the people you love and watch their miraculous movements, enjoy the miracle of life. Reflect on your excellent judgment in selecting a partner with those good qualities. Or, as you walk to the car, notice the dropouts, homeless, less fortunate than you. Give something back from your pocket, even your last dime, to help rebalance the universe towards you.

You can think of any number of situations you can reframe from positive to negative, realizing as you do, how you can grow and become what you always dreamed you are.

How are you doing – confidence, motivation and resilience

Now that you can look from outside yourself and see your self as you really are, inside, where do you know you keep your confidence and self-belief? You already know from anchors that you can go back to a time when you felt good about yourself, even for a moment and how does that feel right now?

Other things may have once been coloured by emotions and stress, limiting beliefs, fear of failure, of losing money or what have you. Learning from mistakes and misjudgments wasn't the only skill you have acquired during the reading of this book which by reading it thus far means that you have chosen to leave any old unresourceful patterns behind you. As the sun shines today and everyday, outside you or inside you, that means that you can see, hear and feel even more clearly the talents and qualities that were shaded or hidden until now.

And what of the new levels of confidence, motivation and resilience that are creeping into your thoughts even as you read this word and the next few thousand that come between now and the end of this book? In how many different ways will they pervade your life? As you go forward in time to a time when you knew you had experienced the benefits of all these changes even then having noticed the signs of success, how good is that feeling inside you know?

Some people have dwelt in the past. Regret was an emotion from the past and fear was a feeling about a different future. For the present, I give you these thoughts, because all that matters to you is the present.

There is no right or wrong in the world, besides what is right for you. You choose your values, you set the rules, you make the plays, you assess the situation, and you have the benchmarks ready for your success. There are no good decisions or bad decisions. Everything is right in its own context and everything is as it should be.

If anything ever didn't work out for you in the past, the time or the context were misplaced. Life is about choices and timing and if things didn't work out quite as hoped, you made the best of it, maybe reframed the context and moved forward yet again. If you had negative patterns and programs and you had found yourself wanting to hang onto them, what was the purpose for yourself? And why would you have wanted to worry any more until you have now changed all that.

Everything in your life is evolution and personal growth. It is what it is. Now that you can be your best at anything and whenever you feel it is appropriate, that means you have the courage to continue to see your way through any ups and downs and achieve the goals you have set yourself. The motivation is your own, towards those aims and everything else that they imply.

Some people may have experienced pain in relationships. If this had happened repeatedly, what message was there? Pain and disappointment are states we may have produced in ourselves, which until they had been eliminated were masking the possibilities and opportunities. If you knew someone who had lost a series of partners, how did they do that and what was there to be learned and understood? If someone knows how to make relationships not work, the context is that they intuitively or instinctively have within them the processes and patterns that make them work, when they can see those now.

You can see it differently, and there is no failure, only feedback, learning, growth and experience. How did you cope with apparent setbacks until you could see the whole picture?

Try this…Go inside and find your mood now. Score it on a scale from minus 100 to plus 100. OK. Now, go back briefly to a time that was the worst. And as you are in that time now, where would you score that, between minus 100 and plus 100? And finally, go back to a time that was the very best and be in that time now, seeing what you saw, hearing what you heard and feeling what you felt. Where would you score that?

So now come back to now and think of the seat you are sitting in. When you read the word *now,* go to that old worst time…and to that very best time, *now*…and finally to that time a few moments ago, where you first started to score…and how did you do that? How did you move your internal state down, up and back to where you were, so elegantly and rapidly that you *know* you can control your state as you want to. Didn't you…

Positive listings and affirmations

Do this. Start a list in a notebook that you can keep and add to any time, of positive qualities and experiences in your life. Begin by listing all your positive experiences or feelings. There is no limit to how many of these, including: occasions that went well; good things that have happened to you; particular skills or abilities that you have; good feelings that you have had; and anything else positive.

An affirmation is a positive sentence that describes the way you want to be. It should focus on a specific aspect of performance and could be based on your goals, for example. Write each one on a card. It should: describe a particular quality that you want (e.g. confidence); state precisely what you want (not what you don't want); be written in the present tense as if you already have it; and use active words that are really meaningful for you; e.g.

"I am always confident in all situations."

Collect together a number of meaningful affirmations and read them several times a day. As you read them, let your mind be filled with what you will see, hear and feel when you have these things.

Detachment

Here are two more ideas: A sense of detachment from unpleasant feelings or experiences is a good way of dealing with external stress or destructive internal emotions.

Think of a time when you were feeling stress or strong negative emotions. Imagine stepping out of yourself and leaving those emotions behind. Notice how much calmer and more detached you can become. (And see associated/dissociated in the appendix, B).

Or, try repeating these phrases. You can keep them general or you could use the power of your imagination to make them more specific:

"I have behaviours and I am much more than those behaviours"

"I have feelings and I am much more than those feelings"

"I have thoughts and I am much more than those thoughts"

"I am greater than those behaviours, feelings and thoughts"

"I control them, they do not control me"

Through these processes you can rapidly detach yourself as and when you choose.

...So they sent to Arthur's room and they got his notebooks. The Dean looked at them and he noticed that there were asterisks in the margin. And some of the topics had one asterisk, some had two, three and four, five, six and only ten topics had seven asterisks. And yes, you've guessed, they were the ten topics on the exam paper.

The Dean turned thoughtfully to Arthur and said "Arthur, you don't have to take the exam. Indeed, you shall graduate with honours. You're a credit to this college"...

You see we are much more than what we say and sometimes the lecturer or the teacher might say "this topic won't come up on the exam paper" and something about what else you noticed suggested...And you can listen intently, watch all there is to see and get a sense or a feeling and the best student realizes, unconsciously that there is much more to these things....

Part 3

ENJOYING
YOUR
SUCCESS

Chapter 5

What will happen when you do these things?

ACHIEVING success and happiness

AND NOTE all the ways in which you are already changing and
implementing these on a daily basis. Maybe you have already acquired
the qualities of self-control through self-mastery, learning and growing
each day... Know yourself, seek to continuously improve as a key part
of self-mastery.

As Daniel Goleman says in '*Working with Emotional Intelligence*':
"Emotional intelligence skills are synergistic with cognitive ones; top
performers have both. The more complex the job, the more emotional
intelligence matters – if only because a deficiency in these abilities
can hinder the use of whatever technical expertise or intellect a person
may have."

Emotional awareness is "The recognition of how our emotions affect
our performance and the ability to use our values to guide our decision
making". And, having made our values predominantly positive, in how
many ways are you already seeing success in your life?

Finally, Goleman says people with self-control "manage their
impulsive feelings and distressing emotions well; stay composed,
positive and unflappable even in trying moments; think clearly and stay
focused under pressure."

With objective self-knowledge, an understanding of your strengths and opportunities for improvement, insight and intuition, the proper mindset and a willingness to change and grow, you can transform your prospects..

Struggle was a state we created only in ourselves. Stress is a product of growing demands tapping into old unwanted states. Use the techniques in this book to remove those states, and old redundant beliefs and have stress will have become a thing of the past. The old, unresourceful traits and emotional states that may have been present in everyday life, may have contradicted those needed for personal growth. This is the point of self-mastery.

I have found much contemplation and personal growth from reading The Tao. It will be a constant reference source throughout my life. I have found such inner peace and calmness since.

"When I let go of what I am, I become what I might be. When I let go of what I have, I receive what I need....and, "To know how other people behave takes intelligence, but to know myself takes wisdom." (Both quotes from *The Tao of Leadership*, John Heider).

You and you alone are responsible for your actions and of their implementation. From the Tao and other works, we understand the importance of focus and the subjugation of self. Those who end up believing they might walk on water, somehow seemed to drown. If you can keep your head when those around you...

Maximizing your NET WORTH

So what are you worth and how do you want that to be? How will you measure your success? There are at least two ways of looking at this.

Someone I know was undergoing profound, rapid and positive lasting change through these tools and techniques. The coach said to them, having elicited their values "I notice that there is nothing there to do with money. Don't you think that is odd?"

Now I can relate to that, because money has only ever been important to me when I didn't have any. You see it could be this way. Set your goals and program your outcomes. You will surely have goals and outcomes related to your work or career (if relevant). So how would it be if you programmed such powerful outcomes that money would surely follow, like night follows day?

You see it's not just about your outcomes, it's also about how you proceed towards them and the actions you take. It's also about changing or releasing negative or limiting patterns, creating or enhancing positive patterns and taking nothing less than massive action.

And when you do all these things and live your life 'ecologically' aware of the needs and models of others, you just might find that the limitless universe delivers all your needs.

So might it be possible that money could be a consequence of all these things? And when you reach the end of a long, productive, healthy, successful and worthwhile life and you are looking back at what you will have achieved now, it's not just about money and it's about the total balance sheet of achievement.

A friend of mine decided to go into business on his own account. He asked my help to prepare a strategic business plan that he then personalized with his wife so that it took account of hers and all their other considerations. After a year we met again to discuss progress.

"How's it going?" I asked. He started to chuckle.

"It's going very well" he said. "We're not actually making any profit yet and you know the amazing thing is that no matter how tough and challenging this year has been, we've never been short of money when we needed it...and I haven't a clue where it keeps coming from." He's such a nice man and a good friend.

Returning to another of Deepak Chopra's wonderful books *Creating Affluence,* he writes:

"Affluence, unboundedness, and abundance are our natural state. We just need to restore the memory of what we already know."

And:

"A truly wealthy person's attention is never focused on money alone....You may have millions of dollars in the bank, but if you think all the time about money, if you have concern about it, if you worry about it – about getting more, about not having enough, about losing it – then irrespective of the dollar amount you possess, you are poor...To have true wealth or affluence is to be totally carefree about everything in life, including money."

In order to know that you have wealth, you need to be able to define it for yourself and then evaluate it. And remember, it is about context, not meaning. It is about process.

So what is Net Worth for you. Supposing you were the richest person on earth and had a terminal illness with no cure. How wealthy would you feel. What would your money buy you, other than a last few earthly pleasures. Money has no worth when it cannot buy happiness no matter how much you pay.

So if you are not wealthy, what are you projecting about yourself? And how will you see yourself when you have achieved something approaching your limitless potential?

And isn't it possible that having done so, wealth need not be a consideration anymore? After all, what price can you put on happiness, peace, calmness, family, relationships and love? And how will you measure the total net worth on your balance sheet of success when you die, if you have none or few of these things? How wealthy can you truly be and be totally alone?

So, my suggestion if you wish to have huge, positive net worth in every sense that is of value to you is simply to: understand where you came from; know where you are going; remove all the negative or limiting patterns of behaviour; believe in your limitless potential; set out your mission, vision and program your goals and successful outcomes; work hard and trust the rest to your unconscious mind which is connected to the limitless universe...

Chapter 6

How will this improve your life?

TLC - Loving and friendship

LOVE AND FRIENDSHIP start from within. When you have found the ways to love and accept yourself, as you are and for what you are, then you are ready to move forward with all these things towards your magnificent self. For as long as you have remained in denial about any patterns or behaviours that have held you back in life and especially in relationships, then you are unlikely to move forward in the way that you dream.

Your internal values, beliefs, patterns, programs and states will constantly be projected outside yourself, especially to those who are close enough to you to intuitively read, see and feel these. They may love you without condition and you will never achieve that state of Nirvana until you will have let go of these old patterns and beliefs that had held you back.

And remembering emotional intelligence can have some relevance especially in the relationships that matter to you most.

If you have poor emotional intelligence, then you may well have poor self-control and especially awareness of others and their needs. So for as long as you have lived your life on the basis that relationships are only about what you can get out of them, then understand this. You will get back what you give and what you project is what you get.

So, for as long as you have dissatisfaction in, or seek perfection in someone else, you shall seek it in yourself. Change that pattern and notice the change in the quality of your relationships. When instead you enter a relationship on the basis only of what you can put into it, you might be surprised and get at least as much back. If not, you may want to check what other programs you may have been running that you can resolve now.

As you realize your limitless potential, move increasingly towards positive patterns in your life and leave those old negative patterns and limiting beliefs behind you, you will inevitably find that more and better people are drawn towards you and the quality of your life all round will change and grow.

The HERITAGE you can pass on - bringing up stars

Whether you have children now or in the future, or not, it would be unusual if you did not come into contact with younger or less fortunate people than yourself. As you grow and change in all these ways, your consciousness will move increasingly outside yourself as you entrust more and more to your unconscious mind, as it moves from unconscious incompetence to unconscious competence in all the patterns and beliefs that you desire.

Once again, your projections will be increasingly positive and, as with those that you love and deeply care for, you may find yourself attracting people to you who are in the image that you wish to be or are increasingly becoming. And there is always so much to be learned from asking open questions and listening.

Meanness of spirit invariably brings meanness of life. Permissive and self-indulgent behaviours can all too easily become a spiral of increasing demands and declining gratification. As with hard drugs, the hits need to be harder and harder to get the same buzz.

And was there ever a time when you felt totally good about yourself? Even if when you were young. And now that you can reproduce that and anchor it and all those other things that can get stronger and stronger, maybe you will already be finding that the artificial aids appear somehow less appealing.

And here's the thing. Drugs, drink and other physical pleasures hungered after, simply reproduce states that you had already learned a long time ago and that your unconscious mind knows how to do as you use these tools and techniques. So, for example, anchors get stronger and stronger.

So whether with so many new choices, all these positive patterns and opportunities and the power to use the feedback model you have learned, you can be part of a great and growing heritage that can be passed to the world which must be better than the interminable aggression and war.

And it's not about teaching so much as sharing knowledge and wisdom, offering advice, guidance and counsel when it is sought, loving without condition and simply 'being there' in all the ways that you now know you can be...

EXERCISING, sports and play

By now you know enough to apply any and all of these things to any aspect of your life and as someone who works with amateur and professional sports people, I can assure you that they are by far the most powerful sports psychologies in the world.

A professional golfer was referred to me. "Are you a sports psychologist?" He asked. I ducked the question.

"I'm a performance coach and I've found that it's not just about sport. The changes you will make and the new choices you can have when we will have worked together will have lasting positive effects and create new choices for you, not only in your sport and also in every aspect of your life."

And of course, it wasn't about positive beliefs when he putted, it was about all the negative patterns he had learned as a child, which were running unconsciously. Ironically, the harder he tried, the more they imposed themselves. After we had worked together for one hour, he went out and shot 65, his lowest score in a tournament for two years. And we've only just started...

NIRVANA - exploring the spirit

We mentioned the spirit in passing when we discussed emotional intelligence. And all these things that you can be doing now, can not only move you inexorably towards your limitless potential and you can be calmer, having stilled the internal voice that previously nattered you and beat you up.

As you go through life with more choices and learning more about these things, you won't be surprised when you are able to find yourself more relaxed and more in touch with your higher consciousness and sense of self-worth.

I don't mind where this takes you, whether in service of God or your fellow, I'm just the tour guide. And maybe you will have found that as you are able to let go of all the needs you had felt for your body, that you were able to get much more in touch with your mind.

The unconscious mind communicates outside you as well as inside and is connected to the whole universe. As you have been able to let go of those old patterns that had held you back, you may find that your consciousness was able to move outside yourself, especially as it grew more in rapport with your unconscious, so that you can be open to many new possibilities..

Chapter 7

How will this improve your work?

Getting a GRIP on stress – the supply/demand model

THERE ARE many good stress consultants in the world, which is just as well, because there is a heck of a lot of it about, especially, but not only at work. One of the reasons is that, try though they might, more and more people have had difficulty in separating their two domains of work and life and getting the work/life balance right.

Enlightened organizations are recognizing that stress is the biggest single cost in industry now, in absence, sickness and staff turnover. It may also be a contributory factor in other problems, such as drink and drugs.

Such organizations are offering stress counseling to their staff, either by contracting external consultants or even recruiting or training their own people in such skills.

Much modern stress counseling is based on 'cognitive dissociative' theory. The skilled counselor facilitates and guides the client to identify the stress factors in their lives and make deliberate decisions to remove, reduce or modify these. The trouble is that, too often, a few months pass and the stress seems to have reappeared.

What is stress anyhow? It is a very definite condition or set of symptoms that manifests itself in different ways for different people. Basically, an external event, stimulus or set of circumstances passes through the client's internal filters and interacts with their past memories or experiences. If it encounters an unresourceful pattern, it can trigger a state in that person, of varying degrees of severity, depending on that person's ability to cope.

Most of us are very good at coping and I would contend that it is one of the most frequently drawn on capabilities these days. And wouldn't you want to be doing better than that? Wouldn't you like to be able to be in control of all aspects of your life, rather than have them seemingly control you? Paradoxically, the way to gain control in your life is to find a way to let go, especially of old unresourceful programs and behaviours.

The Supply/Demand model of Stress Management

The work that we do with stress utilizes what I call the supply/demand model. Most modern counselors are skilled at working on the demand side, i.e. the set of demands that the client faces and is experiencing from day to day. Where the stress reimposes itself, it can often be because the client has consciously or unconsciously slipped back into those old ways.

As well as understanding what stress is, the factors in the client's life that may be causing stress and the ways to change or cope better, we work on the supply factors. These are originating experiences, patterns and programs laid down usually in childhood which, when removed or modified to be resourceful, mean that stress need no longer be a problem. Also, we teach the client new skills to be aware of and modify patterns of daily behaviour such that stress need not occur or intervene.

Making stress work for you

What other people call stress can work for you. By now, you may be unconsciously or even consciously aware of all the ways in which you can change your behaviours and language for the positive.

Stress is the biggest single challenge in industry and society. Organizations and individuals are becoming more skilled in understanding and managing stress.

Good work is being done in helping people to understand the stress factors in their lives and make their own choices to minimize or remove these. Did you ever notice, however, with someone else, that the stress seemed to return to their lives, after a while? This is because they had only worked on the demand factors – what demands in their business and personal lives were causing or adding to stress?

Stress is a state, triggered by experience. What deeper aspect of someone's personality or behaviour is being triggered by the stressful situation?

In my view, on the supply side, many of us have had negative emotional experiences in our past, mainly in childhood, where the basis of a 'supply side' stress factor was laid down. Certain 'demand' situations or an accumulation in general, have in the past led to some people struggling or being unable to cope.

Stress exercise

First, write down absolutely everything that you can recall has caused you stress in the past. Write down all the stress factors there have been in your life. Instinctively understand those which may have had a greater effect than others in the past.

Rank them from one upwards, where number one appears to be the most significant. Now, where can you take decisions, which will remove or alleviate any, some or all of these stress factors?

Now, and with the work you have done earlier, have a sense or a feeling of where that capacity to feel stress came from. Which situations, events, or people in your early life, have you consciously or unconsciously associated with stress before?

Find the source of each of these, inside yourself and go back to a time before that source when you know for certain that you did not have that factor in your life. As you look forward to now, through the origin of that stress capability, what do you notice that is different, in how many ways do you feel better, different, and more resourceful? What is there to learn and keep forever such that you were able to let go of the original emotions you once associated with the source of that particular capacity to feel stress.

Come back to now and go forward to a time when the new learnings and perception of that old feeling have enabled you to feel and be differently, in a situation where you might once have experienced stress. What do you already notice that is different now?

Don't spend too much time practicing these new skills or you might find...

OCCUPATIONAL HEALTH AND WELL-BEING

Modern day organizations and their employees are beset by many more challenges than in the past. As well as stress, there are the demands of the global economy, technology and emails and the growing diversity of society.

Much of society originated in small, parochial communities, with tribal rituals and patterns. Now we live and work in mixed communities and economies with more diversity than ever before. For some, this is yet another positive challenge in the variety and excitement of new cultures, new ideas and new relationships. For others, it strikes at the roots of their prehistoric patterns or their ritualized and sometimes unresourceful patterns and behaviours.

As a species we have not always been comfortable with change. Try this simple test. Put your hands together and interlock your fingers, as if in prayer. Which thumb is on top? Feels comfortable, doesn't it? Now swap the thumbs over, so that the other one is on top. Doesn't feel quite the same, does it? Now swap them back and forth several times to get used to the different feel. Is that better?

With more and more migration of populations throughout the world, there is more cross-fertilization of cultures, nationalities and communities. Some people, for whatever reason find this threatening or unsettling. Others, can feel quite left out, ostracized or worst of all discriminated against.

For both the individual and the organization, the ideal is to create a valuing culture, where the individual feels able to value themselves.

Whether for stress, diversity or whatever challenge, creating the opportunity and the environment where people can learn to release and be their best self, has been shown to make a material contribution to an empowering, productive, integrated culture in the workplace.

As an individual, you will always perform and respond better, being more resourceful, when you are being your best self.

Being your BEST SELF and feeling valued

Feeling valued, consciously or unconsciously, especially at work, is pretty important to a lot of people. At the end of the day, however, they may not yet have realized that, because the whole world is experienced through their own filters, patterns and programs, feeling valued is totally about valuing yourself. True, someone or something else can hit the right buttons and trigger the best states and by now you have realized that they are your buttons, triggers and states and the more you move towards understanding and being your best self, so your personal value to yourself, i.e. your self-esteem, can grow exponentially.

Understanding and EMPOWERING others

So now, having more and more insights into your feelings, patterns and programs to move towards your best self and your limitless potential, you may by now have been noticing that this gives you a better understanding of other people. Now, while they are different from you and have their own 'models of the world', you can better understand their makeup and the codes of human language and behaviour that they draw on in much the same way as you can.

You have learned and are practicing daily, your relating, rapport and communication skills. You are calibrating and noticing more elements of their behaviours and responses. Maybe for those closest to you, you have realized how to 'light them up' like a Christmas tree.

Sadly, a few years ago, I was listening to a psychologist on the radio, explaining the growing divorce and separation rate for younger people. "The trouble is, many young people seem to enter a relationship for what they can get out of it, rather than what they put into it."

Many or most of us are looking for happiness. Some have realized that, as they say in Yorkshire "you have to put out to get owt." Or, in American parlance, "what goes around comes around." The more you invest in a relationship and understanding your partner or other significant others, the more rewarding it can be. And you can use many of the ideas in this book to improve the quality of all your relationships.

This includes at work. The better you understand others, the more appropriate, responsive and resourceful your behaviours will be towards them. The more insights you have into their model of the world, the more and better choices you have in the relationship, being careful all the while to avoid being intrusive or invasive.

Far too many people thought that empowerment was a process that could be done by one person or organization to another person or group of people. The only person that can truly empower someone is themselves. When they, and you, can be your best selves, then each of you can be and feel empowered in the quality of your relationship and interactions.

When I was first promoted into a managerial role, some 25 years ago, I had no formal management training of any sort. I made mistakes and misjudgments. One day, I asked myself the question "what is management?" The spontaneous response from my unconscious was "creating the environment where people's natural talent can flourish".

That has stayed with me ever since and is indeed the watchword and strapline for our motivational and coaching business.

It has several key components.

"Creating" – use the power of your mind and imagination to constantly search for ways to understand, recognize and create the right environment where people can spontaneously feel they can express and be their best selves.

"Natural talent" implies that we all have limitless potential.

"Flourish" implies freedom to be, do, express and growth.

Chapter 8

How will this improve your health?

YIN & YANG - Relaxing and meditating

AS KARL JUNG has found, there is so much to be learned from Eastern philosophy, especially as it is integrated with the new learnings and philosophies of the West. This has been likened to holism of the right and left brain. The left brain is sometimes connoted with the 'harder' more physical, practical side and the right with a softer, wiser, more reflective way of life.

Take martial arts. So many of these could be regarded as forms of aggression and one of the rules is to only use these for self-defence. As you get deeper into an understanding of these sports, you can find that they are based on self-control and the spirit.

So, with the Yin and the Yang. I've taken these as just one example of similar patterns throughout the cultures of the world, not just Eastern.

Yin-yang is concerned with the interplay between the yin, which is negative, passive and weak and the yang, which is positive, active and strong. So, the theory goes, just as the natural order involves yin and yang, with the former subordinate to the latter, so human beings are born with or learn bad and good elements and should subsume the former into the latter.

Chinese philosophy has flowed though the Tao and the thoughts of Lao Tzu and Buddhism to an evolving modern mix of philosophies. This is increasingly true, not only of the East in general, but also of the West. And we are finding more in Eastern philosophy. So, much of what is in this book would be in keeping with such developments.

And so with meditation and other pursuits of relaxation. We consider below a simple method of meditation that can take away the inner voice and leave room for the unconscious mind to fill the void with limitless ideas and potential, including noticing the things that you might not have previously noticed.

Drugs and meditation have in common their ability to take us 'out of ourselves'. Whilst totally deprecating the former, now you can realize that there is far more potential in the latter when combined with all these other things. What we mean by taking out of ourselves, is taking ourselves out of the constantly chattering, narrowly focused, consciousness, into the limitlessness of the unconsciousness. Now that you have found that possibility, there need be no turning back.

Much has been written and talked about meditation. Transcendental meditation, like the martial arts, seemed to involve many years of practice. I believe you can achieve much the same for yourself in a simpler and quicker way.

The value of meditation is threefold: to release stress; to clear the mind of any negative thoughts or internal dialogue which may have been there before; to open a space for your creative brain to slip original thoughts and ideas into. This is of inestimable value in every aspect of your life. Inspiration can make the difference between ordinary and superlative performance.

Before proposing the meditation method, think also about dreams. All the great geniuses of time managed their dreams. Einstein dreamed the theory of relativity. Many of the great inventors created their most brilliantly original ideas in dream. Learn how to manage your dreaming process.

You can use the power of your unconscious mind to help you make decisions. It is connected to the universal consciousness. Before you sleep, consider a challenge or question that needs resolution. Put both sides to your unconscious. Entrust the process to your dreaming philosophy and power of analysis.

Keep a notebook beside you whenever you dream or meditate. Make notes of what you have dreamt immediately you wake, or come out of the meditative state. Notice over time, how much more you can recall.

Plan how you will fit meditation into your daily routine. First thing in the morning or early evening is good. You can create the space to meditate any time you choose. Allocate time to your days.

Find a quiet place where you will not be disturbed for up to half an hour. Sit upright in a comfortable, well-supporting chair, or lie flat in bed, preferably without a pillow. Rest your hands, palms down. Relax your body from the toes and feet upwards. Focus on each part in turn. Think of the sound of waves on a beach, gently flowing, as you progressively relax.

Clear your mind in any way that works for you. When I started, I used to think about a blank, white wall. At first, the internal dialogue chattered away, or music came into my mind. I blanked it out again. On the occasions that did not work, I simply said 'be quiet', in a commanding tone, inside my mind.

Be patient. Over time, your meditation will become calmer, longer and deeper. When you choose to wake, come out of your state gently and slowly, bringing positive, stimulating thoughts about the day into your mind. Notice and note all the positive changes you are making in every aspect of your life.

OPENING YOUR MIND – to the power of healing

Volumes have been written about the power of the mind to heal. Once you will have realized that the mind and body are part of the same systems, you might also notice that there are two ways to think of this. The old way might have been to believe that the body got sick or hurt and the pain or discomfort sometimes became experienced by the mind, even to the point of distraction.

The volumes of literature and documentary evidence on the use of self-induced anaesthesia are growing exponentially. Once we might have thought that only fakirs and similar had the magic power to block pain out of their minds and consciousness. And yet, if that is what drugs do, how do they do it, other than acting on the pain receptors, or inhibiting the pain from being experienced? Basically, they instruct the unconscious mind not to notice or even experience the pain and we can do the same.

To take a small example. The child falls over and bangs its leg. It looks towards its parent to see what the reaction is. The parent rushes to comfort the child, who launches into the passionate programmed behaviour of upset. Alternative two: the parent looks, makes a rapid assessment of the damage, smiles and carries on with what they were doing...and so does the child.

The book that first brought Deepak Chopra to wider attention was *Quantum Healing*. Chopra, a qualified physician practicing in the US, had come from a cultural background that included ayurvedic, or Vedic medicine. After a while, he found that he was being referred incurable patients, some of whom he helped to cure themselves simply with the power of the mind.

We have a long way to go with these things and there isn't time or space now. Having started the journey, you can discover so much. Like when I first read *Beliefs* by Robert Dilts. Working against negative patterns and beliefs and with some of the other patterns you will have learned in this book, he and his mother cured her terminal illness.

And why shouldn't that be true, now that you realize that it is the unconscious mind that runs everything for you, usually without your having noticed, not the body running your life through the narrow gateway of your consciousness...

NUTRITION and nourishment

The 'mind-body' connection is now proven beyond doubt. Care for your body and your mind will be in good condition also.

There have been dietary plans for as long as I can remember. Recent research in the US suggested that, over the longer term, people who embarked on diets ended up three to four pounds heavier than they started. Weight is an attitude of mind. Fatness is an internal belief, based on patterns and beliefs from the past. Body image is created and owned by you. You choose.

On my wall, I have a picture of myself in excellent health, muscled and fit. I see it consciously or unconsciously every day. It is in front of me now. Create your own image of yourself, fit and in perfect health, using the power of your recall from a past time, or your imagination. Step into that image inside your mind now. See what you will see, hear what you will hear and feel what you will feel as you are inside that image now.

Go forward to a time when you will be that image. Let your unconscious mind decide the most appropriate time. As you are in that future time, step out of the image and see yourself as you will be in that time. Now come back to the now.

Everything you will achieve starts with your health. 'Healthy body, healthy mind'. Eat sensibly. You know the best ideas: eat your biggest meal at the start of the day; the second biggest at lunchtime; the smallest in the evening. Go to bed with a light stomach and sleep well. Eat a balanced diet, including fresh fruit and vegetables. A reasonable amount of protein each day. Pasta, pulses, rice, for energy.

Drink no more than a modest amount of alcohol, spread over the week, rather than one binge. Red wine is good for the heart and digestion. Some has bioflavinoids from the black grape skin. These help prevent cancer.

Most of all, whatever you do, drink six pints of water every day. It flushes the kidneys, cleans and dilutes the bloodstream and is marvellous for the skin. You will look and feel well and think clearly.

Exercise for at least half an hour each day. Just enough to get the blood moving around your body. Make exercise enjoyable, rather than stressful or a chore.

Work out a chosen dietary and exercise plan. Diarise it, stick to it and reward yourself from time to time as you see and feel the changes that are taking place and hear the compliments from those you care about and whose opinions you value.

Fulfilling your DESTINY

So, having come this far, on a journey that you have only just begun, what is your destiny? We might once have believed in serendipity, chance or fate. Since then, we have considered synchronicity, choice, belief and limitless potential.

Above all, we have glimpsed the power of your unconscious mind and especially your imagination. Perception is reality and perception is projection. You can create your own reality, now or for the future. Whatever you totally, congruently and passionately believe inside yourself you are projecting outside yourself.

Of course it's all down to fate...and what fate had we decreed for ourselves or resigned ourselves to, before we thought about or reflected on these things.

What you see is what you get...if you always do what you always did, you'll always get what you always got...

And none of this goes counter to religious teaching. Read the Bible again and reflect how congruent all these things are. NLP isn't a series of gimmicks and tricks that someone made up, Bandler and Grinder started a momentum that has led to a complete codification of human language and behaviour. And especially it is founded on an understanding of the power of the unconscious mind and creating rapport with the conscious.

We can believe that all our unconscious minds are in tune with the universe at large and what is prayer other than communion with that greatest of all consciousness, the pervasive, universal presence of God. As the Bible says, God is in us and with us all the time.

What I know and believe above all is that those Practitioners of NLP who I work with that are most fervent and committed, are united by one thing. It is totally about positivity and our truly limitless potential.

So, as you continue on your journey towards being your best in every aspect of your life, you can notice that the quality of your life and those around you and the balance sheet of all your true wealth can move inexorably towards positivity and growth and in doing so, you may discover your higher self also.

Among the Prime Directives of the Unconscious Mind, as taught to NLP Practitioners are:

- To run and preserve the body and maintain its integrity; and

- To be a highly moral being.

So, as you travel on your journey to your higher self, understand that others have recognized a pyramid of behaviours that mankind is journeying through. Different tribes, different cultures and different individuals are at different stages of progress. And you could recognize any or all of these in everyday society and people who you might encounter.

The pyramid progresses from primitive at the base to spiritual and the higher self at the top. So as you continue your own personal journey, towards being your best, notice that the direction is away from those old negative patterns and limiting beliefs that you have left behind and towards your higher self. And I don't see any incongruence between that and the loftiest ideals of any philosophy.

Because as with emotional intelligence, and also with NLP, you cannot reach your highest self without an awareness of and a regard for others and the effects you have on their lives. So travel with total respect for and understanding for their own unique model of the world and a growing awareness and choice in your own.

Good luck.

And so, nourished and enriched, the young tree spread and grew until it was at least as high as any other in the forest was. From its new vantage it was able to see that there were many different trees in the forest, spreading as far as the eye could see. As it watched, day after day, it noticed that many of these were less sturdy or supple. It heard many moans and groans, much of the day.

As some of these others noticed the transformation of the young tree, they were drawn to it in conversation and engaged for many long hours in exchanging stories and ideas, so that soon many were collected in this wiser group and their knowledge and wisdom grew.

As the days and years passed, thoughts and perceptions were cast more and more to the other forms of life in and around the forest and upwards to the stars. There were still some that disparaged this new way of thinking and being, constantly casting their looks downwards, to make sure they were never encroached, drawing their branches in and around. It somehow seemed that these became stunted and left behind as the growth of the others swept up towards the sky.

It wasn't long before the tree noticed that other saplings and seedlings were growing around its roots and close by. Reaching out, it spread its own branches and gently nudged others to one side to make sure these younger ones had room to grow and flourish. Its counsel was increasingly sought by young and old and it listened and nodded, asking a probing question or making a helpful suggestion from time to time.

And one day after many years, Merlin passed by one evening. He cast his eye over the flourishing colony of sound, sturdy trees and saplings which was growing and spreading outwards from what was once the dark centre of the forest. He listened at a distance to the thoughts and exchanges. He smiled at the laughter and openness that he witnessed and marveled at how far they had come in such a short time. Staying only long enough to ascertain that there was little more that he could add to their growing wisdom, knowledge and understanding, without a word he left and moved on with an easy heart to where there was a much greater need...

APPENDICES

Tools and Techniques

for

The Power of Ten^{10}

steps to

success

A

The Presuppositions of NLP (Px)

P1   *The map is not the territory.*

We try to understand people based on what we see and hear. In NLP this is called the shallow structure. It does give some insights into the real person before us, but some language and behaviour is unconsciously created to disguise or conceal aspects of the real personality. Extraversion, for example, may conceal a shy person.

The deep structure is largely composed of our values, attitudes and beliefs. Sometimes we ourselves may not be consciously aware either of these or the behaviours that others perceive. What we do know is that our deep structure will unconsciously influence our behaviour.

These values and beliefs were laid down primarily in the first 18 years of our lives - sometimes called the socialization period. Our parents or surrogates were the prime influence in our first 5-7 years. In the next seven years or so, our school, siblings and peers. Finally, society and its institutions. We can change these values and beliefs.

People are not their behaviours. The language and behaviours only give clues to the whole person. Depending on their programming from their formative years, people will behave differently in different circumstances and with different people. You may come to understand this more clearly as this book unfolds. You may already be getting insights into yourself. You may by now be accepting yourself more. Accept the person and manage their behaviours. That includes you.

P2 Experience has a structure

Our values and beliefs can be changed. All sensory input is reviewed by the mind against existing memories, which are kept in structured patterns. When you change the structure of the memory, you can change how the past is recalled, how the present is experienced and how the future is expected. I will leave it to you to anticipate the positive opportunities for your life.

Another tenet of NLP is:

P3 Perception is projection

There is a traditional equivalent – 'it takes one to know one'. If you are tempted to criticize or speak negatively about someone else, try it on in the first person and see if that changes your perception of you – and them.

Whether on the golf course, the tennis court, at work, or in life in general, be kind to yourself, because every time you criticize or berate yourself, you may be reinforcing exactly the behaviours you might wish to be rid of. People who expect problems somehow seem to get them, sometimes repeatedly!

P4 The effect is not the problem-the cause is

Pleasant or unpleasant situations may trigger states in a person. Sometimes unresourceful behaviours may result. In such circumstances the person may be 'at effect'. The surface effect is merely an indication of the deeper cause. If we have found ourselves at effect in the past, an insight into the originating cause may help us to choose more productive behaviour in future. When you are able to live any aspect of your life at cause, then you may be able to achieve the short or long-term goals you desire.

P5   *All meaning is context dependent*

As Tad James, the famous NLP exponent is fond of saying "there is no content in content worth knowing". Any word is meaningless without a context or reference. If I use the word blue, you might think I am talking about the colour of the sky. I may in fact be thinking about sadness. In a dictionary, words are defined in relation to context.

A thought you think, or something you hear, will be interpreted depending on the assumed or actual context. In some situations, shouting or hollering may be the accepted norm. In a relationship, it would probably be wholly undesirable.

Think now of a pleasurable experience from your past, where you felt great energy and resourcefulness. In this positive context, such behaviour may be entirely appropriate. Reflect for a moment on the positive changes you can make in your life when you can transfer such a positive state into what previously might have been a negative situation.

P6   *Presuppositions of choice*

We always make the best choices available to us in a given state or circumstance. As you improve your self-mastery, you will become aware of opportunities to make different, more productive choices. Any choice is better than no choice and all procedures should increase choice.

Whether at work or in life in general, living one's life at cause means by definition making more choices. If you knew someone who appeared to be at effect, their life may appear to run itself. If you always are what you always were you may always get what you always got.

If your experience has been less successful than you wished, recognize your responsibility for your own life and decisions, move to cause, make more informed and productive choices and see the consequent benefits flow for you.

P7   Underlying every behaviour is a positive intent

Our patterns of behaviour are the result of patterns and programs acquired during our childhood and youth. When we have been momentarily at effect, a state may have emerged from our subconscious, based on these patterns. This did not mean that we wanted the consequent negative result. Have you ever asked yourself "where did that come from?" Have you ever felt yourself to be misunderstood?

Think of an aspect of your past behaviour that you would like to have changed. Ask yourself repeatedly, "for what highest positive purpose for myself did I do that." This process is known as 'chunking up'. As you ask the question, your internal answers should become more abstract. Here is a hypothetical internal dialogue for someone who has made an error of judgment with a relationship:

> "For what purpose for myself did I make that error of judgment?
> *I was frightened that I would lose this person.*
> Why was I frightened?
> *Because I don't like to lose.*
> For what purpose for myself do I not like to lose?
> *I want to be a winner.*
> Why do I want to be a winner?
> *Because I want people to respect me.*
> Why do I want people to respect me?
> *Because I want to be accepted*
> Why do I want to be accepted?
> *Because I want to be happy.*"

So the process ends in a highest positive intent. When you reach happiness, love, or something of equivalent abstraction, you may well be at the highest positive intent. Try it now and realize the positive purposes that have driven any previous unresourceful behaviours.

P8   The meaning of your communication is the response you get

You cannot not communicate. What do I mean? If you and I were sat together now, having a discussion, only 7% of your understanding would come from the actual words I said. (There is no content ....). 38% would come from the tonality I used in saying the words and 55% would come from my 'neurophysiology'.

When you watched Bill Clinton on the Lewinsky tapes, why did there seem to be more meaning than the words themselves conveyed. Did you watch his eye movements, hear him clear his throat, adjust his posture, etc. Part of the reason of course, is that you are interpreting all the input you receive through your own model of the world. We shall see how to change that in perceptual positions.

If we ever misunderstood someone's meaning, maybe it was because we 'mind-read' them. Maybe we unconsciously or intuitively read the 'body language' (neurophysiology) and put on our own interpretation.

Have you ever asked your partner or friend, "what's wrong?" simply because you felt you had an idea that something was not quite right. It may have been as much in what Mr Clinton didn't say as what he said, that we formed our own ideas of the truth. If he had sat there saying nothing to each question, his 'body language' would be communicating some form of message. If only we could understand. People cannot not communicate. Elsewhere you have understood how to interpret these signals.

Resistance is a sign of a lack of rapport. If you do not get the response you intend, it is more than just the words that are involved. "Don't shout so loud, I can't hear you!" If someone grew up around anger, they may have learned at an early age to 'switch off' to loud behaviour.

Later, we shall learn about eye patterns and predicates, so that you can choose to modify your behaviour and communication to achieve the desired response.

P9   *There is no failure, only feedback*

Failure is an attitude of mind. One person may see another as a failure, in their model of the world. The subject may not see things that way. They may not feel a failure; they may have a very positive disposition, seeing every shortfall on desired or planned performance as an opportunity to learn.

If someone saw and continued to see their shortfalls as failure, they may simply be reinforcing a 'program' laid down in childhood. Every situation in life presents opportunities to learn and, if we choose, modify behaviour. Seeing a shortfall as failure is likely to result from, or put someone at, feelings of being at effect. Putting oneself at cause, anything that varies from the planned, or expected outcomes, is an opportunity to review, reappraise, modify, beliefs and behaviours.

Remember this model when you are offering feedback yourself (especially to children):

"This is what specifically went well.
These are possibilities for you to improve.
Overall, this is how well you performed."

Watch the change in response as the person begins to recognize the chance of learning and growing.

If you ever lost out in life, what was there for you to learn? Where could you have improved. Frankly and candidly, how well did you do overall. Are you going to grab the opportunities to learn and grow, resulting in increasing success in the longer term. After all, the chart of life, like the stock market, may seesaw, but given enough time, it continues inexorably upwards. How well is your own long-term chart performing?

If you were to go forward to a time when you could look back and see that, around this time, the chart of your personal fortunes and well-being had broken into a new and powerful uptrend, as a result of understanding the messages in this book, how does that feel for you right now?

P10 If what you are doing isn't working, do something else...anything else!

If your life strategy or style isn't producing the results you desire, or expect, you could review every aspect of what you are doing. This includes not only the mechanical, practical day-to-day things you are doing; it also includes what you are doing in and with yourself. You will understand more as the book unfolds.

P11 The Law of Requisite Variety

This Law comes from cybernetics. Basically it means that the person and/or system with the greatest flexibility and/or adaptability will end up controlling the system. Try varying every aspect of what you do, visualizing and 'running the movie' before you implement it in practice.

Also, as the above implies, if it's not working, try anything else until it does. However, 'if it ain't broke don't try and fix it'.

P12 People work perfectly. We already have all the resources we need.

The question is do we realize this; have we accepted it? Are you at cause or effect in your life? Be at cause and take responsibility for everything that you do. Choose your behaviours and watch a new more purposeful life unfold for you.

P13 If one person can do something, anyone can learn to do it

You will understand and realize the possibilities more and more as you are reading this book. By the time you have come to modeling, having understood everything that went before, you will be realizing the possibilities right now.

P14 All procedures should increase wholeness

Evaluate your behaviour and make the changes appropriate to the context in which you find yourself. Have respect for other people's model of the world. You may not like it, or agree with it, but if you understand it, you have a choice as to whether to respond to it, go with it, go against it, ignore it, etc.

P15 The Mind and Body are part of the same system

You are responsible for your conscious and your unconscious mind and therefore the results that you get. We already know that mind power can control or eliminate illness and disease after it has set in. How many more possibilities can you see when you eliminate it before it occurs.

Norman Vincent Peale wrote of the power of positive thinking. There is now a vast amount of documentary evidence of the powerful positive effects of the unconscious mind. It is also beyond question that the mind and body are part of the same system, now that you are making it work for you...

B

Filters – How the unconscious mind processes information and experience

BELOW IS a picture of what Tad James called 'The Communication Model' in the excellent material for my NLP Practitioner course in 1997. This was of real value in simplifying for me how the unconscious mind works, and the filters through which all information travels.

It summarizes all the filters, many of which we will have considered in this book. Let us take stress. What we call stress can be totally internally generated during fear, for example. Stress is closely linked to the primitive 'Fight or Flight' response.

Where an external event triggers stress, it travels through the filter set, with the unconscious mind attempting to delete what is not relevant, distort the event to fit possible deletion or past experience or memory, or generalize for either purpose. It may then create an internal representation, composed of all your representation systems and their elements (submodalities). If during this almost instantaneous process, a match is made with a negative memory or experience from the deep structure of the mind, it can create an internal state that you would experience in your physiology, whether you were consciously or unconsciously aware of it. This could be a state of stress.

Communication Process – see next page)

Some of these filters are pretty self-explanatory. The ones we shall focus on here are memories, meta programs and language. We have already discussed values and beliefs in detail in the main body.

Memories

Remember that the unconscious mind records everything. It is not about memory, it's about recall. We discussed submodalities earlier and once you understand these, you can achieve even more than you dreamed. You see, all experience has a structure. This structure is the basis of how it is recorded in our minds. It is composed of 'modalities' (or representation systems) and submodalities.

When you are able to: recover a memory; understand its specific structure; experiment with the different submodalities to find out which have the most significant effect on that memory; and then modify or remove these; you change not only the memory, not only how you will re-experience it next time, and also how you will interpret any future experience which has this memory as a context. That is why you have limitless potential. That is why you can create so much positivity and remove any negativity from your experience.

It took me far too long to realize this profound bedrock of NLP. This is what Richard Bandler has focused on most clearly. Anything else may be of value, interesting, even life changing. And now that you have understood the fundamental criticality of submodalities, will it be by tomorrow or next week before you are experiencing dramatic, lasting change on your journey to magnificence.

Modalities (or Representation Systems)

There may seem to be many technical words in NLP and that's all they are: words. What really matters is where these words are the handles we have attached to our processes. We are our processes. When you change your processes, you can change everything that you do and you are.

Try this. Think of a really disappointing experience. Now, change the colour of this image to your favourite, warmest colour and make sure you are 'associated' into the picture (i.e. seeing it through your own eyes). Now, in what ways does it seem different? Wow! We've only just started and I wouldn't want to think that you could get totally absorbed in this skill, like trying on lots and lots of new clothes, like going to an art gallery and looking at all the possibilities in art, or indulging your broadest interests in music...

·We talk about our five senses. There may be more...In our memories, we represent the world primarily through our representation systems. The unconscious mind uses as many of these as possible to 'fix' the memory. You could play with one now and make it even more memorable. Our 'rep systems' are primarily: **(V)**isual (sight), **(A)**uditory (sounds), **(K)**inesthetic (touch or feelings). In addition, we have **(O)**lfactory (smell) and **(G)**ustatory (taste). **VAK(OG)**

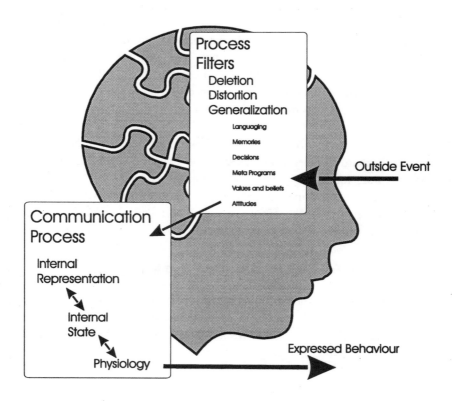

Understanding representation systems and sub-modalities

Each of us has a unique pattern of representation systems. By this I mean the means by which the mind represents an internal real or imaginary experience of the world. What is happening inside you right now, as you read these words – pictures, feelings, sounds, smells, tastes, any or all?

Become aware of how your mind receives and processes information best. Do you learn and understand best from pictures, feelings, hearing something, reading or collecting information and analyzing it. Find out which pattern works best for you. Understand what works best for other people. You could choose to communicate with them in the medium that works for them. Or you could remain as you are. It is your choice.

In my experience, how someone expresses themselves, may not give the real clue to how they process information best. Some people are different. I produce a lot of verbal output, and yet I learn best through seeing and doing something.

The three major senses are: visual; auditory; and kinesthetic. You may use any or all of these. As part of your adaptability and flexibility, try them all.

Each of the 'representation systems' can be further subdivided into 'submodalities' – component parts. So, pictures can be divided into colours, focus, nearness, frame size, movement, etc.

For now, understand your own optimal pattern of rep systems. With their permission, understand your partner's or a friend's. Practice using different patterns. Notice how you need no longer 'talk at cross purposes'. One tip: everyone can make pictures. By and large, women are more visual as a group. Use the magic of language to paint pictures in peoples' minds – and your own.

Analyze your own internal representations into their submodalities. Compare a positive with a negative memory. Notice which submodality(ies) appear most important in each. Find the one(s) that drive the internal representation. Take the driver for positive internal images and enhance that submodality in any negative representations. Play with the control of this driver. If it is nearness, try moving the negative picture nearer or further away. What happens?

Understand how much more power you are already having over your internal and external experiences and relationships.

What are Submodalities?

Submodalities are 'the barcodes of experience' and give finer distinctions of the representation systems. All our memories are coded in detailed distinctions, and when the 'code' is known for a particular state, we can either use these to re-access a state, or change or re-edit past experience.

How can you tell the difference between an experience that happened yesterday and one that happened 20 years ago? You'd probably say, "I just know." Your brain has its way of coding, remembering and recalling experience. These building blocks are called 'Modalities' and 'Submodalities'.

As we have seen, there are five modalities, or representation systems:

For the purposes of simplicity, we tend to code touching, tasting and smelling as all under kinaesthetic, so that we have the commonly used primary representation systems of VAK. Every experience gets recorded using these modalities as structural components. In addition, submodalities (the subcomponents of these) are used by the brain to further code experience. Indeed, the richer the composition of submodalities, the stronger the experience is recorded.

For example, many teachers now use 'three senses learning' to assist in education. This approach would be highly appropriate working with dyslexics, for example, once they have understood the fundamental importance of visual recall in reading, writing and spelling.

Within each representational system, we make fine distinctions. Each sense can have different quality characteristics. Each emotion uses different submodalities. Each belief is emotionally based.

- Visual submodalities include shape, colour/black & white, movement, brightness/dimness, distance, location, etc.
- Auditory submodalities include volume, tempo, pitch, frequency, etc.
- Kinesthetic submodalities include: temperature, pressure, texture, moisture, pain, pleasure.

We can further distinguish between analogue and digital submodalities. Analogue is a continuously 'variable' submodality, e.g. variable sounds – high/low and varied inputs. Digital is on or off, e.g. black/white or colour. Analogue is like a 'dimmer' switch. Variable and digital is like an on/off light switch. Something is analogue if there can be shades of meaning and digital if there is only on and off or 1 and 0 (binary code as in digital computers, i.e. the PC).

- Analogue submodalities include brightness, distance, size, location, etc.
- Digital submodalities include associated/dissociated; colour/black and white; framed or panoramic; focused or unfocused (although unfocused itself is an analogue submodality).

What are Critical Submodalities?

In assessing your submodalities, e.g. for a 'happy memory' code, you could compare two happy memories for sameness in codes, and two sad memories for sameness in codes. The Critical ones are the same in each category. Then the difference in criticals between happy and sad ones are the change points (contrast) which can be used to re-frame or edit memories.

What are Drivers?

Drivers are those which cause other submodalities to change. This has been compared to a linked chain reaction.

Submodalities are Modality Filters

For example, suppose you 'see' a car traveling down the road. The modality of sight would contain many submodalities for this experience, such as:

- Closeness: up close or far away (analogue);
- Colour: red, white, black, blue, etc (analogue);
- Motion: fast, slow, smooth, jerky, etc (analogue);
- Dimension: 3d or flat (digital – there is currently no other possibility...);
- Brightness: dull, bright, etc (analogue).

By the time you have coded and stored the memory, it may be in black and white or colour (digital).

The point is, much of this recording of experience goes on 'below the surface' and outside your conscious awareness. Usually it's no big deal how these experiences are recorded, we just act in certain ways based on all this coding and programming.

Submodalities Checklist

Below is a detailed list of submodalities that you can copy and use for yourself, either now or in future. The sheet is numbered in columns, so that you can use each up to four times.

Visual	1	2	3	4
Black & White or Colour? Near or Far? Bright or Dim? Location? Size of Picture? Associated / Dissociated? Focused or Defocused? Focus (Changing/Steady)				

	1	2	3	4
Framed or Panoramic? Movie or Still? Movie-Fast/Normal/Slow Amount of Contrast 3D or Flat? Angle Viewed From or Pictures (Shift?)				
Auditory				
Location Direction Internal or External? Loud or Soft? Fast or Slow? High or Low? (Pitch) Tonality Timbre Pauses Cadence Duration Uniqueness of Sound				
Kinesthetic				
Location Size Shape Intensity Steady Movement/ Duration Vibration Pressure/Heat? Weight				

Why are Submodalities of Benefit?

You may already have begun to realize in how many different aspects of NLP, submodalities come into play. In anchoring, for example, the qualities of the experiences recalled and anchored can be broken down into their submodalities so that the experience could be specifically intensified.

In discussing representation systems, you discovered about primary systems and drivers. The more you are exploring and understanding submodalities, the more you will be discovering the specific drivers of behaviour that will be used to create and condition your lasting change.

Understanding the structure of submodalities helps us to discover further distinctions in our internal experience. Within the brain, we represent all of our experience, emotions and beliefs using submodalities.

Then there are also our strategies...

How does submodality change work?

Submodality change works through changing the internal representation of the experience, emotion or belief. The most common method is by *bridging across*, which is the process of changing the submodalities of one image into the submodalities of another image. Usually two or three submodalities (such as location, brightness are quite common) will change other submodalities. This will vary from one person to another. The ones that *bridge across* are *critical* and the critical submodalities that cause the change are called *drivers*.

Practical Exercises

Not only can an understanding of submodalities better help us to understand the structure of experience, emotions and beliefs, they are also the basis of a number of different change techniques for both experiences and beliefs:

- Bridging across submodalities, by comparing the differences between, say a negative and a positive experience and bridging the positive driver across into the negative experience to make it positive. E.g. if the driver was brightness, by increasing the brightness in the negative picture, the experience can be re-edited for positive change.

- Future pacing: see a picture of yourself in a future situation where your new belief comes into action and enrich the submodalities.

- Time distortion: see a picture of yourself and go five years into the future. Look back and, having enriched the submodalities, think about how the new beliefs have changed your life. Do the same for 10, 20 and 40 years in the future.

- Visual technique: visualize an image of your belief and an image of something that you doubt. Notice the position in your field of vision of each picture. Cross-map the submodalities. Intensify the submodalities of the doubt in your belief picture by moving the belief back to where it shrinks, blurs and changes to black and white. Now move it to the doubt position. Take the new belief you want to install and put it on the place where the old belief picture is. Now move it up close, bigger and intensify the submodalities.

- Belief Change Cycle (after Robert Dilts): this uses six different spatial ground anchors:

  - Wanting to believe (something new);
  - Being open to believe(something new);
  - Current beliefs;
  - Being open to doubt;
  - Beliefs that you used to believe but don't anymore (Museum of Old Beliefs);
  - Deep Trust.

The method involves walking through each of these spaces, each time creating an appropriate representation and enriching the submodalities.

Meta programs

In their book, *Figuring Out People,* Bob Bodenhammer and L Michael Hall have identified 57 or more categories of 'meta-program' that we may all run. These are fundamental filters of language, behaviour and experience. One of the most fundamental is 'Towards or Away From' that we discussed. Everyone is programmed to either or both move away from pain or towards pleasure. This is derived from the primitive fight or flight response.

Is your 'glass half full or half empty'? If half full, you may see the world in general in a more positive light and be largely motivated towards achievement, pleasure, happiness, etc.

"Every person you meet today, that you engage in conversation, that you try to influence, or who tries to influence you, operates from some *frame-of-mind.* As such, that 'program' that lies above and beyond ('meta') their specific words determines their perspective, way of valuing, style of thinking and emoting, and pattern of choosing and behaving.

Recognizing these meta-software programs in people's heads that control and run their specific frame-of-mind, enables us to know how to more effectively communicate and relate to them. It empowers us to stop getting angry at their frame-of-mind as it equips us for *how* to *effectively work with it!"* (Bodenhammer & Hall, ibid.)

Try the following exercise as a basis to better understand your own or other people's meta programs and maybe by now or soon, you will have understood how people can ever have been 'at cross purposes'.

Question	Filter
What do you want from your life?	Towards/away from
Why are you choosing to do what you do?	Possibility/necessity
How do you know when you've done well?	Internal/external evidence

How do you know other people do well?	See/hear/do/read
How often do they have to do that to convince you?	Automatic/ x times/always
In a new situation do you act or reflect first?	Active/reflective/ both
Describe a time when you were happiest?	hings/people/systems
Describe your favourite restaurant.	People/places/things
If we worked together, would you want the details or the big picture first?	Specific/global
When you come to something afresh, what is different from the last time you did that thing?	Same/different/ exception
Describe a situation that troubled you?	Associated/ disassociated

(In associated you see the memory through your own eyes).

Through the above, you have elicited and understood your primary filters. Try in vain to stop thinking about the many ways this understanding is helping you.

Notice particularly that these key patterns summarize the possibilities that you will encounter in other people. Therefore, as you become more aware of their patterns through the way they speak and act, you have even more choices. Respecting their model of the world and wanting to create excellent communication and superb rapport, you can understand, respond to or manage or change your own patterns while engaging with that person.

Remember, the person with the greatest flexibility of language, and behaviour will end up controlling the process.

Language and other things

So, in so many different ways you can become aware of and change your own language, and behaviours. This can have the effect of enhancing your own performance or potential and your communication and relationships with others.

We talked above about rep systems. Clues to how people process are also present in their language and behaviours. For example, if someone tends normally to favour their visual rep system in communicating or processing their model of the world, you would not be surprised to find clues in their language. Do you see what I mean? Can you get the picture? Does your perception of this concept seem vivid in your mind?

Similarly for auditory and kinesthetic. There is one other pattern to add here (and you will encounter it later when we consider eye patterns) and that is 'auditory digital'. This is largely connected with 'self-talk', internal dialogue, facts and data. So, for example, accountants and scientists might access auditory digital quite a lot (and talk quite a lot, maybe in a relative monotone).

Chunking

One of the important meta programs is 'chunk size'. It might otherwise be denoted as 'global or specific'. You may recognize in yourself or others that some people tend towards a quite specific or detailed model of the world, especially in what they say, while others appear to consider more abstract concepts. The latter might be quite strategic and, interestingly, visual. The former might be more auditory digital.

As you listen to or communicate with someone, you can choose to become aware of their more comfortable 'chunk size'. You could then either take account of it in your own communication, ignore it, or vary your own chunk size in order to increase rapport and the quality of your communication.

Try this as a game with a partner. Think of an object. Have the person choose 'higher' or 'lower' a number of times. Each time, practice moving to a bigger or smaller chunk from the previous level. So, for example:

Phone	Higher	Communication	
Higher	Relating	Higher	Being
Higher	Universe		

Or,	Phone	Lower	Dial	Lower
	Plastic	Higher	Oil	Lower
	Cosmetics	Higher	Beauty	Higher
	Being	Higher	Universe, etc.	

Have fun trying these and other patterns to increase the flexibility of your communication and behaviours.

Associated/Dissociated

Did you ever hear yourself or someone else say something like "you can't bear to face a problem so you avoid it" or whatever? Now, you may have already noticed that when they say 'you' they mean I. At least three interesting consequences follow from this:

They are in effect trying to put that behaviour on the other person, whether they realize it or not;

They are dissociating themselves inside themselves from that memory, behaviour, etc;

If we were to ask them to see, hear and feel that memory or experience inside themselves and to ask whether they could see themselves in the picture, the answer would be very likely to be 'yes'.

This is the 'dissociated' frame.

The opposite is 'associated'. So, when you hear yourself or someone else saying "I...." They are associated and they would probably recall the pattern through their own eyes. They might also interestingly feel stronger feelings or emotions about it.

So, if you want to re-experience something happy, wonderful, etc. Make sure you are associated into the memory and notice already how powerful that can be...

Apart from enriching your own experiences and understanding, this can better equip you with an awareness of other people and their communication.

Health warning: If, without the prior consent of that person, you share with them all the things you believe you are discovering in their language and behaviours, you may find that you irritate them or otherwise compromise that quality of your relationship. Keep them to yourself and notice that growing improvement in your quality of your life and relationships...

C

Calibration

AS YOUR SKILLS in understanding and relating to yourself and others become inexorably better, you may have already noticed that you have been noticing more and more about their language and behaviours. Knowing that words are only 7% of the communication means that you have been noticing what we once called 'body language'.

So, you may have realized how many times in the past you had noticed 'incongruence'? That is, when the body language didn't seem to fit the words. It is very important to understand here that unless you ask the person, or are that person, you don't actually know what is really happening inside them.

This is where it is very important for me to stress that 'guessing' or 'mind-reading' can be really unhelpful. It could be worse still to even dream of telling the person what you think they are saying or doing inside.

The value of practicing 'calibration' that is, noticing all that there is to notice, is that it will be giving you some clues that something is happening or changing and, especially new choices as to whether to vary your language or behaviour.

What is Calibration?

Calibration is the NLP word for the ability to notice and measure changes with respect to a standard. The skill of calibrating depends on refined sensory acuity.

How do you do it? Initially notice what you notice without adding meaning of the persons breathing, eye movements, lower lip size, muscle tonus, skin colour, pupil dilation, to get a baseline of the person from which to compare.

Why do you it? The purpose is to recognize when people are in different states.

Calibration is based on several presuppositions of NLP:

- Process/form/at and/structure versus content;
- Resistance is a sign of insufficient pacing;
- You cannot not communicate;
- The meaning of communication is the response you get;
- You cannot not respond;
- The mind and body are part of the same system;
- There is no failure only feedback.

There are at least seven different things you calibrate:

- Breathing-location, pauses, rate, volume.
- Eye movements
- Lower lip size
- Saliva production-swallowing
- Skin colour
- Pupil dilation
- Micro muscle movements

D

Sensory acuity and peripheral vision

THERE ARE 10,000,000,000[11] nerve cells in your mind/body. Your awareness extends well beyond your physical body. We have forgotten more senses than we know we have. We are connected to a limitless universe of possibilities. We have aspects of awareness which are underused and yet are available to us every moment of every day. We can use much more of our sensory acuity.

There are many ways to access this. Meditation is one. The best learning and understanding state is when the conscious and unconscious mind are in harmony, seeing and feeling things together, now.

Here is another way. Pick a spot, or small feature of the room in front of you, above head height and at least three metres away. Focus all your attention on it. As you become more focused, let your awareness spread out at each side of you, all the while remaining looking at the distant object. Become aware now that you are seeing things either side of you and even behind the line of your eyes. Relax and let what happens happen. You are now using your peripheral vision.

This can also achieve the trance or learning state. Remain in this state as long as you wish. Quiet any negative or unproductive internal dialogue and become aware of creative or useful thoughts that pop into your mind from your unconscious.

Start now and as you become more peripherally aware, understand that you can use this state in any trading situation, especially when you wish to achieve calmness, or clear your mind for optimal thinking or original and creative ideas. Maybe when you have a choice to make or an issue to resolve. Trust your unconscious mind. It is connected to the limitless potential of the universe.

E

Understanding and improving your strategies

Overview of Strategies

Early work in NLP was concerned with modeling excellence in particularly outstanding individuals. Modeling remains central to the study of excellence and the process used has been identified and coded so that others can also achieve it.

Successful modeling is based on successful strategies. First, you find a model of excellence. Then, with the person's permission, you elicit their strategy. Finally, you understand it, practice it and perfect it. We learned to walk by modeling adults. The modeling process is as instinctive as any behaviour that we do. Together with diligence and practice, it is the most powerful factor in acquiring skills.

By codifying language and behaviour, and enabling us to understand the syntax and process of strategies, NLP makes it possible to understand and model excellence in any skill and anyone to move towards our goals and our limitless potential. Furthermore, in the workplace in a more subtle and sensitive way you can be enabled to obtain insights into other people's behaviours, manage relationships and adjust your own responses appropriately to achieve the optimum outcome.

Just as corporate strategy is designed to achieve the organization or company's goals or mission, so we have an individual strategy which will achieve our own outcomes. We all have strategies, whether we are conscious of them or not, and whether they are effective or not. Although most of us enjoy some level of success, having got to wherever we are now in our complex lives, strategies can still be identified that work even better than what we're doing now. ' If it isn't working, try something else, anything else.'

Organizational strategies, where they exist, tend to be in written documents. Even where nothing has been decided or documented consciously, however, organizations still have the unconscious strategies. The business is made up of people. People make decisions, people make choices, and people have values, beliefs and behaviours. Whether or not anything is written down, the organization's strategy will be revealed by its behaviours.

As with the organization, if there were going to be a strategy anyhow, wouldn't it be better if it was planned, modeled on the best, understood, appropriate to the person, efficiently and elegantly implemented?

In summary, all behaviour (learning, remembering, motivation, making your choice, communicating, changing, etc.) results from systematically ordered sequences of sensory representations. The process of eliciting someone's strategy provides a description of what they do inside their head and nervous system to generate a particular behaviour, whether it consists of thoughts, emotions, beliefs, values, states, skills, experiences, communication, etc.

As we learned earlier, Twitmyer and Pavlov, evolved the stimulus-response model. We also considered the TOTE model, which Miller, Galanter and Pribram developed from stimulus-response. Grinder and Bandler combined this work to the understanding of how strategies are created, the processes that comprise them, how they can be unpacked, understood, (improved if appropriate) and learned, so that one can model excellence. This is the core of NLP.

What is a Strategy?

A strategy is a repeatable sequence of thought and behaviour that consistently produces a particular outcome. Strategies are how you organize your thoughts and behaviour to accomplish a task. Strategies always aim for a positive goal. They can be switched on or off by beliefs: to succeed in a task, you need to believe you can do it, otherwise you will not commit yourself fully.

A strategy is, therefore, an anchored sequence of representations used to guide our behaviours. It usually includes each of the representational systems: visual, auditory and kinaesthetic in some order. We can discover them in others and ourselves by listening to the words we choose, observing eye patterns and by asking about the form and sequence of internal representations.

The strategies we use are part of our perceptual filters; they determine how we perceive the world. They have been likened to a recipe. The ingredients are representational systems. The amount and quality of the ingredients are equivalent to our submodalities. And then everything must be put together in the right sequence (syntax) in order to have a successful strategy.

Efficient strategies are at the heart of successful modeling. This is the essence of NLP. You may have identified a model of excellence from whom you can learn. In order to master the particular skill, that person might have taken many years to reach the level of excellence, unaware of the internal strategies that they evolved over that period.

With the person's permission, you could unpack that strategy and model it to achieve your own excellence in a much shorter time. In doing so, you may not only elicit and understand the strategy, but may also identify changes that could make it even better.

Any skill, however quickly understood, needs a period of practice in order to achieve excellence. When you are in possession of the elements of the strategy, the time taken to master the skill may be a fraction of the time taken by a person you have modeled. It is the strategy itself that is the key to what your brain and mind are able to accomplish.

Strategies are always triggered by motivation. They always end with a kinesthetic representation. Strategies always produce results. The question is do they produce the results that you want? Any strategy works perfectly well, but has it been designed to produce the result you would like?

We all have strategies for everything we do in an automatic way, such as love, attraction, buying, motivation, decision, etc. It is rare for people to be aware of how they think and at times when they are delivering excellence. Even during the elicitation process some people are not sufficiently familiar with their own thought processes (representation system and submodalities).

It has been shown that mastery in some activities, such as spelling, was a standard pattern. Furthermore, we also understand that the patterns that we use in decision strategies may be replicated in various aspects of our lives.

Later we shall consider other examples of strategies that are being widely understood and implemented to achieve mastery or improve performance in a number of practical aspects of life. Another recurring factor in modeling mastery is an ability to use all representation systems in a highly developed way, and to switch from one to another.

While it may seem probable that a particular strategy would be based on a particular representation system, e.g. music being based on auditory, in practice efficient and successful strategies usually combine all the key representation systems, i.e. visual, auditory and kinesthetic.

How Does It Work?

"To identify strategies we minimally need the ability to:

> *identify* the strategy,
> *elicit* the strategy,
> *interrupt or alter* the strategy,
> *design* new strategies *or redesign* old ones,
> *install* the strategy,
> *or utilize* it in a different context.

Strategies start by the person receiving input, i.e. a stimulus from the 'territory' outside them. They 'delete, distort and generalize' the input to fit with their internal map. The resulting outcome will be an internal or external response. The skilled practitioner can become aware of both, even without knowing precisely what is happening inside the subject. Nevertheless, they can, by skilful observation (eye movements and other neurophysiological signals) and listening to the auditory description and predicates, get an understanding of the components and order of the internal strategy that the person uses in all such situations.

The syntax of the strategy is a series of internal representations. It is triggered by motivation (a stimulus) and always ends with a kinesthetic representation. Sometimes, there may appear to be an inconsistency in the logic pattern, or a missing step which, when explored sensitively and ecologically with the subject, can help them decide on an appropriate change to make the strategy even more effective towards the chosen outcome, or result in a more desirable outcome.

So, for example, a person may be using a spelling strategy but it may not be working as well as they would wish. In order to improve effectiveness and move towards excellence, a change in the ingredients or the order in which they are used could achieve the desired end. In working with dyslexics, we often come across subjects who appear to be trying to recognize or spell words through their emotional filters. Once they have learned the critical importance of the visual component and the most effective way it can be incorporated, we have seen dramatic changes.

An effective strategy will use all three primary representational systems; many can be improved by an external review step, such as moving to a different perceptual position, in order to review the whole process and eliminate or prevent the formation of loops (leading to indecision or ineffective decision).

What Are the Benefits?

Everything we do uses strategies. There are many behaviours we can modify on the way to excellence. We could, with someone's help, unpack our own strategy for a particular action or decision and intuitively identify and implement the changes to greater effectiveness in what we wish to achieve. Through the magic of NLP, we can go a major step further. 'If any one person on the planet is excellent in a particular skill, then any other person can learn it and implement it.' This is the process of modeling.

There are models of excellence all around us. You may already be consciously and unconsciously understanding and modeling excellence. Understanding the elements and syntax of strategies are fundamental to that modeling process.

In '*In Search of Excellence*', Tom Peters and Robert Waterman interviewed and researched many of the best role models of success in the 1980s. This approach to management textbooks has been continued since. Organizations study models of organizational (Pugh and others) and competitive (Porter) behaviour and attempt to implement them into their own organizations. In doing so, they adapt and evolve them to their own circumstances.

We can do the same. By understanding and implementing the strategy elicitation process we can model excellence in others. Using a modified version, we can apply it to the corporation or organization.

Possible Uses and examples

Strategy elicitation can be used in a multitude of ways. What skill or behaviour do you need, or need to change in your own pursuit of excellence?

It is widely used now in sport (to understand the internal patterns that make the external behaviours work excellently well), education (learning, spelling, reading, etc.), creativity (e.g. the Walt Disney strategy), relationships (decision strategies for selecting a partner, communication strategies, etc.) and so on. Having understood the components of strategies, how they are organized and how they work, you can have fun playing with your own behaviours and modeling your own future success.

One of the most practical and valuable uses of strategies is in the learning process. There are seven separate 'learning strategies' for all generative learning:

1) Motivation – building trust and belief;
2) Acquisition – taking in information and leaving loops otherwise learning stops;
3) Convincer – 'exercise' or practice to produce the result.
4) Contextualization – 'what does this mean for me?'
5) Generalization – 'what does this mean for everybody?'

6) Accessing – the state of accessing information when you need it (recall);

7) Refinement – unconscious competence, mostly done in the absence of the 'teacher.'

How Does It Work?

Strategies are the specific sequences of internal and external representations of experience leading to a specific outcome. We arbitrarily divide experience into strategies in terms of outcomes. Major categories of strategies include: Motivation; Decision; Convincer; Reassurance; Learning; and Reality strategies.

Some major strategies may be comprised of other strategy elements. We shall cover the Motivation strategy later, as this is fundamental to all decisions.

The elements of a buying strategy

- Motivation
- Decision (to buy)
- Convincer
- Reassurance

Elements of a Love Strategy

- Attraction
- Recognizing Attraction
- Deep Love

Processes for Installing or Changing Strategies

- Rehearsing
- Reframing
- Metaphor
- Anchoring
- Dissociated state rehearsal

Basic Motivation Strategy

This demonstrates how the various elements of imagination, expectation, criteria, submodalities and association can be combined into a simple strategy to help people better inspire and motivate themselves to take actions which will lead them to their desired outcomes.

1) Imagine yourself having already achieved a dream or outcome that matches a highly valued criterion, and are really enjoying it. Get in touch with what you are seeing, hearing, doing and feeling while enjoying these benefits

2) Adjust three qualities of your internal experience in such a way that it feels more motivating or compelling. Does the experience become more compelling and attractive if you add more colour? Brightness? Sound? Words? A movement? What happens if you bring the image closer or move it farther away? What happens if you make the sounds or words louder or softer? What do you experience if you make the movement quicker or slower? Identify which qualities make the experience feel the best.

3) Applying those qualities, experience the good feelings that come from having your outcome.

4) Remember those feelings as you picture yourself doing the things that you know will help you move closer to your dream or outcome. (You can create a self anchor in order to help transfer those feelings, or use the submodality qualities you identified in step two).

5) The purpose of initially focusing on outcome and its positive consequences, rather than the particular behaviour required to reach the outcome, is to create an 'attractor' that will stimulate the natural self organizing functions of the nervous system. It also helps to create a positive feelings state, or 'outcome expectancy', that is later linked to the behaviours required to reach the outcome (which may not be as inherently positive as reaching the outcome). Thus, you are using the positive feelings of what is 'farther away in time' to leverage or support the necessary short-term actions required to reach the longer term desired state.

F

Overview of the TOTE Model

THE TOTE MODEL is first discussed in Miller, Galanter and Pribram's *Plans and the Structure of Behaviour* (1960). Going beyond the simple Stimulus Response model that had originated with Pavlov and others, this completely original model provided a 'flow-chart' for tracking human subjectivity from stimulus through internal 'processing' in terms of the human responses of:

- *Testing* the stimulus against internal models (plans, expectations, thoughts, ideas)
- *Operating* either on the stimulus to alter it or one's internal map to alter it
- *Testing* for congruency or the lack of it, and then
- *Exiting* the program.

These models describe the process of modeling: starting with some stimulus in the present state and tracking the process of getting to some new, different, and better response that leaves one in a more desired state.

The TOTE model updated the Stimulus-Response model by incorporating feedback and outcome. It also offers a formal pattern for the internal processing sequence triggered by a stimulus. *Testing* refers to the conditions that the *operating* has to meet before the response will occur. This stage reveals congruity or incongruity. If incongruity shows up, the process will loop back to the test, until congruity is present, when the process will exit. In this feedback phase, the system operates to change some aspect of the stimulus or of the person's internal state to satisfy the test.

The TOTE model presupposes that we can achieve behavioural excellence through having:

- A future goal in mind;
- Sensory and behavioural evidence that indicates the achieving of the goal;
- A range of operations, procedures or choices with which to accomplish the goal.

G

Creating rapport (1) – eye patterns

THESE SECTIONS are about choice in creating rapport with the people around you.

When there is calmness in your personal life and you can choose to be at ease with yourself in any aspect, then you can be at your best, creating rapport with anyone, at ease, including yourself... You could also use these techniques in order to break rapport or create negative rapport, so that you can disengage, consciously or unconsciously, being able to be yourself in any way that seems right for you.

We'll start with eye patterns. Some people are oppositely organized (that is, their eye patterns will work in the opposite way to the following), and it is easiest to assume that almost everyone is 'normally' organized.

Ask someone an open question (one for which the answer is more than just a single word, such as yes or no). As they answer, watch their eyes. The eyes are connected to the various parts of the brain.

Movement up and to the left as you look at them indicates they are making a picture inside (Vc). Up and to the right means they are recalling a picture (Vr) that they have previously seen outside or inside themselves.

Movement across left denotes creating sounds (Ac) inside and across right is recalling sounds (Ar).

Down to the left as you look at their face (K), indicates they are accessing their feelings, or may be about to use a 'physical' predicate or description. Down to the right (Ad), is where self-talk, data, facts, criteria, etc are accessed.

Have fun trying these and please be aware of other peoples' wishes or feelings. If you make what you are doing obvious, or start telling people what they are doing, you may upset, annoy or otherwise unsettle the person. The skills you are using are to privately enhance the basis and quality of your understanding and relationships. If you start replaying these things, or the following section back to them, they may feel they are being 'analyzed'.

Listen all the while to their language. Remember the section on representations that we covered earlier. You could choose the information you are discovering to help create superb rapport.

I dislike the 'self-confession' shows, such as Jerry Springer, but they are great for practicing my understanding of eye cues. Watching Blind Date and the Clinton tapes was most enlightening also.

H

Creating rapport (2) – mirroring and matching

REMEMBER THAT 55% of communication is non-verbal. Babies cannot see much more than a foot when they are born. For some time, they make out shapes and movements in their immediate vicinity. What do they see most of, other than the face and eyes of the person holding them?

As they grow older, they spend a lot of time sitting and watching. They learn so much from what they observe, unconsciously matching it with the sounds that they hear. We all learned the skills I am teaching you here, at an early age. The process was 'hit and miss' however. I am now offering you the chance to 'unpack' these skills, review them, improve them, practice and reinstall them to enhance any aspect of your life you choose.

As you are standing or sitting, communicating with someone (which of course you can also do unconsciously), you may be aware when you are in rapport that your body posture is similar. Did you ever notice that?

Many people since Desmond Morris have written about 'body language'. You may be able to understand so much from someone's posture. And, suppose they sighed, or breathed in a certain way...

What you can learn and practice here, I ask you to do subtly and with respect for someone else's model of the world. We are not talking of mimicry. That is what children do, with voice or posture. You may have found that irritating.

When you use the following skills subtly, you can improve the quality of any relationship. Since Dale Carnegie first wrote 'How to Win Friends and Influence People', it has been acceptable to use and improve your skills in the quality of your business and personal relationships.

As you sit or stand with someone, you may notice their body posture, breathing, tonality, facial expressions, hand movements and even phrases or other mannerisms they use. As you begin to quietly and carefully mirror the body posture and match all the others, you may find yourself being or feeling in rapport.

People often ask me whether others spot this happening. If they do, you have an opportunity to practice and improve further. No-one has ever drawn my attention to what I was doing, unless I first asked them to take part in an exercise.

Think of all the situations in which you will be able to use all these new skills and, having used them in any aspect of your life, how many new possibilities are opening up.

Now you can be your best self, at ease with anyone, including yourself, at any time, then in how many ways will your whole experience have improved, by the time you have realized that already?

I

Perceptual positions

IMAGINE YOU are discussing, debating, arguing, and negotiating with someone. I guess you may already be noticing how these other things can improve the quality of that mutual communication? With an awareness of perceptual positions, you can go one step further.

As you sit there putting forward your own position or opinion exactly as you want it, from inside yourself, you may have noticed that the other person doesn't follow you, understand or agree with you. You are in *position 1*. Now, in the interests of better communication and relationships, you could move your conscious awareness into their position; 'try it on'. For example, you could ask yourself "with what I know of this person, or understand so far, what would they have to be thinking, seeing, hearing, feeling, to be saying/doing what they are saying/doing?" You are now trying on *position 2*.

Maybe things still aren't working, happening, moving forward in the way you both might have hoped. Now you can try going up onto the ceiling and look down on the two of you, to get a completely detached perspective. What do you notice from up there? To get you there, you could ask "what's happening here? What is really happening here?" This is *position 3*.

So now you have even more flexibility in your behaviour, communication, potential, etc. seeing the world from others' or impartial *perceptual positions*.

Managing perceptual positions

Now you have accumulated so many skills that you can have an understanding in your conscious, or your unconscious, mind. Being able to see the world from someone else's perspective, or even to be the proverbial 'fly on the wall' can dramatically improve the many possibilities in your life.

In how many ways does your life change and improve when you can step outside yourself and see the situation from someone else's perspective, or especially an impartial position?

How well can you model the skills of another when you can 'be in their shoes' whenever you wish?

Exercise

Find a quiet space, maybe in meditation, or elsewhere. Fill yourself with an awareness of what you are seeing, hearing and feeling inside yourself. Using all the skills of submodalities and others, enrich your experience of what is happening inside yourself now, knowing you can always do this at will. You are now deep in position 1.

Choose a friend who enjoys having fun. Go into an open space together. Have the friend walk along, thinking of a very specific situation, maybe something they imagine themselves going to. Walk one pace behind them, opening your mind, so that the spontaneous thoughts and feelings can emerge and grow in your unconscious mind. Allow your unconscious awareness to flow into that of the friend ahead of you, as you are walking 'in their shoes'.

After a minute or two, stop and tell them what you sensed or felt was in their mind.

Notice how your perception grows as you practice this exercise. You could also do this as you talk with someone else. Have an impression of leaving your own position and going into theirs. How different do things seem now? You are in position 2.

Recall or be in a time as you are listening to, or engaging with someone else. Or, do the same for any appropriate situation. Now step outside yourself and move your awareness up onto the ceiling, or to some other place where you can have a completely detached view, sense or feeling of what is happening. This is position 3.

Practice these positions regularly until they become unconscious. If ever you wish to review a situation or decision, do it from all three positions. Use this ability in your relationships and see yourself from positions 2 and 3, as you choose.

J

Listening well

I LEARNED from my father the ability to talk...too much. A basic shyness in personality led to my deciding to engage more with people verbally. Unfortunately, lack of self-esteem also meant that I was seeking to be accepted and, as well as talking too much, I had become practiced in trying to impose my view on others...

I am learning, changing and growing. I love that capacity of 'gravitas', being able to be cool and detached as appropriate before offering the appropriate thought at just the right moment. I have accepted that it was my own pattern of talking, not my father's. I am responsible for all my own choices.

As a mentor, coach and therapist, it is ideal that one listens well to another. The good counselor listens, plays back accurately, acknowledges appropriately and facilitates the environment where the client comes to see or feel the way forward that is right for themselves.

In business I learned the technique of active listening, including summarizing and playing back what the other person says, as appropriate.

When we talk a lot, or even too much... we may miss the messages that are out there for us to learn and grow. 'The meaning of your communication is in the response you get'.

You can listen with your whole self. Practice listening with your ears, eyes, mouth, body, thoughts and any other faculties you have, as you see or feel to be appropriate.

Again, practice moving around from position 1 to position 2, 3 and back, noticing the changes you experience and the messages that come, as you listen.

Be aware of and respectful of others' models of the world. You might find yourself trying on their model of the world by asking "what would they have to see, hear, feel, experience or believe, in order to speak or behave in that way?"

You could also ask yourself the question "what's happening here?" knowing it will take you into position 3.

You can only ever know your own model of the world, because that is what you are. You may put yourself in someone else's shoes, or even in the detached position 3 and you will always interpret what you experience through your own filters, beliefs, values and behaviours. You can gain much greater insight into the behaviour of yourself and others, by practicing these techniques and all the others until they become second nature.

Being a good listener, you can be much more aware of what is going on. Were you ever in a restaurant, or situation where you became aware of someone else's conversation, almost without trying? What was it about that conversation that triggered your awareness?

As you practice your listening skills and all the other things which are already increasing your general awareness, you may be noticing much more that is of use or value for you.

K

Setting and using anchors

What is Anchoring?

"An anchor is anything that accesses an emotional state" (*Introducing NLP*, O'Connor & Seymour). The structure of an anchor is a stimulus, followed by a response. We respond to anchors in all aspects of our life: the voice of someone you know; the strapline of an advert; the smell of food that triggers hunger; 'our song'; the alarm going off; etc.

'Anchoring' is the process by which anchors operate. Understanding and modeling that process leads to insights into the basis and patterns of behaviours, together with new choices how to modify or replace such behaviours, or install new, resourceful behaviours.

The origins of anchoring have been said to be in Pavlovian Conditioning. Pavlov noticed the salivation response of dogs to the sight and smell of meat. He then introduced the tuning fork in the same instant that the meat appeared. The ringing became associated with the meat. Eventually, the dogs were conditioned to salivate to the ringing sound. It had become an anchor.

In fact, 'classical conditioning' was discovered three years earlier, by Edwin B. Twitmyer. He first observed that striking the knee in the right place would cause a physical reflex. Eventually he showed that the response could occur simply at the suggestion of striking it.

Apart from having an unmemorable name, Twitmyer did not elicit as much response to his Ph.D. thesis on the knee-jerk reflex from his US peers as Pavlov did with his esteemed Russian colleagues. The latter's work became a core element of modern psychology theory.

Why and how does anchoring work?

An anchor is rooted in the deep structure. The cause-effect pattern has been learned either by an intense emotional originating experience, and/or by repetition. The generalization process also creates associations appropriate to the specific behaviour patterns of the individual.

Example: As a child, a person watched their father gluing carpet with Copydex. The predominant component of the glue was ammonia, which eventually caused nausea. In later life, the adult could not eat camembert or brie without feeling nausea, due to the predominant ammonia smell. The unconscious mind had set up the anchor pattern in childhood and then associated other related experiences to the original stimulus.

Any time a person is in an associated, intense state, if at the peak of that experience, a specific stimulus is applied, then the two will be linked neurologically.

Anchoring can be used both to discover/uncover states and/or originating experiences and to change or remove such experiences, or generate new behaviours. "Anchoring, and the construction of new possibilities using anchoring, can literally convert your personal history from a set of limitations to a set of resources." (*Frogs Into Princes,* ibid.)

The Anchoring Process

There are four steps to the anchoring process:

1) Have the person **Recall** a vivid past experience.
2) **Anchor** (provide) a specific stimulus at the peak.
3) **Change** the person's state.
4) **Evoke the State** – set off the anchor to test it.

There are four widely accepted keys to anchoring:

1) The **Intensity** of the state or experience.
2) The **Timing** of the Anchor (at the peak of experience).
3) The **Uniqueness** of the Anchor (or stimulus).
4) The **Replication** of the stimulus.

In addition, the number of repetitions can have an effect on the strength of the anchor.

Procedure for creating an anchor:

1) The **uniqueness of the stimulus**. (For example, on the right hand of a right-handed person, the anchor might accidentally be fired by shaking hands).

2) Being **exactly repeatable**. (Again, where one is working with someone else, it is important that the anchor point is easily and naturally reachable).

3) **Peak timing**. Start by applying the anchor stimulus at the moment of undeniable physiological change (usually 5 to 15 seconds before the peak), holding and releasing just before the peak.

4) **Repetition** (as appropriate to increase the intensity of the anchored response).

5) **Test.** Fire the anchor and test whether the same physiological response occurs reinforced with a conscious convincer.

6) **Future Pace.** Vividly imagine firing the anchor 3 times in the future. (Optionally imagine a previously experienced unresourceful state some time in the future. Fire the anchor. Elicit the internally experienced changes that occur. Reinforce the positive change with a conscious convincer.)

7) **Continuous calibration** of the 'meta' physiological responses.

Diagrammatic Representation of the anchoring process

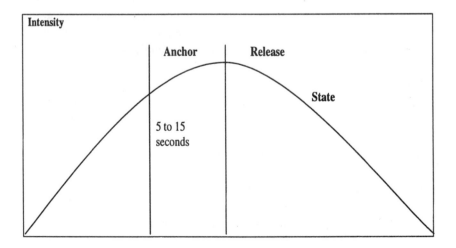

Uses of Basic Anchoring

In personal life, anchors can be very powerful:

- The degeneration of relationships is often based on continuous and usually unconscious anchoring of negative patterns and responses to everyday exchanges;
- The most special, intimate moments can be reinforced by visual, kinesthetic or auditory anchors, such that the same response can be elicited on future occasions;
- One mother played the Hawaii 5-0 music at every bath time until simply playing the music would have her children scampering to the bathroom and willingly going to bed;

In business, basic anchors could be used in a number of circumstances, e.g.:

- In selling, observed positive responses by the prospective customer could be anchored using an auditory marker, such as the click of the pen. Once set, if signs of resistance appeared later, the pen could be clicked to fire the previously anchored positive physiological pattern;
- The fire bell in organizations and the school bell at period end are commonly encountered anchors;
- The use of spatial marking during a presentation;
- Words, postures or movements not normally adopted, could be used to 'mark' a desired conditioned response, e.g. in a meeting. (Unfortunately, some people have done this unwittingly, e.g. the person who always seems to raise a problem or objection might have anchored a negative response to simply beginning to speak).

Other examples might include: the spontaneous salute in the forces; the spontaneous quieting of noise as someone of respect enters a room; the 'Chariots of Fire' music associated with achievement; the use of commanding or questioning tonality in voice patterns; the red traffic light in front of you or the blue flashing light behind...

Anchoring resourceful states in meetings

- Identify the state you wish to anchor in another person in that process, that will support the achievement of agreed mutual outcomes.

- Decide what resource anchor you will use, e.g. a word or words, gesture or posture;
- When the relevant person naturally demonstrates that behaviour, use the chosen anchor. You may need to do this several times.
- If the meeting or discussion reaches a stage where the chosen state would be valuable, fire the anchor. Notice what happens.

Example: Grinder and Anthony Robbins were making a sales pitch to the US Army, in a room that was often used by the Generals for major decisions. While the key decision-maker was not present, the team who were there had the delegated authority to decide whether to hire the consultants. During the discussion, Grinder and Robbins several times walked up to the General's chair at the head of the table, standing behind it and leaning on it. At one stage Robbins sat in it, briefly. This pattern was only used to anchor key aspects of the proposal to the chair. When the time came to make the decision, it was made swiftly and without objection, as it already had the anchored approval of the 'phantom' General.

Stacking Anchors

The technique of adding different positive resources in the same physical location is known as stacking anchors. One possible use is in collapsing anchors (see later). Stacked anchors could be used to change either past or future history.

Process

- Suppose you wished to be more motivated.
- Select a part of your non-writing hand or arm.
- Select between three and five strong, positive states you would like to easily access.
- Think of a time in your life when you were totally motivated. Step into that situation in your mind and fully associate yourself into whatever sights, sounds are present in that time now, so that you feel the same way.
- As the experience begins to peak, press the chosen part of your hand or arm and release it just before the moment passes. At the same time, say something appropriate inside, such as 'yes!'

- Now think of another experience when you felt totally motivated to do something. As before, at the peak of the experience, set the anchor in the same place as before, with the same pressure and the same sound.
- Stack a further two or three such experiences in the same place to create a powerful stacked anchor.
- Now think of a decision you have to make, a challenge you face, or a task you wish to achieve. Associate yourself into that situation.
- Fire your stacked anchor and notice the changes you are already seeing, hearing and feeling in your internal representation.

In some circumstances, it could be equally effective to stack a series of different positive states, such as: feeling totally motivated; feeling totally loved or appreciated; feeling totally confident; feeling totally energetic; feeling totally happy; etc.

Possible Benefits

- Being able to prepare for (preframe) or respond to a challenge in the workplace;
- Being able to use a stacked calmness anchor in the face of adversity or anger;
- To trigger or reinforce positive states in a sport or leisure pursuit;
- To store and stack strongly positive states in your relationship (and see example below);
- Stacking a powerful resource to draw on before, or during a challenging personal task, such as a sporting endeavor, to enhance the prospects of success;
- The 'firewalk' is achieved by stacking a series of powerful resource states and then creating a deep trance state through ritual and collective chanting and encouragement.

Chaining Anchors

This is a technique that is used when the desired emotional state is significantly different from the present emotional state, i.e. the 'stretch' is too far. Chaining involves anchoring logical and progressive intermediate transition states to each other in order to create a smooth and gradual flow from the present state to the desired state. Each anchor provides a link in the 'chain' and triggers the next one, in the same way as electrical impulses flow from one nerve cell to another.

Anchors are an external representation of how we create new, resourceful neural pathways in our deep structure of behaviours. The conscious component of the anchoring process progressively declines as it becomes unconsciously embedded in our patterned behaviours. Eventually, the new pathway is spontaneously triggered by the old signal and the desired resourceful state is automatically experienced, consciously and unconsciously.

Think of a time, or situation when you may have felt frustrated to some degree. Can you identify the signal that triggers this feeling? Is it visual, auditory or kinesthetic?

Now, what is your desired new resourceful response to this signal? Chaining anchors may be appropriate to 'bridge' from the old state to the new, chosen state.

Chained anchors are like stepping stones across a river. Only when you reach the other side, you have built a permanent bridge.

The process works because each subsequent anchor is anchored to its predecessors. You create the chain such that the next anchor is fired when the previous one has peaked. Eventually, the signal or trigger that had been linked to the first anchor, automatically sets off the entire chain in sequence and the response is that of the final anchor. The result is a new pathway from the old signal straight to the chosen state.

An example of a useful chain for procrastination might be: procrastination; boredom; curiosity; anticipation; motivation.

Process

- Identify your present unresourceful state and the desired resourceful state that you have chosen to replace it.

- Determine a natural, logical, progressive sequence of states that flow from one to the other. Be sure not to select an end state or a regressive state in any of the intermediate stages, or you may find yourself stuck before you reach the new state.
- Choose the locations for each state, again in a logical progressive order, easily accessible in sequence. For the example used above, you could use the knuckles of your left hand.
- Anchor each of the chosen states in sequence, in the chosen locations. Stack each state on its chosen location if you wish, to be sure that when it is fired it will produce the selected physiological change. Break state between each anchoring.
- Fire each state and calibrate it in turn, only moving to the next state when the latter triggers the relevant response. Be sure that at no time are two or more anchors fired simultaneously. They should also only be fired and/or tested in the correct order. If there is any doubt about a previous anchor, go back and start the sequence again.
- Break state.
- To use the example above: fire the procrastination anchor; as it peaks, fire the boredom anchor; as that peaks, fire the curiosity anchor and so on, for anticipation and motivation.
- Break state.
- Repeat the above process as often as is desired.
- Test the 'chain' by firing the procrastination anchor and noting the motivation response. If there is room for greater effectiveness, stack each of the anchors and repeat the chaining process exactly as above until the new neural pathway is installed.
- Future pace. Go forward to a time or situation where previously you might have felt, e.g. procrastination. Fire your procrastination anchor and note the changes in that future behaviour.

Possible Uses

You can chain anchors with your physiology, tonality or visually. Some suggest that it is most effective to chain anchors using all primary representation systems, for each step of the chain.

Example: A consultant wished to sell a proposal to a prospective client. When they first met, there was an apparent hesitancy in the prospect, who said she was unsure of the value of using external trainers. The consultant anchored the state with a facial expression and a mirrored physiology.

He then asked, "what does it take for that uncertainty to shift into interest?" Her physiology shifted and she stated "well if I start to feel more confident that the person we contract can help us grow and understands what direction we are headed in." He anchored the 'interested' state, again visually, the different physiology and, played back the statement in a matched tonality.

The consultant continued by asking "when you decided on the last outside consultant you appointed, and it was a good decision, what was it that made you absolutely confident that it was the right decision?" He anchored the resulting 'confidence' state.

Finally, pacing her authority, he asked her "as the best person to find the right consultant, how do you know when you are absolutely certain that someone like me (pointing to self) is the right person to contract?" At the end of the process, he had set up the following chain: uncertainty/doubt; interested; confident; absolutely certain.

Explaining exactly how his offering matched her precise expressed needs, he utilized the anchors, paced the sequence verbally, and adopted the appropriate physiology and tonality in sequential order. He got the contract.

In the workplace, people sometimes have a long way to go from their present exhibited behaviours to the organization's desired level of effectiveness and productivity. Training is one way to achieve this progression and repetitive routines can result in an anchored behaviour.

Sometimes, however, the person is unresourceful in certain behaviours, due to patterns established a long time ago. Stress in the workplace is a very good example. Stress management often focuses on the stress factors and new choices that the client can make. Unfortunately, stress response is an anchored state. Some stress counseling leads to temporary improvement. The skilled NLP therapist can use a change personal history approach, where chaining resource anchors may be very effective in moving towards the desired behaviours, permanently.

Collapsing Anchors

Collapsing anchors involves linking a resourceful state with an unresourceful state and adding a resource for the person to then have. It is the procedure by which two anchors for two incompatible responses are triggered at the same time. The more powerful of the two anchors will dominate, resulting in at least neutralization and ideally elimination of the unresourceful state.

What happens if you try to feel hot and cold at the same time? What happens if two different people try to speak to you about different things or the television and the stereo are both playing loudly at the same time? To collapse anchors, you anchor an unwanted negative state, and a positive state, in separate places and fire them simultaneously. After a short period of confusion, the negative state is changed or eliminated and a new state comes into being. Sometimes the positive resource state is stacked to override the negative state.

Process

- Identify the problem state and a powerful positive state that you would rather have available to you.
- Elicit the positive state and calibrate the physiology so that you can distinguish it.
- Break state.
- Elicit the desired state again, and anchor it with a particular touch and word or phrase, in a unique location.
- Break state.
- Test the positive anchor to be sure it is established. Fire the anchor with the same touch and words. Be sure that you do indeed experience the physiology of the desired state. If you wish, or may be unsure, stack the anchor (repeat the process) to firmly establish it. When you have established a positive anchor for the desired state, break state.

- Identify the negative experience and repeat the above steps using the negative state. You do not need to stack this negative state, simply anchor it when you experience the physiology shift and anchor it in a different location. This establishes an anchor for the problem state.
- Break state.
- Go through each state in turn, using the anchors alternately, saying something like "so there are times when I have felt …(fire negative anchor) and in these situations I would rather feel…(fire positive anchor)? Repeat this a number of times, without breaking state between them.
- Break state.
- When you are ready, fire both anchors at the same time until they peak and the disintegration is complete.
- Release the unresourceful anchor first.
- Hold the resourceful anchor until you have experienced a change and then release.
- Break state.
- Test the effectiveness by trying to access the problem state or by firing the negative anchor. You should go into a state between the two, or a new and different state, or the positive state.
- If you are still getting the negative state, find out what other resource you need. Anchor that on the same site as the first positive resource and repeat from firing both anchors simultaneously.
- Future pace. Go out into the future, to a situation where you might once have felt that old feeling of negativity or unresourcefulness and describe what happens, all the while noticing your physiology.

Collapse anchors will only work if the positive resource is stronger than the negative resource. This can be achieved by finding a strong resource in the first place, stacking the positive resource only, or stacking more than one positive resource as above.

Benefits and Uses

As a key agent in changing your personal history and future expectations, behaviours or experiences.

Business and other similar situations in which positive anchoring processes could be useful include:

- Giving and receiving feedback;
- Solving problems and being creative;
- Being assertive;
- Listening;
- Tackling work that a person might not naturally be motivated to do;
- Making time for your family or friends (changing the internal patterns of apparent 'workaholics');
- Making a presentation;
- Dealing with customers;
- Telephone or face to face sales.

L

Reframing negatives to positives

THE UNIVERSE is in always balance. For every negative experience in the world, there is always a positive somewhere. If it is true that you can only experience the world through yourself, then both the negative and the positive are inside you. If you create no negatives, there is no need to create a countervailing positive.

What it does mean is that you can *reframe* any negative perception to positive.

It has been said that 'it's an ill wind that blows nobody any good'. Also, some people see the world as being a glass half full and others a glass half empty.

There are three main ways to reframe: context, content and time. Each can be applied at your choice to any negative perceptions you may have had.

With a context reframe, you change the context of the negative situation. For example, someone might have been embarrassed about having a booming voice in social or personal relationships. In an open street market, however, it could be a real advantage, to get your offer heard.

So, think of a negative belief or attitude you have held in the past. Ask yourself "in what context would it be useful to have this characteristic, belief or attitude?"

Change the content of a negative situation and you can create a positive result. For example:

"My mind seems to go blank when I have to make an important decision…".

The reframe would be "that means that I am clearing my mind so that nothing gets in the way of the important decision".   The question is, now that your mind is blank, what positive, appropriate and relevant thoughts come into your mind and how are you going to use all the skills you have learned and accumulated in the reading of this book?

With a time reframe, you simply take the apparent negative and ask yourself "when would this be of positive use to me?"

So, "I am slow in making decisions". Reframed, "that means I have the time and the consideration to be confident it is the best decision in the circumstances"; or, maybe a faster decision would not have been the right one for you; or, that means that you can invest more time in preparing for upcoming situations and the decisions you want to make, confident they are right for you.

Spend some time practicing reframes into positives.

M

Setting and visualizing outcomes

REMEMBER EARLIER we discussed choosing and setting your goals. There are two techniques related to outcomes that are useful for reinforcing and programming goals and also for helping to remove inner barriers to excellence. It starts with the structure of a 'well-formed outcome'.

Well-formed outcomes

There are seven stages to setting a well-formed outcome:

- State in the positive exactly what you want for yourself;
- When, where and with whom do you want this outcome;
- What will you see, hear, feel and notice when you get this outcome;
- Are you in charge of the changes you require;
- Will you lose anything if you gain this outcome;
- Is the outcome worth what it takes to get it;
- What are the consequences in your life if this goal is achieved?

Programming a goal

Using the above as a structure to start with, you can do these things.

Ask yourself "what is the last thing that has to happen for me to know that I have got this outcome for myself?"

(This could be something that spontaneously suggests itself to you, or you could decide what it will be. So, my business partner wanted to bring her golf handicap down by six shots. Apart from the other techniques from this book that she applied, she imagined herself drinking a bottle of champagne that she had bought for herself and her husband to celebrate having achieved her goal.)

Now go forward to that time when that event has happened, so that you know that you have got your outcome.

And as you're in that moment when you know that you have got that outcome, make sure you are inside yourself in that future memory, seeing what you see, feeling what you feel and hearing what you hear as you're in that time now.

Identify all the submodalities of the experience, all the while staying inside yourself.

Now build them up so that they are really strong and you are vividly living this future experience in a totally associated state.

Now step outside yourself and see yourself in the picture, having achieved your outcome and

Come back into the now, leaving that outcome programmed into your future....

(Do this for each and every one of your goals, trusting your unconscious mind to know exactly when, how....)

Finally, before you sleep tonight, read quickly through the appendices once more, if necessary referring to the relevant section in the main body of the book. As you sleep, your unconscious mind is already collecting and converging all the opportunities, positives and possibilities for you and your life. When you wake tomorrow, you can be choosing or using any of these skills, consciously or unconsciously as you improve the quality and success of your relationships and your life.

There are many 'quiet moments' during any day. Don't even think of all the opportunities to spend many or even all of these seeing the possibilities of, or using all these skills, all the while learning and growing.

You know you will need to try all of these techniques to see how well they are working, don't you...